WHITEFELLA COMIN'

WHITEFELLA COMIN'

Aboriginal responses to colonialism in northern Australia

David S. Trigger

Department of Anthropology
The University of Western Australia

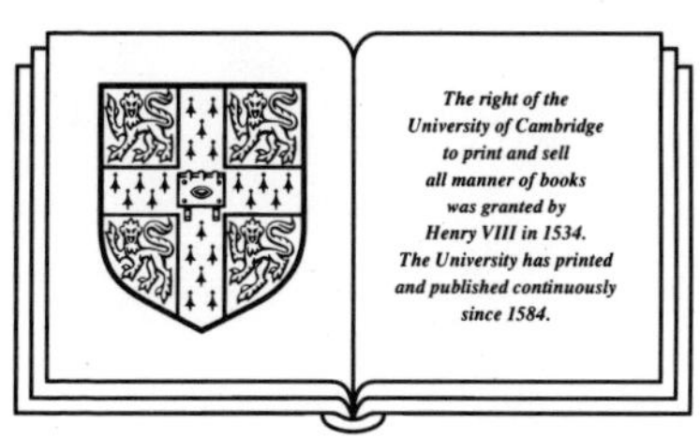

CAMBRIDGE UNIVERSITY PRESS

Cambridge

New York Port Chester Melbourne Sydney

Published by the Press Syndicate of the University of Cambridge
The Pitt Building, Trumpington Street, Cambridge CB2 1RP, UK
40 West 20th Street, New York, NY 10011-4211, USA
10 Stamford Road, Oakleigh, Victoria 3166, Australia

First published 1992

Printed in Hong Kong by Colorcraft

National Library of Australia cataloguing-in-publication data:
Trigger, David S, (David Samuel), 1953–
'Whitefella comin' : Aboriginal responses to colonialism
in northern Australia
Bibliography.
Includes index.
ISBN 0 521 40181 X
I. Aborigines, Australian — Queensland — Doomadgee
Aboriginal Reserve — Social conditions. 2. Doomadgee Aboriginal
Reserve (Qld.) — Race relations. I.
Title.
306.089991509437

Library of Congress Cataloguing-in-Publication Data:
Trigger, David S. (David Samuel). 1953–
'Whitefella comin' : Aboriginal responses to colonialism in northern
Australia / David S. Trigger.
Includes bibliographical references and index.
ISBN 0-521-40181-X
I. Australian aborigines — Australia — Queensland — Government
relations. 2. Australian aborigines — Australia — Queensland —
History. 3. Queensland — Race relations. I. Title.
GN667.Q4T75 1991
305.8'991509437 — dc20

A catalogue record for this book is available from the British Library

ISBN 0 521 40181 X hardback

In memory of Johnny Watson, a great singer.
And for Vicki, Benjamin and Rebecca.

Contents

List of maps

List of figures

Preface

This is a study of power relations and social action at Doomadgee, an Aboriginal settlement on the Nicholson River in the far northwest corner of Queensland, Australia (see map 1). My interest is in how Aboriginal and White people in this relatively remote setting have operated within the political and economic structures of colonialism. If the laws and policies of the state have historically promoted coercive local administrative practices, what have been the responses of Aboriginal people? Has there been resistance as well as compliance? What counts as resistance, and what counts as consent, among subjugated Aboriginal people encapsulated within colonial social relations in northern Australia? Has there been ideological incorporation of Aboriginal people to the extent that they come to attribute legitimacy to the state-sponsored system of administration? And if so, have particular material and social conditions engendered this form of accommodation to a system of colonial domination?

I regard these as questions with complex answers, best addressed by detailed ethnographic and historical research. My study of colonialism, resistance and consent focuses on the period between 1978 and 1983, during which I carried out fifty-four weeks of fieldwork, visiting the settlement and the surrounding region every year except 1981. Aboriginal people at Doomadgee have traditional and historical ties across a region encompassing areas in both Queensland and the Northern Territory, and the study includes investigation of the history of this region prior to the establishment of Doomadgee Mission in the early 1930s. This historical research relies in part on much unpublished archival material, as well as on Aboriginal oral historical accounts.

The country from Burketown in the east to Borroloola in the west has always been populated fairly sparsely. During the period of my research, most of the pastoral leases were owned and managed by non-Aboriginal people, although Aboriginal stockmen worked at some of these cattle stations. Just over half of the 212 people living at Burketown, some 90 km east of Doomadgee, were of Aboriginal descent, according to 1981 figures from the Australian Bureau of Statistics. To the north lies the more populous Aboriginal settlement of Mornington Island. Indeed, you have to drive some 400 km to the south, to Mt Isa (a town of 24 500 with an Aboriginal minority of only 7 per cent), before encountering a centre that is predominantly comprised of White people. The officially recorded Aboriginal population at Doomadgee itself increased during my fieldwork from 885 (DAIA 1978: 26) to 1083 (DAIA 1983: 46), although there is some evidence (DAA n.d.*a*: 5) that these were over-estimates of the number of people actually resident there at any one time. Most importantly for this study, there have also been up to eighty non-Aboriginal Christian Brethren missionary staff and their families at Doomadgee, a small minority, but one that has exercised colonial influence over the nature of settlement life.

The quotation in the title of this book, 'Whitefella comin', is a statement I heard often during fieldwork, as Aboriginal people commented apprehensively on the approach of a White staff member. Rarely was it said with malice, and on occasions the tone was affectionate. By including this phrase in the title, I mean to invoke the image of the White presence in this remote settlement as simultaneously peripheral to much of Aboriginal social life yet also highly influential over certain aspects of Aboriginal action and consciousness. An understanding of Aboriginal people at Doomadgee requires an understanding of various aspects of non-Aboriginal society. For to borrow from Genovese's (1974: xvi-xvii) similar point appropos north American slavery, Aboriginal and non-Aboriginal peoples in north Australia have shaped each other in important ways, and an adequate study of their situations cannot treat each in isolation.

Most of the fieldwork for this study was undertaken while I was a doctoral candidate at the University of Queensland and simultaneously an employee funded to carry out research on Aboriginal sites of significance and traditional systems of land tenure. Since completing the PhD dissertation in 1985, I have returned to the Gulf Country for a number of short periods of research.

I wish to acknowledge intellectual and social support from staff and student colleagues in Brisbane during the main period of fieldwork; in particular, my debt to Athol Chase, Chris Anderson and Ian Keen is considerable. I am grateful to Paul Memmott who generously gave me access to historical records held at the Aboriginal Data Archive, University of Queensland. The opportunity to carry out the research was made possible by grants from the Australian Institute of Aboriginal Studies, and I wish to thank Bruce Rigsby for assistance in maintaining the continuity of this funding. More recently, comments from Jeremy Beckett have been constructive and, since my move to The University of Western Australia, Bob Tonkinson, Michael Pinches, John Stanton and John Gordon have given much helpful advice as my manuscript has taken shape.

Without the support, collaboration and interest of many Aboriginal residents at Doomadgee, the research could not have been carried out. Several missionary staff also assisted me hospitably. While the Aboriginal people to whom I am indebted are far too numerous to name, I wish to express my gratitude to the community as a whole, and to make special mention of my close friendship with the late Neville Ned and his wife Alice Ned. My residence during much of the fieldwork was at the home of Alan and Cathy Jupiter (and family) to whom I am particularly grateful.

The people of Doomadgee have enriched my life by sharing their experiences with me, and I have attempted to portray my understanding of these experiences both sensitively and accurately. Nevertheless, this book is written for a wider audience, in an attempt to provide an informed analysis of Aboriginal/White relations. As in any study of politics and power, it would be naive to expect that all the people about whom I write will agree completely with my analysis, although I am confident that there will be no lack of such agreement. I ask simply that this study be received in the spirit in which it has been written, which is to improve our understanding of the process of colonisation and its aftermath.

Abbreviations and conventions

DAA Commonwealth Department of Aboriginal Affairs

DAIA Queensland Department of Aboriginal and Islanders Advancement

QGG Queensland Government Gazette

Field tape recordings are referred to in parenthesis by reference to the number of the tape following the letter 'T', for example (T1). The tapes are lodged in the archives of the Australian Institute of Aboriginal and Torres Strait Islander Studies.

References to unpublished historical and archival materials are listed separately in the bibliography; these are referred to in the text using the full date (day, month and year) where it is available.

I know these old people, if they're sittin' round in a group, if they ever see Mr. . . ., Mrs. . . . [the manager and his wife] they'll say: '[whispering] *Mandagi* [Whitefella], *Mandagi, Mandagi* . . .', and get up and run away then . . . [and the young child] will know what to do when he see a White man — he'll learn that habit . . . from an early age.

A comment from an Aboriginal resident of Doomadgee

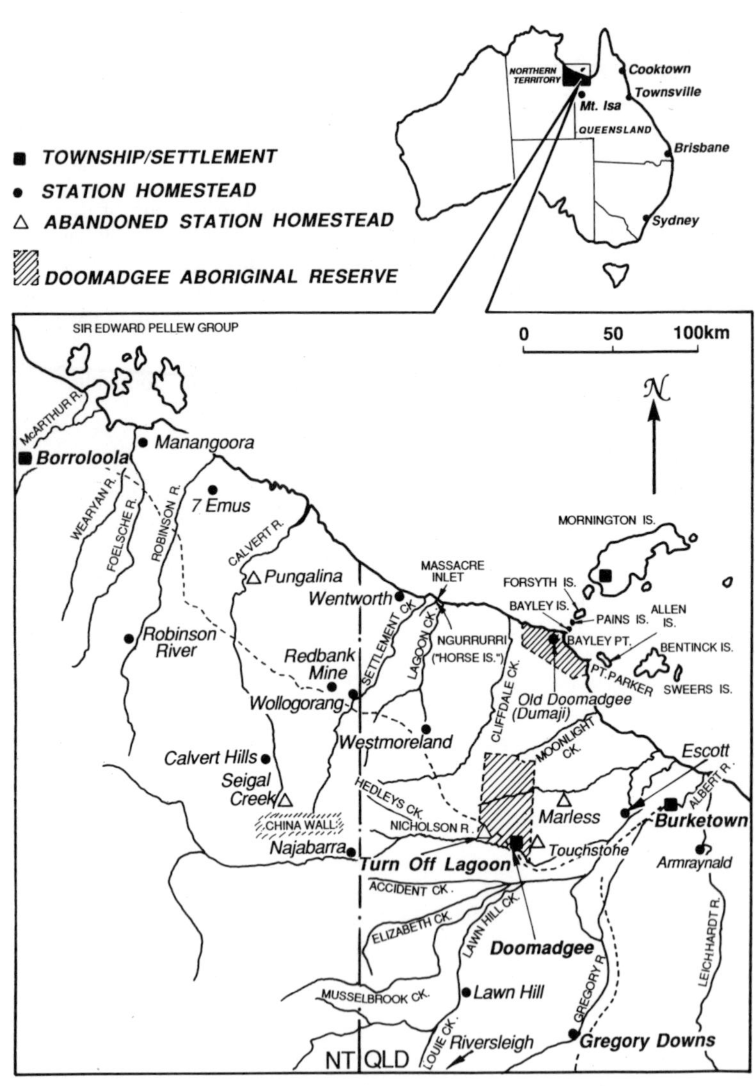

Map 1 Southern Gulf of Carpentaria region, northern Australia

CHAPTER ONE

Doomadgee: the politics of colonial social relations

By the time I reached Doomadgee on my first visit in May 1978, I had recorded conflicting fragments of folk knowledge about the place and its people. In Mt Isa, one view described the Aboriginal residents of Doomadgee as largely 'having no minds of their own', as 'like children to a father', the father figure being the long-serving manager of the settlement. This perspective was put to me by a White lawyer who had worked with the Aboriginal Legal Service, by several Aboriginal people who were not from Doomadgee, and by an Aboriginal man who had left there some years previously. The general feeling among these people was that Doomadgee Aborigines lacked a full awareness of their own oppression, and that both political motivation and sophistication were lacking in their response to their circumstances.

Yet I was also informed by the representative member of the National Aboriginal Conference (a now defunct commonwealth government advisory organisation) that there was some interest in 'land rights' at Doomadgee, and in teaching 'culture' to the children. Several Aboriginal people in Mt Isa told me that some of the older Doomadgee residents were very knowledgeable about the history of a wide region, including the settlement. One woman of Aboriginal/European descent asked me to find out from certain old people what I could of her mother's mother's connections to kin and country. Her grandmother had looked after her on a mainland cattle station until 1929, when as a child of nine years she was taken by the authorities, with her siblings, to Mornington Island. This woman regarded certain of the older residents at Doomadgee as custodians of valuable historical information about her family. Another Aboriginal man, who was originally from Mornington Island, explained that many people at Doomadgee had much knowledge of the country;

his work as a government ranger involved recording archaeological sites in the Doomadgee area. These views countered the image of Doomadgee people as childlike inmates of an authoritarian institution.

I had also gleaned some information about the place from an earlier interview with a recently retired long-serving member of the Doomadgee staff. She had talked mostly about routine aspects of the administration. Although she indicated that some of the old men knew 'stories' relevant to 'initiation', she stressed that Doomadgee Aborigines wished to forget about 'spirit worship and devil worship' practices. Yet, by her own account, the strength of their alleged convictions in this respect remained unclear, for she made the point that anthropologists were dangerous because their questions stirred up the old people's thoughts about the 'old ways', and thereby made them sad. Another (younger) staff member, who had spent only a comparatively short time at Doomadgee, had complained of authoritarianism on the part of senior members of the administration, and (although she eventually changed her mind) she said in early 1978 that she would not return to work 'under the present administration'. Hence, on my first visit, I did not expect uniformity of views among the non-Aboriginal staff.

Little research had been done at Doomadgee. One researcher carried out substantial linguistic fieldwork there in 1970, mostly consisting of intensive work with a few of the remaining fluent speakers of one of the Aboriginal languages spoken in the settlement. In her view the mission 'stepped on the people very hard and [beat] out a lot of their spirit and self-respect . . . it's preposterous what's happened in the past' (S. Keen, personal communication 4/4/1978). Another colleague, who had spent a brief period conducting anthropological research at Doomadgee in the early 1970s, also mentioned the authoritarian nature of the administration, although he was not prepared to elaborate and thereby disclose what he regarded as information obtained in confidence. Nor was he inclined to portray the Brethren Mission administration solely in negative terms (M. Calley, personal communication 1978).

Thus, my expectations on entering Doomadgee were of a relatively isolated and socially closed authoritarian mission settlement. In addition to my broad concern to understand the nature of social life there, I was employed to research Aboriginal relationships to land, and to document 'sites of significance' in terms of Aboriginal traditions. How much 'traditional' knowledge would be held, perhaps having survived zealous missionary opposition over decades? Was the idea of serious research on traditional knowledge of the landscape really as futile as had been implied by a young (non-Aboriginal) DAIA clerk in Mt Isa, who sarcastically identified one of the centrally located bars in town (the 'Snake Pit' in local parlance), as an 'Aboriginal site'?

My first encounters with Doomadgee people, in Mt Isa and on the drive northwards, had provided little evidence to counter this young man's portrayal of Aborigines in the region as hopeless drunks. I met drunk people from Doomadgee at the Gregory Downs and Burketown hotels. And as I finally slowed the vehicle to a stop at the crossing of the Nicholson River just east of the settlement, a very inebriated middle-aged man climbed up on to the running board and tried to hold a disjointed conversation, while attempting to focus his gaze on my face by peering in the open side window. After a short time, aware that I was trying to drive off, one of the women with him (also very drunk) sought to persuade him to get down, using vigorous verbal abuse. When words failed she punched him, and I drove off leaving the pair struggling by the side of the road. The approving reports several individuals had given me about Doomadgee being something of a Christian haven away from the damage caused by over-consumption of alcohol had apparently portrayed only part of the reality.

In hindsight, my first period of fieldwork (six and a half weeks) was full of extremely intensive experiences, during which the question with which this volume is primarily concerned gradually coalesced in my mind. Field notes and diary entries indicate my constant awareness of the politics of social life. Things were far from completely serene, stable or cooperative. Public drunkenness like that I had encountered at the river crossing on the first day, with its associated loud verbal abuse, violence and intervention by the local Aboriginal police, was one of the obvious indicators of a lack of social harmony. It also indicated a conflict over definitions of appropriate public behaviour. Like the routine gambling activities held 'down the river', public drunkenness contradicted local views (held by some Aboriginal residents, as well as all non-Aboriginal staff) about acceptable Christian behaviour. And this was just one aspect of a broadly contested, complex series of views apparently held about how people should behave and what they should think. From the very early stages of my fieldwork, the prevailing social order appeared to be the result of a pragmatic consensus that was routinely contested in social action, though certainly not always as openly as in the case of public drunkenness.

As I experienced settlement life, I became aware of a complex interplay between different aspects of social action among Aboriginal residents, which appeared variously to constitute both accommodation and resistance to the wider society within which they were encapsulated. In one sense, their situation was clear. Aborigines' material circumstances were much poorer than all but the most destitute of non-Aboriginal Australians. Their residences were inferior to those of the White staff, who lived in a separate part of the settlement, where essential services such as the store, school and hospital were also located. The routine material conditions of physical existence indicated an entrenched Aboriginal passive dependency on the remote industrial economy of modern Australia. For while there were some hunting, fishing and gathering activities, mostly on weekends, Aboriginal residents were clearly dependent on the regular arrival of essential food commodities which were purchased from the store. Many were also dependent on social security benefits for the means to purchase these commodities.

Moreover, people were not seeking to purchase only essential goods. In some respects there was an evident accommodation to a broadly commodity-centred lifestyle. Some non-essential goods were highly desired. My diary records that one of my strongest impressions at the end of the first day was that many motor vehicles (some very dilapidated) were regularly and speedily driven around the settlement by young men; and it did not take long to realise just how widespread was the desire for access to a vehicle. Indeed, I soon learned that even the children's play incorporated the 'motor car' as an important focus of settlement life. They used wire and old tin cans to make what they called 'tin trucks', and spent much time vigorously pushing these around in the red dust, emulating the sounds of roaring engines and changing gears as they changed direction and speed.

However, if there was accommodation to a commodity-centred lifestyle, people were not complacent about their capacity to obtain desired items. There were complaints about what Aboriginal residents saw as their material poverty, especially in comparison to the perceived material wealth of the local White staff. A particularly forceful complaint concerned the lack of hot water facilities in the Aboriginal houses, in contrast to the staff homes. The most common expression of dissatisfaction was that the settlement store would not sell tobacco (because of the religious convictions of the local mission staff). On most days I would hear people saying 'we buggered for smoke', as they commented on their lack of tobacco and sought to borrow the makings for a cigarette. Other complaint was directed against White governmental authorities; indeed, the most bitterly contentious issue concerning material interests was that Aboriginal employees on the settlement were not paid award wages.

However, not all Aboriginal residents were entirely sympathetic to these sentiments of complaint. The Christians largely supported the mission decision not to sell tobacco. And while all of those who held jobs thought they should receive award wages, some employed Aboriginal people spoke disdainfully of others' lack of commitment to a regular working lifestyle. In the words of an Aboriginal policeman at that time, and his wife: 'The people can get jobs if they try'. Some of the older people were more likely to complain about the behaviour of the 'young generation' than about whether they had hot water taps, a refrigerator or a washing machine; and many were more likely to express affection for various White staff, and gratitude for the way they had been 'looked after' by the mission over the years, than to complain about the wage rates of Aboriginal workers. In fact, old men who had worked for long periods in the pastoral industry regarded most young people as comparatively poor workers; the young men were said to be 'always chasin grog' or 'thinkin about that dress [i.e. young women]'. The Aboriginal population was certainly not united in an articulated opposition to the local missionary administration or the broader Australian society.

My enquiries concerning the complexities of settlement politics soon became focused on the issue of 'culture', for not only did both Aboriginal and White residents learn quickly of my interest in this subject, but also, I found that this had been a contentious public issue for some time prior to my arrival. About two weeks earlier, the school had begun a 'culture program', to teach what both Aborigines and Whites were calling 'culture' to the children. A small number of residents had successfully sought funding from the Aboriginal Arts Board (a commonwealth government agency) to form what they termed a 'culture company'. At least, the idea of a 'company' had apparently arisen because only a legally incorporated organisation could receive the available funds and make sure that control over this money remained in the hands of the group of Aboriginal people who had held the initial discussions with the Arts Board. I was informed that this was a stated objective of both the Aboriginal group and the Arts Board itself. However, the White teachers had instead instituted a 'culture committee', which was expected to advise the school staff about what should be taught. The committee was made up of the older Aboriginal residents who were employed casually to teach 'culture' in school hours. The school principal reported that he had pointed out (to the Arts Board, as well as to the members of the proposed 'culture company') that without assistance from White bookkeepers, the company would be unable to organise such administrative procedures as the purchase of equipment and payment of wages. He thereby implied that such assistance would not be forthcoming for a legally incorporated Aboriginal body that was to be formally independent, not only of the school administrative structure, but of the Aboriginal council as well.

Other missionary staff appeared unhappy with any kind of 'culture program', whether controlled by the teachers or not. While the school principal said that his aim was to show the children that their people once had a viable Aboriginal culture, some of the non-teaching staff asserted that it was not possible to separate the acceptable aspects of 'culture' from the many parts that are unacceptable from a Christian Brethren viewpoint. The principal's claim that 'sinister' beliefs and practices would be excluded from the 'culture syllabus' was rejected as naive by some of the non-teaching staff. It was said that there was no 'scriptural authority' for the 'separation' of cultures which was implicit in such teaching of Aboriginal 'culture'; e.g. the manager's wife stated that: 'We'll all be together in heaven so why separate now?'. The manager felt that the 'culture program' would lead to 'racism', presumably because it would emphasise differences between Aboriginal and non-Aboriginal people. Furthermore, his view was that the 'old ways' were gone, and the strength of his belief was made clear to me on my first day at the settlement, when four Aboriginal councillors met me in the manager's office to discuss my plans to carry out research at Doomadgee. In response to my statement of interest in traditional culture and knowledge of country, the manager incredulously posed a question-statement to the council chairman: 'You didn't have any of that culture, did you [X]?'. He thereby elicited agreement from the chairman with this proposition, and with the fact that 'Aboriginal culture' was now simply part of 'history', though I noted that the other councillors appeared non-committal about this point.

It was soon clear that Aboriginal opinion on these issues varied. For example, the 'culture teachers' seemed happy enough with the school 'culture program', though there was complaint that the wages were not high enough, and that the children were 'too stupid' to learn; several people described the pupils as 'lost, poor things' and 'spoiled by White man'. Some older residents expressed the view that not only should 'culture' be taught to the children, but also that 'Blackfella law' should be revived and boys should once again be initiated at Doomadgee. I learned that for many years only a small number of youths with ties to kin and country to the west had continued to be sent to Borroloola to be initiated. The viewpoint arguing for re-establishment of initiation ceremonies at Doomadgee was opposed quite vehemently by a committed Christian Aboriginal minority, as well as by all the White staff. Indeed, in June 1978, a group of Christian Aboriginal councillors notified those planning an initiation ceremony that they were not allowed to hold such activities anywhere on the Doomadgee Reserve. This occurred the morning after a 'practice' session of dancing and singing had been held in preparation for the planned ceremony. On that morning, the councillors met with the manager and, after communicating their decision to the main 'law man' organising the ceremony, came to my camp to warn me not to 'encourage' people in these activities. Among their arguments were the propositions that the majority of Aboriginal residents did not want such ceremonies to occur at Doomadgee, that the ceremonies were based on fear, and that people were typically coerced into participating.

This event, which occurred just prior to the end of my first fieldwork period, highlighted the problem of accommodation and resistance in Aboriginal social action. The struggle over definitions of appropriate worldview and associated practices appeared to be a fundamental aspect of settlement life. Certain staff and Aboriginal people held formal offices that allowed them to wield legally sanctioned power. Moreover, the brief accounts of the settlement's history I had obtained indicated that the threat and employment of coercive force had played a critical role in reproducing the historical domination of Aboriginal society. Several people had pointed out the heavy mesh covering the windows in the old boys' dormitory building where, it was said, the inmates were once locked up every night. Yet Aboriginal compliance in 1978 could not be characterised solely in terms of a passive response to the formal state-sponsored power of the staff. There were ways in which some Aboriginal people appeared actively to attribute legitimacy to various features of the system of power relations in which they were enmeshed. It was not so much that certain individuals supported the missionary administration or Queensland government policies in any complete fashion; rather, a wide range of Aboriginal residents expressed, in both their reflective and unelicited discourse, an ambiguous agreement with key aspects of White ideology. Some tenets of Christianity were central to this ideology, with even individuals who stated commitment to 'Blackfella law' also expressing belief in aspects of Christian doctrine. Other ideas that were apparently selectively embraced by a small number of people concerned acceptance of a commodity-centred and employment-centred set of economic aspirations, and of the necessity for continued non-Aboriginal tutelage, if not control, in the administration of the settlement.

On the other hand, actual social relations between Aboriginal and White residents were typically strained, with little apparent intimacy and a great deal of evident social distance. In their everyday domestic life, Aboriginal people largely withdrew from close relationships with White staff. It was soon clear to me that this social separation was a very routine aspect of settlement life, and not something that either Aborigines or Whites commonly remarked upon in unelicited discourse. However, this fundamental social distance prompted an important theoretical question. Might it not be regarded analytically as a form of Aboriginal resistance against administrative intrusiveness, even though it did not evoke clear statements of moral disapproval as did such activities as public drunkenness, gambling and attempts at carrying out traditional ritual practices?

Following an initial, intense period of fieldwork, the complex question of understanding the processes of coercion, resistance and accommodation in settlement power relations became a major focus of my research at Doomadgee. The early characterisations I had encountered, of Aboriginal residents as completely powerless and compliant, had proved to be simplistic and naive. Nevertheless, the issue of ideological incorporation of Aboriginal thinking was to become an important area of investigation. The study of social life at Doomadgee thus led me to consider theories of power relations which encompass the nature of both structural and ideological constraints on subordinate individuals and groups.

The problem of coercion and consent

Central to this problem has been the long-debated relationship between voluntarism and determinism. In discussing the concept of power, Lukes (1977: 3) presents this issue in its most general and simple form: to what extent and in what ways are social actors constrained to think and act in the ways they do? The 'voluntarist' or 'anti-structural' view is that the constraints facing choice-making agents are minimal, always external to the agent, and centred upon action as opposed to thought or desire (p. 15). The opposing 'structuralist' (and, as Lukes presents it, Marxist) position emphasises the way structural constraints determine individuals' actions and thoughts. In its most extreme version, this view maintains that the subjectivity or agency of individuals is not the critical factor in explaining social life; what is critical is the way in which individuals are the effects, or 'bearers' of an ensemble of structures (pp. 15–8). With Lukes (p. 29), we can reject both these extreme positions, and recognise that:

> social life can only properly be understood as a dialectic of power and structure, a web of possibilities for agents, whose nature is both active and structured, to make choices and pursue strategies within given limits, which in consequence expand and contract over time.

However, the problem remains of understanding how this dialectic operates between structural constraint and individual capacity for social action.

The Weberian tradition provides a partial answer. Weber deals with 'the authoritarian power of command', by which 'the manifested will' of 'the rulers' influences the conduct of 'the ruled' (Weber 1968 III: 946). Thus domination by virtue of structural authority results in obedience to those whose bureaucratic office or social position requires it. Such powers of command typically exist 'by virtue of law' and are implemented through an administrative apparatus (Weber

1968 III: 948). The importance of structural authority, imposed by state law and consequent administrative practices, operating as a coercive force in the lives of such colonised peoples as Aborigines at Doomadgee, was clear from my earliest fieldwork. Also apposite is Weber's conceptualisation of those aspects of domination that are maintained through 'economic power'. For in the context of the colonisation process, Aboriginal people develop a 'constellation of [material] interests' (Weber 1968 III: 941ff), which typically engenders their dependency on highly regulated access to commodities.

Yet the Weberian discussion of domination does not provide an adequate sociology of compliance. Weber stresses that subordinate people attribute legitimacy to the system of authority relations within which they are situated (1968 III: 952–54). He assumes that people in a position of power or advantage need to justify the legitimacy of their dominance, and hence he gives most attention to the justificatory claims emanating from those 'on high' (Parkin 1982: 77–8). But the question of bestowal of legitimacy 'from below' is not treated fully. Indeed Parkin (1982: 74) describes the Weberian view as being that obedience is given willingly through a positive commitment on the part of the subordinate to the authority they obey. To be fair, if Weber is to be interpreted as stressing voluntarism among the subordinate, his writings also indicate the view that voluntary compliance is derived from people having an 'interest' in obedience that may stem from 'the most diverse motives': '. . . all the way from simple habituation to the most purely rational calculation of advantage' (1968 I: 212). Nevertheless, Parkin's (1982: 76) complaint must be considered seriously:

> Weber makes no distinction between normative compliance that springs from voluntary commitment and that which is grounded in a long term strategy for survival. The questions raised by Marx and his followers concerning the relationship between coercion and compliance are closed off by Weber's approach to the matter. This approach has no place for notions like 'hegemony'.

The concept of hegemony returns us to Lukes' point about the importance of recognising constraints that can structure individuals' thoughts and desires as well as their abilities to carry out actions. Certain Marxist writings, influenced by Gramsci's notion of hegemony, lead us away from considering power relations solely in terms of legally-based structural authority and market-based economic power. Gramsci drew attention to the aspects of class rule in capitalist society that are non-coercive, in that they rest on consent engendered from subordinate groups (Hall *et al* 1977: 51). This occurs within 'civil society': the realm of day-to-day life experience, of moral values and customs, which is analytically separable from both the economic structure and the state, while being constrained by both economic and political structures. As Hoffman (1984) has put it, the 'Gramscian challenge' to structural Marxism has been to redress its emphasis on the coercive nature of politics, by seeking adequate analysis of the problem of consent.

In much writing on this subject, to discuss 'consent' is to focus on the extent to which subordinate consciousness is constrained by dominant ideology. In a major critique of the 'dominant ideology thesis' (Abercrombie *et al* 1980: 29), this notion is presented as over-emphasising the causal efficacy of influential ideas (or the 'super-structure') and under-emphasising the role of economic constraint in the maintenance of power relations. Thus, by this view, we should be careful in a study of colonial social relations not to over-emphasise the constraints on Aboriginal thinking that derive from key ideas imposed by the colonisers. At least, we should not stress this aspect of colonialism without addressing sufficiently the role of economic power.

Nevertheless, contrary to what has been suggested (Abercrombie *et al* 1980: 8), the importance of dominant ideology can be recognised without implying that there can be no resilient subordinate culture, or that the intellectual universe of subordinate groups becomes identical to that of ruling groups. As Rootes (1981: 440) has argued, this attack on the concept of dominant ideology has been too fixed on the notion of ideology as a systematic and coherently articulated body of ideas. He suggests (p. 440) that another level of ideology is 'directly relevant to practice, directly influenced by experience, and unreflectively uttered as "common-sense" '.

Indeed, the concept of hegemony has been developed in certain Marxist writings beyond the notion of dominant ideology as simply an imposed set of ideas. Consider Williams' discussion of the concept's relevance for literary analysis: 'What is decisive is not only the conscious system of ideas and beliefs, but the whole lived social process as practically organized by specific and dominant meanings and values' (Williams 1977: 109). Williams' concept of hegemony stresses processes of 'lived' dominance and subordination whereby, apart from the formally coercive power of economic and political structures, it is broader cultural meanings and values that powerfully constrain individuals' thinking and behaviour.

Fine-grained study of the 'cultural' life of small populations, including ethnographic description and analysis of emic meanings expressed as 'common sense', has long been the hallmark of anthropology. In recent theorising there has been a noticeable focus on the importance of routine 'practices' for the understanding of relations of domination. In her overview of anthropological theory during the past few decades, Ortner (1984: 148) notes that the stress has recently been on how 'to explain the relationship(s) that obtain between human action . . . and some global entity which we may call "the system" '. To use the terminology of one of the key writers in this area (Bourdieu 1977), 'the link between the structuring structures within which the agents practise and the individuated expression of interests is the "habitus" ' (Miller and Branson 1987: 216–7). Bourdieu (1972: 77) defines 'habitus' as the 'systems of durable, transposable *dispositions*' that generate practices; the concept of habitus designates a habitual set of predispositions, tendencies, propensities and inclinations for individuals to think and behave in certain ways (Bourdieu 1977: 214, fn 1). And apart from those aspects of practice that social actors consciously intend, Bourdieu also pays close attention to routinised social action, the consequences of which commonly escape those practising it repetitively. What is important for our analysis is that in continually engaging in these practices, people re-endorse in the world of public observation and discourse the pattern of power relations within which they are embedded (Ortner 1984: 154; Miller and Branson 1987: 219).

However, this literature also recognises resistance within the pattern of constraint. Hegemony is never total, and always more fragile than it appears (Ortner 1984: 154). The system of hegemonic domination has to be constantly 'renewed, recreated, defended, and modified', in the face of continual resistance, which may be conceived as patterns of 'counter-hegemonic' practices (Williams 1977: 112–3). In this way, the Gramscian view of society as an arena of incessant conflict whereby a consensus is imposed but also resisted has encouraged the importance of recognising alternate worldviews among the subordinate. Together with routine practices, such worldviews entail common sense meanings and values that require attention in assessing processes of coercion, resistance and consent in specific ethnographic settings.

The material presented in this study makes clear the coercive authority of the state, through its local agents (variously police and missionaries), in the domination of Aboriginal society. Similarly, the history of domination imposed via Aborigines' economic dependence will become evident. Yet I am also concerned with the nature of resistance to colonial domination at Doomadgee, within the broader pattern of structural coercion and compliance. Assessing resistance has meant careful analysis of a colonial struggle which has taken place in the intellectual arena, as well as in the world of concrete material interests. This has entailed consideration of the problematic relationship between resistance and accommodation in the context of colonial social relations.

Resistance and accommodation in colonial social relations

Cowlishaw (1988) recently raised the issue of resistance in a study of Aboriginal/White relations in rural New South Wales. In considering the history of these relations, she asks (p. 34) whether resistance might refer to all the aspects of Aboriginal behaviour that 'created problems' for settlers, or more specifically to reluctance to change or slowness to adapt. Or should it be conceived only in terms of deliberate attempts to stop invasion and refusal to concede defeat? Cowlishaw (p. 34) concludes that:

> Even though defeated, surely it is possible to resist complete domination? It seems to me that the notion of resistance need not depend on conscious planned campaigns, but simply on denial of cooperation. If the settlers were not being accommodated, they were being resisted, regardless of motive.

However, for this line of thinking to be adequate, the question must be pushed further, to ask what constitutes accommodation.

With reference to his important work on Black American slavery, Genovese (1975: 78) writes of a complementary and organic connection between resistance and accommodation; as he comments, there can be no 'superficial bifurcation of resistance and accommodation'. For we have a 'continuum of resistance in accommodation and accommodation in resistance' (1974: 598). Hence:

> The slaves' response to paternalism and their imaginative creation of a partially autonomous religion provided a record of simultaneous accommodation and resistance to slavery. (1974: 597)

Or as Sider (1987: 3) puts it in his historical study of American Indian-White relations, 'resistance can occur simultaneously with collusion'. In this case, the author writes of new forms of Indian social organisation emerging and flourishing (p. 15), while in that process becoming permeated with 'borrowed symbols of domination and of being dominated' (p. 19). Sider (pp. 17–8) reflects on a 'partial autonomy' achieved by American native peoples, within 'a semi-autonomous field of strategy and maneuver, resistance and collusion' (p. 15).

If resistance among the subordinate is conceived in the terms proposed in Scott's (1986) work on Malaysian peasants, the goal is not to overthrow or transform a system of domination, but to survive within it. Thus, everyday forms of resistance or 'truly durable weapons of the weak' (p. 31), including such unorganised action by individuals or groups as passive non-compliance, feigned ignorance, slander and withdrawal of deference, also represent accommodation in that they only 'nibble away' at the system of dominance and typically do not result directly in substantial social change. Scott (1986: 22–6) does not argue that resistance can be defined with reference to its consequences alone; intentions are built into his definition of resistance. However, he points out that when examining lower-class peasants' intentions to advance their interests or mitigate or deny the claims of the superordinate, we must recognise the element of short-term self-interest typically entailed within such intentions. Moreover, we cannot expect intentions to resist (i.e. typically to survive and persist) necessarily to be revealed articulately:

> Their intentions may be so embedded in the peasant subculture and in the routine, taken-for-granted struggle for subsistence as to remain inarticulate. The fish do not talk about the water. (Scott 1987: 452)

Neither Malaysian peasants nor Black American slaves, nor for that matter colonised American Indians, present a case directly parallel to the situation of Australia's colonised Aboriginal minority. However, similar issues have been raised in several approaches to Australian material. In his study of the Torres Strait Islanders (of Melanesian cultural background, but encapsulated within Australian society in the same way as Aborigines) Beckett (1987: 11) identifies the Islanders' 'custom' as having 'fortified their cultural and political unity'. The parallels he draws are with the way such peoples as highlanders of Papua New Guinea and New World slaves have historically had the capacity to reserve 'an essential part of themselves outside the relations of production and consumption, which constituted the dominant order, and to defend this domain against encroachment' (1987: 10). In part, this defence is regarded by Beckett as against hegemonic control over the common-sense meanings and routine activities of everyday life. Thus, the indigenous system takes on an oppositional character by which people attempt to exert some control over their lives, even if it is only to choose what they have to do anyway (p. 9).

Yet the Islanders' custom results from a colonial history stretching back, in the case of some islands, to the 1840s (p. 32). And this is a case of successful indoctrination by missionaries and government teachers, who inculcated the ideals of spiritual and material progress to the extent that Islanders came to celebrate the anniversary of the coming of the London Missionary Society as the time of the bringing of the light (the Gospel) that ended the darkness (the pre-Christian situation of the Islanders). They regarded themselves as forever indebted to White people for this 'gift beyond price' (p. 94). From the 1930s, local courts made up of Islanders upheld a code of by-laws derived mainly from the teachings of the missionaries, which included such offences as fornication, adultery, message carrying and domestic squabbling (p. 56). During the same period, Islanders jealously fought over the privileges of cleaning and decorating the church, and organising celebrations (p. 57). Beckett says that the achievement of the London Missionary Society was to persuade the Islanders to accept not just the Gospel but the whole colonial experience. He refers to Williams' (1977: 108–14) notion of 'lived dominance' in characterising the Islanders' accommodation to colonialism:

> As Islanders came to live, and, even more, to think with their work ethic, their loyalty [to both the British monarchy and the Australian nation] and their Christianity, colonial culture became hegemonic, 'a lived dominance' . . . (Beckett 1987: 91–2).

At the same time, through ongoing social interaction among Islanders, and in the practice of a creatively constructed Island 'custom', the hegemonic impact of colonial ideology was dulled, and to this extent, resisted (pp. 92–3).

Similar themes were broached in Morris's recent work (1988) on resistance to assimilation among Aboriginal people in the Macleay Valley in New South Wales, during an era (1936–68) when the Aborigines were subjected to much greater institutionalisation than had previously been the case. This historical work deals with a situation parallel in certain respects to Doomadgee. The setting of Morris's study is a 'manager-supervised institution, which was to organise the inculcation of Aborigines with what were regarded as the superior values of the dominant society' (1988: 33). While the White manager and matron were empowered by law to control many aspects of Aborigines' behaviour, Morris focuses particularly on the 'pedagogic or positive aspect of power' (p. 41) by which Aborigines' thinking was to be re-formed so that they were assimilated into White society.

Morris (p. 33–4) identifies 'the emergence of subtle, non-violent forms of resistance' that were 'inscribed at the level of culture', and sought to 'impose limitations on a system of power in which those in authority appear to exercise unlimited control'. Thus, he writes (p. 44 ff.) of the 'emergence of a culture of resistance'. This 'culture' consisted of an emphasis on the distinction between 'blackfella's way' and 'whitefella's way', by reference to knowledge of discontinued male initiation ceremonies and distinctive 'blackfella' and 'whitefella' styles of music and dancing. More generally, the culture of resistance involved 'the remaking of the cultural distance from European society' (p. 47); his point is seemingly that the terms in which Aboriginal people understood this distance constituted part of a culture of resistance.

Morris regards the Aboriginal stations as total institutions (Goffman 1961) and reflects on how Aboriginal 'inmates' would create 'free space', particularly through illegal drinking and gambling, which both subverted the manager's authority and defied what Aboriginal people were supposed to become in terms of the White charter of assimilation (p. 50). Drinking, gambling, excess indulgence and wastefulness thus 'acted as effective statements of opposition to those European values which the Welfare Board sought to cultivate' (pp. 51–2). Aboriginal residents of the stations would also covertly collect information about the characters of managers and matrons, and limit the Whites' access to information about themselves and other Aborigines. This behaviour, he says, 'served a strategic, and hence political, function' (p. 50); furthermore, it generated 'an oppositional sense of identity' (p. 49).

Morris (p. 53) also stresses the importance of not avoiding the problem of hegemonic domination. However, his account of the accommodatory elements in station culture is relatively undeveloped. Aboriginal people (particularly the young) did come to be ashamed of the 'old blackfella ways', such as public use of an Aboriginal language, eating bush foods or dancing in the 'Koori way' (i.e. according to Aboriginal neo-traditional style). As Morris (p. 59) puts it, White racism and paternalism thereby had the hegemonic effect of undermining the Aboriginal sense of worth. However, the concept of 'shame' was also used to direct hostility towards those Aboriginal people who attempted to embrace European values. It was used as a levelling device that constrained anybody who might seek to accumulate material wealth: individuals would be shamed into giving up such aspirations. Morris's study thus tells us much more about what he construes as resistance than it does about what might have been consent or accommodation among the Aboriginal station residents of New South Wales.

Coercion, resistance and accommodation at Doomadgee

This study of Doomadgee describes and analyses many aspects of Aboriginal social action that may well best be understood as resistance, though always within a broader set of dominant colonial political and economic structures. Some chapters deal particularly with Aboriginal strategies to survive and persist, and with Aboriginal refusal to embrace various values and practices promulgated by the White staff and more generally by White Australian society. However, other chapters depict considerable attribution of legitimacy to the White system of law and authority, at least on the part of some Aboriginal residents.

I am mindful of Scott's cautionary comment in his discussion of everyday forms of peasant resistance. Not everything that subordinate people do can be understood as resistance. Much of it is best regarded as compliance, or at least, as Genovese has put it, as resistance within accommodation. To the extent that beliefs, values and practices among some Aboriginal people can be construed as operating against broad Aboriginal interests, they may be regarded as indicating consent among the subordinate, that is, hegemonic control. Thus, while focused on the issue of resistance, my study also deals with the complex question of how much ideological containment has been achieved at Doomadgee. This treatment of resistance and accommodation is set within an investigation of the practical constraints deriving from the political, legal and economic structures of Australian colonialism.

CHAPTER TWO

'Wild Time': a history of coercion and resistance

My aim here is to discuss the historical development of Aboriginal/White relations during the first forty or so years of colonial impact. Aboriginal oral history designates 'Wild Time' as the beginning of the colonial encounter. Prior to (but also coterminous with) Wild Time there was '*Wanggala* Time' or 'Dreamtime'. This latter concept entails the earliest of all known time, the creative period when the major features of the physical and social universe were shaped. When interpreting local conceptions of *Wanggala* Time, it is difficult to separate the temporal dimensions of the period from the notion of imperatives still stemming from it. The spiritual imperatives understood to derive from the concept of '*Wanggala*' are conceived as continuing beyond the creative era (cf. Stanner 1965a). However, accounts (from older people particularly) indicate that it is the disruption of social and spiritual order which occurred during colonisation that marks the end of *Wanggala* Time.

Those older people oriented towards what is known as 'Blackfella law' (the inherited body of traditional knowledge) are perceived to be closest to *Wanggala* Time. Occasionally, very old individuals who are known to have learned little about White Australian society (e.g. who speak little English) may be referred to as 'belonging' to *Wanggala*. References to *Wanggala* Time often emphasise the relative strength of 'law' then, as compared with the present. When given the opportunity to record on tape a statement about regional Aboriginal history, two older men explained how people 'sat down with' (i.e. obeyed the requirements of) *Wanggala* for a long time, and that only for 'lately generations' is '*Wanggala* gone now'. This is because the young generation is 'mad' (*murdu*) — '*migu yaji guwarda*' or 'nothing ear', they cannot 'hear'; which is to say that they cannot listen to or understand proper custom and 'law' (T77). In the view of these old people, imperatives still stem from *Wanggala* Time, but no longer properly control Aboriginal society. Thus, while the notion of *Wanggala* encompasses all chronological stages of the rich oral history held among Aboriginal people, *Wanggala* Time is recognised as having been severely displaced through the colonial experience.

Violence on the frontier

In Aboriginal discourse, the phrase 'Wild Time' describes the period from before White incursions through subsequent phases of interaction with Whites, until people were 'quietened down'. The period is also referred to as 'early day' or 'young day'. Extensive violence in the bush is the focus of the discourse about Wild Time. Aborigines of the time are known as the 'old people', who were 'wild' in that they 'belonged to bush' and did not know about or understand White people, their material goods or their customs. The bush people are recognised as having become 'quiet' with their semi-sedentary location at camps near cattle stations and police depots. When this happened varied greatly throughout the southern Gulf region. May (1983: 65) notes remote Gulf Country squatters (in the Burketown area) using local Aboriginal labour from as early as 1867, while a policeman on patrol as recently as 1944 (Bowie 28.4.1944: 3) reports at Redbank Creek (in the Northern Territory not far from the Queensland border) a 'large tribe' of about eighty Aborigines 'practically in their native state'.

The policeman probably encountered people who in fact had considerable contact with surrounding cattle stations, but Wild Time did continue into the twentieth century. Early mainland exploration began in 1845, and the first phase of pastoral invasion occurred from 1864, then was abandoned, and re-established from 1874 onwards. With the introduction of the Queensland Mounted Native Police in 1889 and the early infiltration of large numbers of cattle and sheep, violence between Aborigines and Whites continued through the 1890s and into the first decade of this century (Dymock 1982). Wild Time may be viewed as having extended at least up to 1910.[1]

There was reportedly a short period of Aboriginal/White interaction prior to the occurrence of violence on the frontier. The Aboriginal account of the earliest period of contact comes from an old man, told by his father about the first time Aborigines in coastal Yanyula country (see map 2) encountered Whites. They perceived them as their deceased relatives returning from the domain of dead spirits, located in 'the middle of the sea'. The Whites are remembered as coming in boats from the west. The Aborigines cried with sorrow for the Whites, calling out kin terms for father and father's brother;

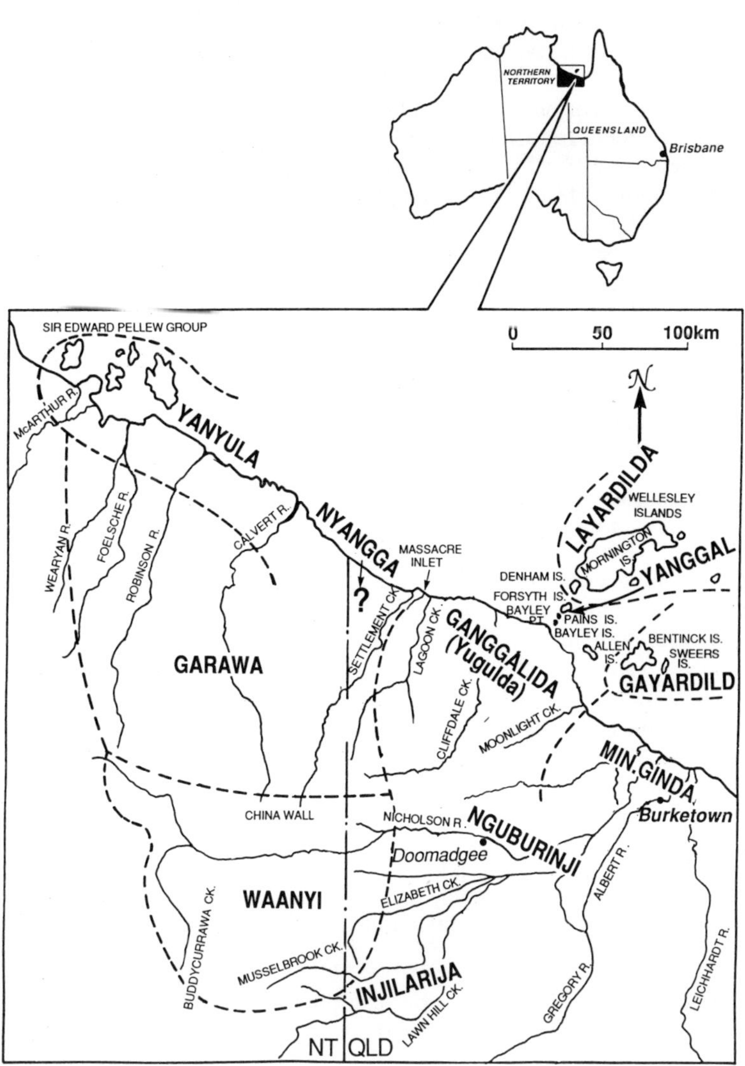

Map 2 Linguistic territories

they fed them with high status marine meat resources (such as dugong and sea turtle), and then 'hand[ed] them over la nother lot tribe', until the Whites returned westwards. They 'helped them all the way' (T73).[2]

It is unclear how long this illusion about Whites was maintained. It has been reported for other parts of the Australian frontier (Reynolds 1981: 25–32), as have initially friendly encounters where Aborigines offered Whites hospitality and assistance (Reynolds 1981: 20–1). For the east of the study region, Dymock (1982: 18) quotes a newspaper source indicating friendly relations between Aborigines and Whites in 1866 and Bauer (1959: 22) comments more generally that by 1862 advancing Whites had found Aborigines numerous but not hostile. The early pastoralists Little and Hetzer (8.6.1868: 1) provide a general comment consistent with these reports:

> Outrages by the blacks are seldom committed in the earliest stage of the settlement of a new district, and this has been particularly the case in this district of Burke, where for the first two years the blacks were quiet enough to make many settlers believe them incapable of violence and to consider them quite harmless.

Conflicts of interest soon arose. Aboriginal oral accounts describe vicious killings of Aboriginal men, women and children by both Whites and members of the Queensland Mounted Native Police Force. Recounted attrocities by native police include smashing children against trees and rocks 'so their brains came out' and, after shootings, cutting up bodies, burning bodies, and hanging up parts of corpses in trees where other Aborigines would later find them. People were often shot at daybreak in camp. One older woman explains certain Aboriginal tactics to avoid police:

> When *Mandagi* [Whites] come this way, y'know look about want to shootim down people, my dad and mum used to go that way, behind their back [to elude them], all the way like that now, my mum used to tell me. (T66)

She also describes the tactic of hiding beneath 'bush passionfruit' vegetation,which afforded good cover. Others make references (e.g. T73) to those who were fleeing from Whites and native police having to leave children hidden amid the foliage of trees in beach areas. People lit fires in some circumstances, to create conditions that would assist them to avoid Whites, although in other circumstances Whites used fires to force Aborigines to leave hiding places. It is also said that certain Aboriginal people would 'sing' the firearms and bullets of Whites so that they would not work properly, then move in to spear their adversaries (T52).

Specific shootings of certain relatives at known places are remembered in oral tradition. However, many old people are not sure of what happened to their grandparents; some simply surmise that they 'must have been shot'. Some assume that certain kinds of country would have provided relatively safe hiding places (e.g. in reference to the 'cave country' in the vicinity of the China Wall escarpment in the upper Nicholson River area: 'I think our people been more safe here hey? — not like on that plain country'). Doomadgee people see themselves as descended from the survivors of very violent times. Those who survived were made 'quiet': they came to an accommodation with White settlement. As one senior woman recalled in reference to coastal Ganggalida country (see map 2):

> them White man now cheeky one where they been killim 'bout people — most they been killim now, old people they been killim, some of them young people they been killim . . . some what sit down with them [i.e. remain under control], they take'em, quieten'em make'em work . . . some woman too. (T78)

In the Aboriginal view, part of the evidence for the deaths of many of the 'old people' is the large amount of country for which 'Blackfella all finish'. While evidence of previous Aboriginal occupation is often clear in the form of stone tools, old campsites, rock art, marked trees, and so on, and the totemic and subsection affiliation of areas may even be known, the earlier land-owning groups are known to have died out.[3]

Cattle spearing by Aborigines is said to have been a major source of conflict, e.g. oral accounts describe how people were pursued for this reason away from Lawn Hill Station up Lawn Hill and Louie Creeks (see map 1). In one incident, two sisters reputedly hid in the water under lily leaves and Pandanus roots and leaves while native police watched the water to shoot at any movements. While hiding they could see the bodies of those who had been shot being burned. At the Wollogorang station house (adjacent to the state border, in the Northern Territory) the Whites are said to have strategically placed a square of string with attached bells on the ground at night; the openings in the hut walls from which rifles would be fired into the square area when the bells rang could still be seen in the early 1980s.

Oral accounts also describe conflict over Aboriginal women. In a well-known event at Wollogorang, a party of Whites (and at least one man of mixed descent) from the station attacked a large group of people holding a major cult ceremony at a site on Settlement Creek some 19 km from the station house. They shot many and abducted a woman, taking her back to the house. Her husband escaped and came to the house that night. There are different accounts of precisely what happened, but the result was that he speared the White abductor in the thigh, and was himself shot by the latter with a shotgun. Both men survived. As the story is described (T73), the woman was able to get away from the station house, but: 'then [later on] . . . when everything been get settle down, two fella been get friend up'. That is, the husband eventually came, with others, to live a semi-sedentary life at Wollogorang, and establish a relationship of some familiarity with the White station lessee. Indeed, he was made 'king' of that station, a status discussed below. Archival records indicate that the attack at the ceremony site and subsequent violence at the homestead occurred in 1897 (Dymock 1982: 81–3).

The huge impact of the frontier Whites on Aboriginal society is clear. Their agents, the native police, were equally violent but much less culturally alien. They were apparently perceived by local Aborigines as culturally familiar in a general way and yet socially distant because they came from 'another country'. Native police were known locally as *yabayirri* 'because they didn't go through bora' (i.e. they were not circumcised). The term, adapted from languages to the south, was used to refer to young uncircumcised men from elsewhere. Oral and written comments indicate that these native police came predominantly from the Cooktown area in northeast Queensland, and that they came into the study region, under the supervision of White police officers, from the south. Dymock (1982: 39–41) documents their first establishment at Turn Off Lagoon (on the Nicholson River some 26 km west of the current Doomadgee site) in 1889, and it is probable that they had a presence in the area until 1897, when the transition to civil police in dealing with Aborigines throughout Queensland occurred (Rowley 1970: 181).

Apart from the native police, the fact that certain other Aboriginal men from outside the region aligned themselves with the forces of White authority is now usually explained in terms of traditional ethnocentrism. 'Yella Paddy', the mixed descent individual who is remembered as accompanying the attacking party from Wollogorang in the incident recounted above, was referred to in several conversations (T66, T68, T73) as: 'real bloodthirsty — cause he wasn't belong to the country'. A non-Aboriginal history of the region (McIntyre 1921: 8) bears out this description, and makes it clear where this individual's allegiance lay: 'yellow Paddy, the half-breed (one of the smartest and whitest hearted black-fellows that ever [etc.])'. While it is only rarely mentioned as a weapon used against Whites, sorcery is said to have been used routinely against Aboriginal people who are now remembered as those 'who been kill their own colour'.

It has been said of some local Aborigines' historical alignment with Whites that the latter 'made them do it'. However, the more general reason mentioned is the same as that given in response to most questions about why any people were violent during this period of history: 'because the country been wild'. Aboriginal discourse seems to acknowledge that the circumstances were out of control rather than to seek to stress the blame that could be attributed to particular individuals. While some local Aboriginal police trackers are remembered as traitorous, others are recalled as having been 'good men' who deliberately missed when shooting at those still in the bush, warned them of encroaching police parties, and generally tried to defuse the situation by 'quietening down' their relatives in the bush without further violence. The descendants of many of these men now live at Doomadgee and elsewhere in the region.

By 1899, police correspondence states that Aborigines in the Turn Off Lagoon district 'are on the best of terms with the . . . constable and Troopers [i.e. Aboriginal police]' (Ordish 19.10.1899), and that patrols keep 'in close touch with the Queensland Blacks, who are always glad to see the Troopers' (Ordish 12.11.1899). This constable also states that the 'shy' Aborigines further up the Nicholson River 'will gradually come in when they find the others of their tribe on such good terms with the Troopers'. In contrast, accounts of violence and tension predominate in Aboriginal discourse about this period though, as evident from the discussion so far about Aborigines operating as the agents of Whites, the violence is not remembered as a simple conflict between Aboriginal and non-Aboriginal peoples. This point emerges more clearly when we consider that Aboriginal consciousness also recounts the occurrence during Wild Time of violence among Aborigines that did not directly involve Whites or Aboriginal police as their agents.

A most dramatic example of such remembered violent events is the killing of a large number of Aboriginal people on Bayley and Pains Islands, offshore from Bayley Point (see map 1). The mass killing was carried out by Yanyula and Garawa people who had travelled there for this purpose from a long way to the west. Written sources indicate that the event occurred early in 1897. A report in *The Queenslander* newspaper (10.4.1897: 774), extracted from the *Burke Telegraph* (a local Burketown newspaper), gives information consistent with oral Aboriginal accounts:

> During the past week (. . . of 19th March) there has been an invasion of Borrolooloo [*sic*] blacks in town, and they bring with them a gory story of having wiped out a tribe on the islands off Point Parker. They certainly look equal to their yarn, being tall and well-built, with blood-thirsty countenances. They are about 300 strong, including their captured gins

> and pickaninnies and are gorgeously dressed for the most part in a spear and a rag. They have also put the fear of death into the town blacks, who are scared out of their wits . . . Some of these newcomers are magnificent specimens of physical strength, over 6 feet in height and broad in proportion.

Oral Aboriginal tradition remembers the incident in the following way (T30 and T85). A man and woman, both belonging to Garawa/ Yanyula country to the west, 'been run away *gunjiwa*' (i.e. had eloped) and had travelled together to the offshore islands. They were living together on Bayley Island when the man was killed while asleep; his throat was cut (and according to some his body was further mutilated) by a certain local man who wanted the woman himself. Others were present and were subsequently regarded by the victim's relatives as condoning, if not assisting in, the killing. The body was buried on Bayley Island by another local man, and the woman subsequently ran away westwards along the coast and informed the people in her and the murdered man's countries of what had happened. Meanwhile the murderer had gone to live at the Aboriginal camp on the fringes of Burketown. A 'really big mob' of Yanyula and Garawa people (confirmed by the figure in the newspaper source, even if it is an over-estimate) then travelled eastwards for revenge, attracting people as they went. Two men led all the way and when they reached the Bayley Point area they established that the target group was on the island(s) offshore. Members of the revenge party eventually surrounded and viciously killed many people (men, women and children) as they slept in camp. It is difficult to estimate the number killed, and while most accounts say this occurred on Bayley Island, there is some oral evidence indicating there were also killings on Pains, and possibly Forsyth, Islands. The revenge party then proceeded to Burketown, finally killed the initial murderer, and eventually returned westwards. At least two women from the coastal and offshore island area went with them.

A second example is of violence within Aboriginal society in which a White man is said to have been used as an agent by Aboriginal protagonists. A White cook shot an Aboriginal man at a mustering camp (at Dawarrayi, known in English as 'Sampling Yard', on Settlement Creek). The incident probably occurred during the second decade of this century. A number of old people say consistently that certain Aboriginal men were the real killers. Using sorcery known as *wabugamba*, they magically speared the man in the forehead, then masked the scar by use of a certain song. This process of sorcery ensures that some time after the oblivious victim 'wakes up', he will be killed by having a fatal wound inflicted in the site of the initial masked wound. As is usually the case with speculations about sorcery, this version of the death is not held unanimously. Several people attach full blame to the White cook, and state bluntly that he 'got off' by arguing self-defence against an attack with a shovel, and by fabricating evidence of the alleged attack. In contrast to the discourse about sorcery, one old lady (when visiting the site of the killing) left no doubt about who she regarded as the murderer of her kinsman: 'mongrel bastard *Wayjbala* [Whitefella] should be finish [deserves to be dead]!'.

There are further indications that, in general, Aboriginal oral history does not posit that the conflict that characterised Wild Time was solely between Aboriginal and non-Aboriginal peoples. There are accounts of incidents where Whites were saved and protected from hostile Aboriginal individuals by other Aboriginal people. McIntyre (1921: 20) refers to the small-scale copper miner at Redbank Mine who would have been killed by 'Murdering Tommy' if not for his 'own boys' (i.e. those Aborigines living and working with him).[4]

Another example concerns 'Bad Peter' who in 1917 murdered the first missionary on Mornington Island, Reverend R. Hall (Bleakley 1918: 5; Memmott 1979: 252). Peter had been working for various White cattlemen on the mainland, though he had initially come from Mornington Island. He left Touchstone Station and travelled to the Dumaji area on the coast (see map 1), where he told the Aboriginal people camped there that he was going to go back and kill the White station man for whom he had been working. Eussen's popular historical report (published in a Brisbane newspaper, the *Sunday Mail Colour*, 6th June 1976: 6) describes Peter as an excellent stockman and in demand as a drover, but simply says he 'went bad'. McIntyre (1921: 93) says no one employed him for long because he was a 'cheeky nigger', and that he had been punished (i.e. beaten) with a pair of hobbles by his previous boss for having 'spoke decidedly out of his turn'. In any case, the Ganggalida people on the coast told him not to kill the White station man. According to an old woman reflecting on this event, Peter was told: 'hey, we can't huntim away that *Mandagi* [Whiteman], he stay here, work here'. They took Peter to a canoe on the beach and told him forcefully to go back to his country on Mornington Island; they told him not to 'sneak back' and watched to make sure he did not. They are now regarded as having 'saved the life' of the White station man because they knew him and some had worked for him, and because 'everything been settle now' (i.e. they felt that the period of earlier violence was over). They regarded Peter as a 'mad fella' (T81). Soon after reaching Mornington Island, Peter murdered Reverend Hall.

Dislocation of local groups, moving and mixing

A major feature of White impact in this part of the southern Gulf Country was the dislocation of local groups from their territories. While people apparently travelled to attend ceremonies in precontact times, and there was travel and trade between the mainland and the Wellesley Islands (as well as the Sir Edward Pellew Islands), the colonial invasion led to an unprecedented and widespread series of movements. This was generally from west to east, but not entirely. Some Waanyi groups moved west from their traditional territories in the vicinity of the upper Nicholson River to stations on the Barkly Tableland and north to other stations. But the majority moved east down the Nicholson River, Elizabeth, Musselbrook and Lawn Hill Creeks to Turn Off Lagoon police depot and various stations. A considerable number of Garawa and Yanyula people moved east, often along the coast, to stations in Queensland, and many Ganggalida people joined those of other language groups in camps on the fringes of Burketown.

Movements through the bush from the Northern Territory east into Queensland appear to have continued into the first and second decades of the twentieth century, and some old Garawa and Yanyula people can describe their journeys, often completed as children accompanying their parents and other kin. One man (T74) described his trip, undertaken soon after he was initiated, in a dugout canoe using calico for a sail. Six canoes, followed by other people walking along the beach, came east at about the same time. Most of the people had travelled from Borroloola, and they stopped at Ngurrurri (an area on the east side of Massacre Inlet) where many Ganggalida, Yanyula and Garawa people had congregated at a 'big camp' and were holding dances. People also travelled inland to stations (particularly Westmoreland), and east as far as Burketown.

The movements of members of five example groups from different linguistic territories are described in Appendix A. The kinds of movements represented by these five cases are now said to have occurred for two main reasons. Firstly, to escape violence: 'give it [Whites] room y'know — all run away'. For Garawa, Waanyi and some Yanyula people, the 'Wild Time stations' in the east appeared to offer physical safety; initially things generally 'quietened down' earlier on the Queensland side of the border, although violent disputes over cattle continued to occur. The second main reason was the attraction of certain material commodities, particularly food and tobacco. With sentiments of ironic and sad humour, people listen to the stories of old people about how Aborigines at various places initially did not know the uses of various goods: they feared foods were poisons and threw them away, thought flour was body paint and then tried to cook it dry on the coals of a fire. They are now said to have been 'myall' and 'wild'. However, they soon acquired a desire for certain items: iron was obviously useful for various purposes, but tobacco apparently became essential to people's lives (cf. Stanner's [1979: 47] comment for the Daly River area). Some occasional exchange of goods is said to have occurred (e.g. coastal Aborigines provided fish to individual Whites in return for a nip of rum and some tobacco) but Aboriginal access to commodities was predominantly via government-sponsored rations and blankets.

The distribution and movements of Aborigines during the 1890s and the first decade of the twentieth century are also evident from written sources. While information concerning the size of the population varies, it is entirely consistent about the movement eastwards into Queensland of Aboriginal people from across the border. White officialdom was not at all happy with this movement, although it was not all one way. Burketown police correspondence (Old 25.5.1899) mentions 'Carawah [Garawa] blacks' having left Burketown for the border in 1899 (i.e. returning to their country). In the same year, correspondence from the Inspector of Police at Normanton to the Commissioner of Police in Brisbane discusses the need:

> to keep all Northern Territory blacks on their own side of the border line, as I am of opinion if these blacks are allowed to come freely in to Queensland that they will commit depredations sooner or later. (Lamond 7.2.1899: 1)
>
> The Queensland blacks would give no trouble whatever as their numbers are few[5] but when those Northern Territory blacks come over the border to participate in [sic] the Lawn Hill [Station] bullocks trouble may arise at any time. (Lamond 7.2.1899: 3)

The police inspector refers to the impossibility of overtaking Aborigines fleeing into 'almost impassable' country across the border (i.e. west of Lawn Hill). Also in the same year, the constable at Turn Off Lagoon (Ordish 12.11.1899) states that he has had to carry out constant patrols to 'put a stop to cattle killing which was carried on to a great extent by South Australian [i.e. Northern Territory] Blacks', and to keep them on their own side of the border.

However, it is the Queensland Government Northern Protector (Roth 14.8.1901) who presents us with a more informed assessment of these movements (see map 3). He firstly describes how large areas much greater than the legally leased blocks were 'controlled' by cattlemen in Queensland, for they stocked the country according to the carrying capacity of the waterholes rather than of their particular block area. Aborigines were thus excluded from the major water sources, which were invariably enclosed by a block, but also from 'legally unoccupied' land into which the large numbers of cattle

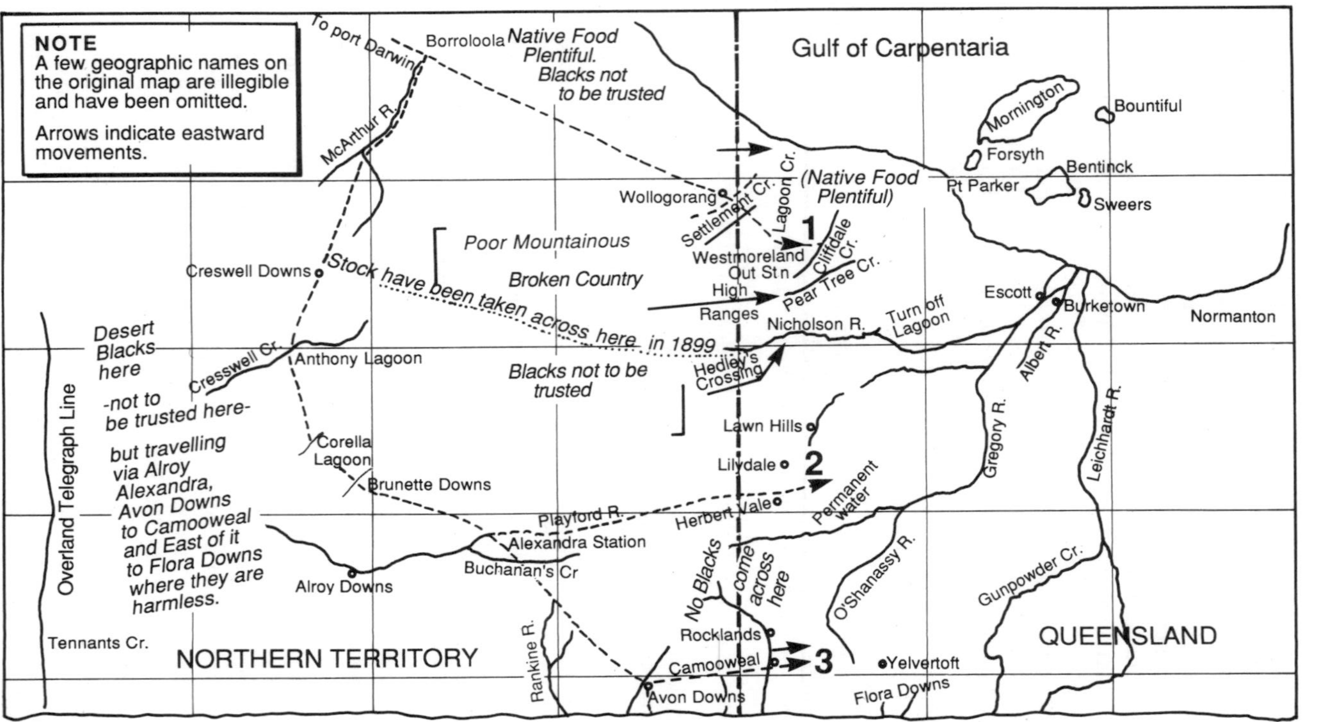

Map 3 Portion of sketch map by W Roth showing Aboriginal movements eastwards into Queensland
(Source 'The Northern Territory — Queensland Border, north of "Urandangie"' 14 August 1901 ms.)

would range from the water, as: 'where the cattle are — and where legally they have not th[e] slightest right to remain — the blacks have to be hunted away' (p. 2). Roth (p. 3) then describes the easterly 'migrations' of 'three main groups' of Northern Territory Aborigines into Queensland (see map 3): the coastal ones, who travelled 'both along the coast-line and behind it as far as Wollogorang, . . . eastwards as far as Burketown'; the mountain ones, who travelled generally parallel to and both north and south of the Nicholson River, crossing Hedleys, Settlement, Lagoon and Cliffdale creeks; and the desert ones, who travelled along a route located well to the south of the Nicholson River. According to Roth (p. 3) these migrations were all along 'trade-routes' that were well established in precontact times because of water and other bush resources along them. During contact times they had thus come to be used as stock-routes, and also 'as avenues of escape for horse-thieves, and cattle-duffers into [the] Northern Territory and for the surreptitious immigration of Chinese [from the Northern Territory] into Queensland' (p. 3).

Roth (pp. 2–3) gives reasons for the Aboriginal 'migration eastwards'. Firstly, he says it was 'due, partly to the desert water-holes giving ou[t] in certain times of the year'. It is unclear, however, to what extent in the post-contact south of the region, the return trip west in such a traditionally seasonal movement was being made. According to Roth the movements were also due:

> partly to the mountain and wilder blacks making descent on the more peaceful aboriginals occupying the plains, [and] partly to the fact of more highly prized articles of barter (iron, blankets, tobacco) being obtained from the more settled (Queensland) districts and partly to other causes.

On the question of Whites' hostility towards the Aborigines coming from the west, Roth's (14.8.1901: 3) evaluation is again instructive:

> The consensus of opinion among the Europeans along the Queensland side of the border is that these Northern Territory blacks are not to be trusted though, with the exception perhaps of the McArthur [River] boys, it would appear tha[t] when they come into Queensland, they do not appear to be very troublesome. That those same blacks have a locally bad reputation, I am not at all surprised, considering — what I have every reason to believe is true — the treatment to which they and their women are apparently still being subjected. Kombo-ism [White men engaging in sexual relations with Aboriginal women] is . . . rife . . . [and]: half-castes continue to be bred into the world.[6]

These are the views of a senior bureaucrat who had considerable influence over official state policy concerning Aboriginal people. Roth sought protection, segregation and control of Aborigines at a time when this was not always a popular view among other Whites throughout the region.

White ideology and practice

The official ideology of protection, segregation and control was embodied in 1897 in the *Aborigines Protection and Restriction of the Sale of Opium Act*, which enabled the formal creation of reserve lands and the removal of Aborigines to them (sections 4a, 4b & 9). While protectionism was by no means supported unanimously by local Whites, support for the creation of reserves appears not to have been entirely lacking in the Burke district. Turnbull (1911 [1896]: 39) was a pastoralist east of Burketown:

> I do not see why the Governments of the colonies should not be compelled to look after the poor remnant left, to give them reserves, to heal their ailments, and generally to smooth the path of the people from whom we have taken one of the finest countries under the snu [*sic*].

Some local pastoralists supported the establishment of reserves more to control and segregate Aborigines away from their cattle than to advance Aboriginal welfare. For example, the pastoralist at Gregory Downs wished to have Aborigines shifted away to a reserve because:

> they are all runaway boys and bad characters; they are continually hunting on my run frightening cattle, stealing from the station when I am away from home, ... also they keep several gins simply for letting to any traveller who may come along, and [therefore there are] usually one or more white men of the lowest order camped with these blacks, and as they give them rum and all get drunk together you can imagine the hideous rows they make during nighttime. (Watson 10.8.1898)

He recommended that a reserve be created further upstream on the Gregory River amid 'good watered hilly country' which was 'vacant and not fit for anything else'. The policeman investigating Watson's complaint (Casey 3.10.1898: 4) reported that it was 'without just foundation', but that the 'Camp tribe' (rather than the 'Station Blacks' — Watson's employees) would be 'more than pleased' to be able to form a camp at the designated site because of the bush resources there: 'it appears they had a fear to go there as they were warned off some years ago' (by local pastoralists who had since abandoned their 'run'). The policeman reports that on understanding they were free to go there they soon moved off but that it was questionable how long they would remain due to their being 'such an unsettled people and of a roving disposition'. While Watson saw the move as further reason to create a reserve (31.10.1898), the Inspector of Police for the district (Lamond 10.2.1899) recommended against this because more than half of it was unoccupied (by Whites) anyway; the 'tribe' did not number more than thirty; 'the Northern Territory blacks would ... take advantage of it and be a great trouble'; and the Aborigines concerned would not stay on it preferring to 'hunt all over that region'. He concludes by stating his view as a local government official, which differs from that of the Gregory Downs pastoralist by virtue of its optimism:

> The squatters treat them well and both black and white will soon understand that the black is to have the unoccupied country and not to go near stations or stocked country.

Contrary views were also held by the Lawn Hill Station owner. These are evident from his open criticism of both police and Roth, the Northern Protector, in their administration of the 1897 Act. In a letter to a Queensland government politician (Macintosh 6.12.1902) he complains as follows:

> You will . . . see the difficulties we are labouring under and how we are simply at the mercy of these nomadic notorious half-civilised blacks under an Act which I consider should be restricted to those parts of the State where the aborigines do not come in contact with stock particularly so, those portions which by nature afford the utmost protection for those blacks of the class referred to above . . . Blacks must obey and be taught to obey otherwise they will, as the saying is, 'ride rough shod over one' — Blacks and Stock in this country will not do together for many years . . . at the present and as the Act is administered under useless unbinding [employment] agreements these people are being schooled to all kinds of trickery which will in a few years require harsh and severe treatment to control.

He complains of horses and cattle being speared, and of not being allowed under the Act:

> either to bring the perpetrators to punishment or chastise them but most unreasonable of all according to Dr. Roth we should not be allowed even to requisition the Police and if these officers or men do come they at their peril correct these people.

Macintosh concludes on this issue:

> the question is one that is becoming almost intolerable and steps must be taken by individuals unless the Police are allowed to use their discretion and bring to justice offenders.

The politician made enquiries (Forsyth 30.12.1902), saying he had letters similar to that from Macintosh 'from men all over the Gulf complaining of the working of the Act', and Roth responded strongly (30.12.1902). He questioned the accuracy of the accusation concerning stealing of cattle and horses, and enquired polemically whether Macintosh could provide 'accurate information as to the number of blacks who have been shot in the neighbourhood of Lawn Hills during the same period'. He argued for Aboriginal offenders to be 'brought to justice', not 'chastised' by police, and stated that until reserves were established there would continue to be trouble.

Among the three reserves later formally requested by Roth (21.4.1903) was the one along the border west of Lawn Hill initially designated by McIntosh, the lessee of that station. However, local attitudes to reserves depended largely on where they were to be located. Dymock (1982: 66) quotes a newspaper source (*Burke Telegraph* 4.6.1897) which argues against a reserve at Turn Off Lagoon because it would attract 'hundreds of myalls from the Northern Territory . . . whose character for bloodthirstiness and wanton destruction of stock is [well known]'. Moreover, these people would have to be fed. This view also argued against a Turn Off Lagoon reserve because, as it was put in the newspaper, Whites believed Aborigines polluted water sources, and thus White people would no longer be able to use the water at Turn Off Lagoon. The item concluded by suggesting that a reserve would be better located in a more remote area like the country between Point Parker and Borroloola.

The clearest contrasting White view again comes from Roth, in his official report as the Northern Protector of Aboriginals for 1902 (1903: 23):

> The time has now arrived when it is imperative that various areas in the extreme Western and Gulf districts be dedicated wholly and solely to the natives . . . The whole question resolves itself into one of either sacrificing human lives, or losing a few pounds derived from rents. So long as the land can be taken up at a few shillings per square mile, and no provision made for the dependent blacks who can and are being hunted off it, there certainly will be trouble . . . The value of one human life, no matter the colour of the skin which clothes it, is more to me than that of all the cattle in creation.

The report then refers to much police correspondence listing complaints against Aborigines by stockowners who invariably request that the Aborigines be shifted away from the waterholes. One policeman states that the Aborigines 'are often dispersed by the station hands' and that: 'Of course, such dispersals are not reported to the police'. The policemen consistently say that reserves are the only answer. Roth's comment (p. 23) on the situation indicates considerable commitment to the improvement of Aboriginal circumstances: 'I blush in shame that I should be personally powerless to remedy such a state of affairs'.

As a senior representative of the government, Roth promoted what he clearly saw as the only rational policy to address the Aboriginal predicament. Nevertheless, it was some time before reserves were established. As early as 1897, a government report (Parry-Okedon 1897) had recommended a reserve over a large area from Burketown to the border, including the Wellesley Islands, and another one adjacent to the border between the Nicholson and Gregory Rivers. However, only a section of the former was eventually declared, and the mainland area of it was not gazetted until 1917 (QGG 1917: 757).

Furthermore, in spite of Roth's genuine humanitarian concern, not all agents of the state sought to maintain the distribution of 'rations' (mainly blankets, tobacco and beef). In 1899 the Inspector of Police (Lamond 7.2.1899) opposed:

> the present system of killing cattle for them [although just where this was occurring is unclear] . . . as the blacks congregate together and some times wait for days for the bullock to be killed . . .

In this correspondence he argues that Aborigines have no shortage of bush food, suggests that the police at Turn Off Lagoon should have sole control over the distribution of tobacco and the killing of cattle for 'Queensland blacks', and recommends that the latter receive these commodities 'as good will offerings' and 'now and again as a reward for good conduct and to show them the Police are friendly and not hostile'. The Inspector appears to have believed that selectively providing for certain desires of Aborigines in Queensland would keep them 'perfectly quiet' and that those from the Northern Territory could be better kept there if they were not given tobacco and beef in Queensland. The Commissioner of Police in Brisbane agreed with him, mentioning in his reply (1.3.1899) the importance of Aboriginal people maintaining their own system of bush food production, and so not coming to rely on regular rations. Later that year, the Inspector wrote again (Lamond 20.11.1899), commenting that Aborigines 'are . . . resuming their old modes of getting food etc. and are in consequence much more healthy and contented than they were when loafing about the townships'.

Nevertheless, government rations continued to be distributed in Queensland. During 1899 (Roth 1900: 3) the lowest estimates of blankets required were Burketown 100, Gregory Downs 50, Lawn Hill 100 and Turn Off Lagoon 100. A later report (Roth 1903: 4) states that only infirm Northern Territory Aborigines were given blankets. For 'purposes of conciliation' a 'small expenditure for fish-hooks' was made at Turn Off Lagoon in 1903 (Roth 1904: 7). In 1905, the constable at Turn Off Lagoon (Smith 31.12.1905) requested more material assistance for the Aborigines there. During the year he had issued: 20 pounds (nearly 9 kg) tobacco, 20 tomahawks, 50 clay pipes, 30 fishing lines, a small box of hooks, and 17 pairs of blankets. This 'small amount of Relief' had been inadequate, and he requested permission to provide 'a few head of cattle', to 'keep them from killing cattle [on their own]'. However, the request was refused on the grounds that 'expenditure on healthy blacks . . . would incourage [*sic*] idleness' and the habit of killing other cattle at their whim.

While individual policemen recognised that Aboriginal people could remain healthy by not becoming dependent on rations, reports generally indicate that their health was rapidly deteriorating. For example, the constable at Turn Off Lagoon who asked for more material assistance (Smith 31.12.1905) also reported that he had 'all the Bush Blacks well under control and they are little or no trouble so far', but that a lot of the 'wanjee [Waanyi] tribe' were suffering very badly from syphilis. Other sources suggest that Aboriginal health was particularly bad at the Burketown camps. Telegrams from the police in 1897 and 1899 (Graham 13.1.1897; Lamond 8.3.1899) state that people were starving there in the wet season, and in need of government rations. A report in 1906 (Progress Report of the Chief Protector of Aborigines, May 1906) observes that they 'are suffering from pose [catarrh, head cold] and unable to walk to the barracks for food'. As Wild Time came to a close, the domination of Aboriginal society had clearly been achieved.

The force of the colonial state

Apart from a brief initial period during Wild Time when Aborigines regarded Whites as deceased kinsmen, there was extensive violence until people were 'quietened down', as Aboriginal oral accounts put it. The conflict was not solely between Aborigines and Whites, for native police were introduced as the subordinate allies of Whites, and local Aboriginal men were also later recruited as police trackers. Explanation of the motivations of Aboriginal men who aligned themselves with Whites (particularly the native police) should make reference to a number of factors: the material advantages achieved through such alignment; the physical prowess obtained through access to White weaponry; and the possibility of escape from certain constraints of the traditional systems of ritual and kinship.

While there was physical resistance against Whites, their Aboriginal agents and their control of critical water sources through the large scale infiltration of cattle, the continuation of internal Aboriginal political life may be regarded as having defused this resistance. Violent encounters between Aboriginal groups, some apparently not related directly to the White presence, continued during Wild Time. At times, Whites were defended by certain Aborigines against others, and were also occasionally aligned with particular Aboriginal individuals in their conflicts with other Aboriginal people. To make this point about continuity of Aboriginal political life is not to ignore that major changes were occurring within it. Colonisation resulted in individuals gaining influence throughout wider social fields than in the past, as the key groupings of precontact social life were dislocated from small-scale physical occupation of territories, and as larger congregations of people formed at places strategically located in the bush and at White towns, cattle stations and police depots.

The selective distribution of certain desired commodities as 'rations' engendered a form of accommodation to the coercive control of the state and the intrusive appropriation of lands by pastoralists. The colonial discourse quoted variously regards these rations as 'reward for good conduct' or 'good will offerings' or 'for purposes of conciliation'. Rations established a material basis for the beginning of a prolonged process of pauperisation among Aboriginal people. Yet within the encapsulating colonial political and economic structures, considerable diversity in degrees of Aboriginal compliance operated. Those who became 'station blacks' during Wild Time accommodated fairly swiftly to the prevailing pastoral economy, and were generally distinguished by Whites from 'bush blacks' or the 'camp tribe', who remained relatively independent of direct coercion. In particular, those coming eastwards from the Northern Territory into Queensland were 'not to be trusted' as compared with those already in Queensland who would 'give no trouble whatsoever'.

Colonial ideology varied among Whites in the region, with control being sought in different ways. Local stockholders were preoccupied with segregating Aboriginal people away from their cattle herds. As with one quoted pastoralist's position: 'Blacks must obey and be taught to obey'. There appears to have been little if any concern with legitimating domination in this view. There was considerable tension between pastoralists and senior local officials (including some police) who were concerned to exercise what they saw as legitimate control on the basis of formal Australian law and through state-regulated bureaucratic administrative practices. While this ideology also stressed control of Aborigines, it included some concern for their material circumstances. The basis of the monetary income and material standard of living of such state employees was not in conflict with Aboriginal interests to the same degree as was that of the stockholders. The process of 'quietening down' Aborigines during Wild Time did not have the same implications for differing sections of White society. However, as with the pastoralist ideology, officialdom at this stage sought control via coercion, not via any attempt to control the thinking of Aboriginal people. There was no room during Wild Time for hegemonic control. What needs to be emphasised for this period is the exercise of power by White Australian society through overt use of physical force and the threat of such use.

Notes

[1] In 1913 the policeman at Borroloola received the following correspondence from two White men at Wollogorang, a station located adjacent to the Queensland/Northern Territory border:

> Blacks are a great drawback [for] settlers in these outside places and we can get no redress. I consider I lose 5 percent of Cattle from niggers and 5 percent from natural causes. I know of several men who have been out this way looking for country recently who would have settled . . . if it had not been for the blacks. I can assure you that the natives are as troublesome now in this District than they were 20 years ago. They walk all over one's holding burning grass, camping at main waters, spearing cattle etc and we can do nothing, and I trust that you having the settlement of the country at heart will give this matter most serious attention it is the greatest drawback we have to contend with. (in Dempsey 8.8.1913)

[2] Several old people now refer to the first contact as with 'Captain Cook'; thus the Aboriginal people of the time are said to have fed Captain Cook and received tobacco from him. In fact, Cook did not travel through the southern Gulf area (Rienits and Rienits 1968). The symbolic significance attributed to the concept of 'Captain Cook' in Aboriginal thought has been discussed by a number of writers (Kolig 1980; Chase 1981: 11; Rose 1984; Mackinolty and Wainburranga 1988).

[3] The traditional system of land tenure stresses the rights of patriclan members in their father's estate, but also recognises individuals' affiliations to a range of other estates. The totemic features of the landscape are conceived partly in terms of non-contiguously distributed parcels of land that are associated with subsection couples (or semimoieties). In some parts of the region, processes of succession are recognised whereby traditional ownership of estates can be taken over by owning groups of nearby lands (see Sharp 1939; Reay 1962; Avery 1977; Trigger 1982).

[4] Extracts from the Borroloola police journals indicate that Murdering Tommy led the 'last pocket' of cattle killing and threatening of Whites at Wollogorang during 1916–19 (McLaughlin 1977: 4, 21–2). Along with others, he was arrested in 1917 for killing fifteen cattle. After escaping from gaol in Darwin, Tommy was described as 'one of the worst natives in these parts', and later assaulted a policeman at Wollogorang, stealing his revolver (while his relatives threw spears at the Aboriginal police trackers). In December 1918, Aboriginal police and 'Station Blacks' were attacked by a number of people including Murdering Tommy near the headwaters of the Robinson River. It appears (see Appendix B) that Tommy was captured in 1920 and sent to Yarrabah, an Aboriginal settlement in northeast Queensland.

[5] The Inspector later states there are no more than 200 Aborigines from the border to the Leichhardt River, although this figure may well have been a low estimate.

[6] White officialdom at this time clearly viewed the mixed-race population as different from that solely of Aboriginal descent, and felt that the former should be separated residentially. Roth (1900: 10) mentions such children

being killed at birth in the Burke district, though he does not elaborate on possible reasons. We are not given any indication of Aboriginal beliefs about mixed-race children, and there is no mention of whether the rape of Aboriginal women by non-Aboriginal men affected these beliefs. Roth suggests (1902: 7) that in the 'far western and Gulf country' it is 'better to remove half-caste girls to the Missions'. (See also Chapter 8 below and Trigger 1989).

CHAPTER THREE

Station and fringe-dwelling life

According to Aboriginal oral history, by the time the country had 'quietened down' large camps had formed at certain stations (e.g. Wollogorang in the Northern Territory and Westmoreland and Lawn Hill in Queensland). Through the 1920s and 1930s people in Queensland also congregated at Turn Off Lagoon, Burketown and the Gregory Downs Reserve, and went from these places to stations for employment, while in the Northern Territory larger groups remained camped in the vicinity of station homesteads. Throughout the region men worked as stockmen, in droving teams, as fencers and in various other manual jobs of the cattle industry; some women also did outside manual work, but most were employed as domestic workers.

This period of station and fringe-dwelling life has come to occupy a major place in Aboriginal oral history at Doomadgee. Historical associations are recognised between categories of people (and/or their descendants) and the places where they (or their ancestors) were based. For example, the 'Burketown mob' or 'Munggabayi mob' are those (predominantly Ganggalida people) who came from the coast country to live in the Burketown fringe-camps (in the vicinity of the site known as Munggabayi); and 'running water people' are those (predominantly Waanyi people) who came east to reside at station homesteads adjacent to the spring-fed 'running water' streams of Lawn Hill, Musselbrook, and Elizabeth Creeks, and the Gregory River. As people moved into new areas, they incorporated traditional knowledge of these landscapes into their own traditions, and passed on this information to their children.

Some people were able to maintain physical contact with their own 'countries' (as the areas inherited from their ancestors are termed), particularly when they were engaged in intermittent or fairly regular work for stations that contained part or all of these countries within their boundaries. This was particularly so for Aborigines based at certain homesteads in the Northern Territory, some of whom later came east to stations in Queensland and eventually to Doomadgee Mission in the 1960s and early 1970s. For example, a patrol officer (with the Northern Territory Department of Native Affairs) reported in 1948 the presence of approximately 170 Aborigines in the areas of Manangoora, Seven Emus, Robinson River and Wollogorang homesteads. They were remaining near to the station enterprises where members of their families were actually 'employed' (Kyle-Little 16.12.1948). The officer also encountered 'a party of nomadic natives' on the 'Fulche [i.e. Foelsche] River' (21.12.1948: 6), no doubt in the process of moving between known homestead locations.

Movements and 'removals'

To some extent, Aboriginal movements in both the Northern Territory and Queensland were made independently of White employers and officialdom. Some places away from the homesteads and towns were used as sites to hold prolonged cult ceremonies (e.g. at Julujuluyurdi on Accident Creek to which people came from Turn Off Lagoon, Lawn Hill Station and stations as far westwards as Alexandria during the 1930s and into the 1940s).[1] 'Burketown side' people did not come to this site; their range of movement was oriented towards the coast (T42). Ritual was also performed very near to the station homesteads, and many Aboriginal men who later came to Doomadgee were initiated at Turn Off Lagoon and Westmoreland. To instigate such initiation ceremonies, *wardanguji* (novices decorated with hair belts) would be sent through the bush (e.g. from Turn Off Lagoon to Westmoreland and Wollogorang). People would respond to their arrival by returning with them to their *jaman.gi* (initiation) ground. Older informants describe how, during their youth, White station managers generally did not 'block' them from moving around the bush, unlike the managers' more recent counterparts. As one woman put it: 'this last lot they cheeky!' (T78). She was comparing current restrictions on movement across cattle properties with her generally unhindered movements as a girl in the 1920s along the coast to the Magundi area, her mother's mother's country, just west of Massacre Inlet.

Apart from this kind of independent Aboriginal movement, authorities in Queensland 'removed' many people. For example, official records (reproduced partly in Appendix B) indicate that, from 1912 to 1936, 116 individuals (including fifty-eight children) plus one family of unspecified size were removed from Burketown, Turn Off Lagoon and various stations. Of these, sixty (including forty-four children) were sent to Mornington Island, one to Old Doomadgee Mission (see below), and the rest to quite distant Aboriginal settlements throughout Queensland. The reasons given for removal (see Appendix B) were: that some individuals were seen as a threat to Whites and/or other Aborigines; or that they were seen to be in need of 'protection' or medical treatment. In the case of the former, people were most commonly sent to the distant Palm Island and, in the latter, to Mornington Island.

The removals from Turn Off Lagoon in 1935–6 were apparently also due to the closure of the police station there. Older people comment that the police said they could no longer give them rations and that the children had to go to school. The policeman told them to go to Old Doomadgee Mission on the coast, but the people said they did not want to go there because they were Waanyi and did not belong to the coast country. So the police sent them to Burketown and from there they were taken to Mornington Island, a journey that most made with reluctance. Some lived on the island for many years, while others returned to the mainland (and eventually to Doomadgee Mission) more quickly (one family did this quite independently by means of a dugout canoe).

Apart from these cases, older informants talk about many other removals, as does the ex-superintendant of Mornington Island Mission, who discusses individuals being sent to the island via Burketown during the 1920s and 1930s (personal communication, D. Belcher 20.1.1980, 27.1.1981). He also suggests that, during 1914–17, Reverend Hall 'took some half-caste children (& F[ull] B[lood]) from Burketown because of their neglected condition'; and that 'The Police tended to send children to Mornington Island without regard to kin factors at Burketown (early 20's)'. Some children were apparently regarded by White officialdom as orphans without adequate family care (see Appendix B for removals from Marless and Augustus Downs Stations); although this may well have been due to White perceptions of the physical conditions in camps more than the real absence of any related adults willing to look after the children. Aboriginal people say that White police invariably wanted to remove children of mixed racial descent. Remembered incidents include mixed-descent children at Riversleigh Station being hidden by their mothers, who feared they would be sent to Palm Island, and two occasions (in 1922 and 1929) when children were taken away from their grandmothers and sent to Mornington Island during what were intended merely as short visits to Burketown.

By most oral accounts, the removals of mixed-descent children were opposed by their mothers, and in some cases by their socially acknowledged non-Aboriginal fathers as well. Chinese fathers are said to have remained with their Aboriginal women and children more often than White men. On some occasions there was apparently hostility from Aboriginal men when their wives gave birth to mixed-descent children. In one event (*circa* 1935) the mother is said to have been attacked by her husband soon after the birth and, despite attempts by his brothers to restrain him, the woman eventually died of injuries sustained (T46).

Liaisons between White (and Chinese) men and Aboriginal women at bush camps and stations were reasonably common, despite the laws in both Queensland and the Northern Territory prohibiting them.[2] The activities of the Whites with cattle and horses were not always legal, and police investigations into both breaches of the law were often combined. For example, an order was issued by the Queensland Director of Native Affairs on 8.5.1941[3] for the removal of a woman and her children to Palm Island during 'the Director's pleasure' for absconding from (station) employment with her children, taking her employer's horses, and absconding with a White man. Aboriginal residents at Doomadgee know the White man to have been the father of two of her children. This family eluded police in the bush until January/February 1943. The Northern Territory policeman who took them into custody (Graham 15.3.1943) reported that he was satisfied 'that a definite cattle-stealing ring has been in existance [*sic*] in the area patrolled', and he mentioned one other White man as having been 'greatly assisted' in this illegal activity by his female Aboriginal consort. This man was convicted of consorting with a female Aborigine. He was fined fifty pounds with ten shillings costs, and allowed a fortnight to pay or two months' imprisonment. The policeman also strongly recommended that the Northern Territory Director of Native Affairs not grant this man permission to marry the woman, which he had requested after his conviction. Another White man was similarly charged and convicted for 'consorting with a female halfcaste'.

The 1948 patrol officer's report (Kyle-Little 16.12.1948) indicates the official concern specifically to investigate the situation of mixed-descent children and have them removed if necessary. At Wollogorang Station, he recommends 'that the half-caste girls . . . be shifted from the area as it is quite apparent that nobody is looking after their interests'. At Redbank Mine near Wollogorang, the old White miner (aged seventy-seven years), who lived in a cave, had a sixteen year old 'half-caste' girl living in an adjoining cave:

> [the White owner] stated that he had taken this half-caste girl from the native camp at an early age and had looked after her interests ever since. He had given her a little education, clothed and fed her. He requested that I remove the girl as the residents of the various stations and people in Burketown claimed that he was living with [her] . . . I am quite convinced that in the past [he] has acted in the best interests of the girl.

In some circumstances non-Aboriginal fathers were regarded as providing an appropriate environment for mixed-race children. The patrol officer discusses three stations where the White lessees had maintained long conjugal relationships with Aboriginal women, and in all cases notes close and caring relationships between these men and their 'half-caste' children. He also notes that the children would probably inherit the stations after their fathers' deaths. It was doubtless more common, however, for non-Aboriginal fathers to be absent or simply not prepared to look after their mixed-race children. At two stations the officer questioned people about the fathers of mixed-descent children and recommended that a certain White man 'be made to pay an amount each week for the upkeep of the child' if he admitted to being the father. Throughout his long report, the patrol officer describes the situation of 'half-castes' and 'natives' separately, and clearly holds the view that the needs of the former, and their capacity for development, could not usually be met appropriately in the 'native camp'.

Other Aboriginal children, usually boys, left their families' camps as 'employees' of White (and other non-Aboriginal) 'bosses'. To refer again to the example groups treated in Appendix A, in case 1 (figure 2, Appendix A), the man shown as *B* was 'picked up' by a White man from Westmoreland Station when he was about twelve years old (*circa* 1914): 'he been pick me up there want to grow me up, for boy for him — take me away' (T71). The two travelled to Burketown, Turn Off Lagoon and various stations. The White man had a small number of horses of his own, and would get work on stations breaking in horses and doing general stock work. After a while, *B* obtained his own station job, while the White man was working at a nearby station. However, when the latter returned to live at Burketown for a while and married a woman of Aboriginal/Chinese descent, *B* again went to live with him: 'you know, just like my home, come up sit down might be here for Christmas — like that' (T71). He took the White's surname as his own English surname, and developed a close relationship with his 'boss'.

Similarly, in the same example group, *C* (who, like most of the children of 'King Peter', was born at Westmoreland Station) was 'picked up' (*circa* the late 1920s) from there by an Afghan hawker[4]: 'he been askim me . . . you want a job?' (T72). They travelled to many stations selling clothes and other commodities, brought originally from Townsville (on the east coast of Queensland). When the hawker returned there to purchase more items, *C* waited for him at Kamilroi Station, was injured when breaking in a horse and spent time recovering in Burketown hospital, then returned to the station to wait for the Afghan boss. As he put it in discussion with me: 'my boss been still away'. He had originally been left simply to look after the hawker's buggy, and on his return the latter abused the station manager for getting *C* to work with horses. The Afghan boss clearly felt he had propriety over his Aboriginal 'boy'. Eventually, *C* and his boss argued over the former being required to cut a lot of wood, the hawker threatened him with a rifle, and *C* reported him to the Burketown police sergeant. The boss subsequently asked the sergeant if he could 'have the boy back', but *C* would not go, and another 'boy' went with him. They then 'had a row' on their first trip and the Aboriginal man is said to have killed the hawker with lightning using a sorcery song. *C* later married a woman who worked as a cleaner at the Burketown hospital. The marriage was opposed by the woman's family because she was promised to another man, but they were married by the police sergeant anyway, thus using White authority to overcome traditional opposition.

After their initial movement away from Westmoreland Station where their families had been based, both *B* and *C* (with their wives and children) lived and worked on many cattle properties. They spent some time in the bush during 'off-seasons' (usually when it was too wet to work), and returned to the Burketown camps for some periods. They also went on long cattle droves. Such movements were the prevailing pattern on the Queensland side of the border,[5] dictated by the availability of work on stations or in Burketown, and the movements of 'bosses' who were themselves itinerant workers. Often the non-Aboriginal boss would tell a young boy's parents that he would bring him back every now and then. One man described such an interaction between his boss and his mother in the late 1920s, at the family's camp in coastal Ganggalida country. The boss said, 'I'll take this little boy, I'll bring him back' (T79).

Some of the older residents of Doomadgee now recognise the impact of these kinds of movements and their long experience in the pastoral industry on their commitment to maintaining traditional ritual knowledge and customary practices: 'I been forget now — too much cattle'n horse been makim me silly'; and, 'we didn't worry for that — work for White man all the time'. However, it appears that many station Whites and itinerant bosses were not particularly concerned with changing such areas of Aboriginal life. Their major concern, and indeed the critical focus of colonial social relations, was obtaining Aboriginal labour.

The negotiation of labour relations

A complex series of laws and amendments provided the legal framework for labour relations between Aborigines and others in this region. In Queensland, *The Aboriginals Protection and Restriction of the Sale of Opium Acts* 1897 to 1934, and successive Regulations under them, required people to apply for a permit to employ 'Aboriginals' and 'half-castes', and then complete a written 'agreement' containing the names of the parties, the nature of the service to be rendered by the employee, the wages or other remuneration, length of employment (although after twelve months a new agreement was required), and so on. Applications for permits, permits themselves, and agreements were all set out on various forms. Police officers and local protectors were expected to oversee and witness these arrangements, and they could (after an amending Act in 1901) receive the wages of Aboriginal workers and manage both this money and the property of all Aborigines. Subsequent Queensland legislation retained the emphasis on 'protection' of the Aboriginal worker through paternalistic management of his or her labour, wages, property, and movement. Indeed, Queensland law generally maintained colonial labour arrangements until the late 1960s. Similar legislation operated in the Northern Territory until the same period (Rowley 1972: chapters 10–16; Stevens 1974; 1980: chapters 3–5).

Long before the Northern Territory (or any other government in Australia), Queensland established special minimum wages for Aboriginal pastoral workers, and by the 1919 Regulations these were about two-thirds of the general Queensland pastoral award wage, on the basis that the value of the Aboriginal worker was inferior because he lacked a sense of responsibility. By 1964 Aboriginal station hands still received approximately the same percentage of the general award rate (i.e. of the minimum wage required by law), and the percentage was less for other jobs in the pastoral industry (Rowley 1972: 237).[6]

Throughout the years, the legally stipulated wages for Aboriginal pastoral workers were always much higher in Queensland than in the Northern Territory. From 1955 onwards the worker in Queensland received over twice the amount paid to his Northern Territory counterpart after 1959 (Rowley 1972: 232). According to Stevens (1973: 159), the first minimum rate for Northern Territory Aboriginal pastoral workers was set in 1928. Rowley (1972: 285) refers to criticism of the fixed rate in the same year. The rate was five shillings per week plus keep, tobacco and clothing, about an eighth of the award rate for White workers (then two pounds per week with keep). There are similar discrepancies in drovers' rates. Furthermore, the Regulations allowed the chief protector in the Northern Territory to absolve an employer from paying any wages if he maintained the relatives and dependants of an Aboriginal employee. The Queensland 1919 Regulations (QGG 1919: 1579–82) give a minimum rate for Aboriginal adult male pastoral workers of two pounds per week. As Rowley (1972: 236–7) points out, however, this difference between Queensland and the Northern Territory looks less impressive after

1934, when Queensland Aborigines made compulsory contributions to various state-administered welfare funds. These contributions were deducted from Aboriginal workers' earnings and placed in a government-administered fund for expenditure on 'general welfare and relief' in relation to Aboriginal communities.

Aboriginal workers were finally included in the pastoral awards of both Queensland and the Northern Territory during 1968 (Rowley 1972: chapter 16). In the Northern Territory after 1953, mixed-descent Aborigines were legally entitled to non-Aboriginal conditions of employment (Rowley 1972: 295–6; Stevens 1980: 64–5) everywhere except in the cattle industry. This was because 'Aboriginals' as defined in the 1918 Ordinance (i.e. including 'half-castes') were excluded from the *Cattle Station Industry (NT) Award* (Sharp 1966: 157–8). In Queensland, while 'Aboriginals' (including 'half-castes') could be exempted from the legislation regulating their employment, they were in any case excluded from the Queensland *Station Hands Award* (Sharp 1966: 156).

Rowley (1972: chapters 10–16) and Stevens (1980: chapters 3–5) refer to many reports of Aboriginal station workers (particularly in the Northern Territory) not receiving the legally stipulated rates of pay and conditions. Rowley's general remarks (1972: 232–3) for Queensland are certainly apposite for the southern Gulf region straddling the border:

> In practice, signing on was an arrangement which a settlement superintendent or a Police Protector negotiated with the employer. . .
>
> In the frontier areas, the police officer had to 'get on' with the local employer. There must have been those who were ready to compromise. The actual procedure, until 1966, was that the Protector kept the bank book, into which a proportion of the wage (which he decided) was paid, irrespective of the wishes of the employee, who could make withdrawals only through him. Especially where the worker is illiterate, such a system is open to abuse, and abuses inevitably occurred.

Nevertheless, a 1949 survey of wages paid to 118 Aboriginal station workers (Davis 19.9.1949) indicates that protectors in this region were operating according to the instruction in the Regulations that they should claim higher rates than the prescribed minimums 'when satisfied the ability of the aboriginal warrants such higher payment'. The wages of individuals surveyed vary considerably, however the averages for both station hands and those employed by drovers were above the minimum rates given in the 1945 Regulations. The average wage was higher under agreements arranged by the Doomadgee Mission Protector (approximately forty-three shillings and six pence per week) than under those arranged by the Burketown Protector (approximately thirty-five shillings and six pence per week), a matter of some dispute between these men. The difference in rates paid under the two protectors is actually greater than these figures indicate, because a larger proportion of the Doomadgee-based employees were aged under twenty-one years and therefore entitled to less pay (28 per cent of those Doomadgee based, 16 per cent of those Burketown based).

The Aboriginal workers themselves apparently knew little about their legal entitlements. Older Doomadgee residents remember, as teenagers, being paid mainly in rations. One man told of how his parents came to camp semipermanently at Gregory Downs Station after he had been taken there as a young boy by a policeman:

> they come down here [to Gregory Downs Station] and they stayed there, they used to come to the station [homestead] and manager give'em tucker 'n flour . . . beef . . . they give'em anything — tobacco — been so pleased to get the kids off 'em. (T23)

Another old man described how, as a boy, he was picked up from the Burketown camp by a White station man. The White reportedly said to the boy's mother: 'You give me the boy, we give you some tucker, clothes'. There was then a period during which his mother was able to obtain commodities from the police station. While some people report unambiguously that they received no wages for long periods, others remember receiving wages as they grew older, particularly those who were working for itinerant bosses with whom they had developed familiar relationships.

Some arrangements not involving wages were apparently regarded as satisfactory. For example, during parts of the dry season Aboriginal people normally based at Westmoreland would move down to the coastal area of Ngurrurri (also known as 'Horse Island'), taking station horses there 'to fatten them'. After some time in the bush they would return to the station homestead with the horses as the wet season began, and then receive rations for a period. In other cases, despite some wages, the 'trade' is now perceived to have been unfair. The following man recalls his fencing contractor boss paying his wages into the bank and providing his family with food:

> I done a lot of that mill work, sawmill, I done a lot of yardwork, and terrible lot of fencing too. No mate, on me own, nobody with me, no offsider . . . me old boss used to just lay down in the shade, I used to make the money . . . old man, he just lay down there while I earn the money for him [laughing] . . . when he die I got an old motor car off him there he had an old Ford car so the policeman said: 'You can have that old car . . . the old man died, he won't be using it'. (T23)

Despite such complaints, long-standing relationships between Aboriginal workers and their bosses were often close and supportive. For example, the man just quoted also relates with fondness how his old boss would usually cook for him.

Such itinerant bosses were often unmarried and without other kin support, and in a number of recorded cases they died at remote bush locations while with their Aboriginal worker(s). Some are now remembered with great affection. The boss was often a father figure to young Aboriginal workers, and many came to be known in English by their boss's name. The support and trust of a boss is now recounted with pride. Thus, old people tell of occasions when, during the manager's absence, they were entrusted with custodianship of station buildings and equipment, and given open access to food and other stores. When they intimated they would soon 'finish up' at a station their boss would say he could not cope without them ('no you can't pull out, you our boy') as their knowledge of the country is said to have been essential for adequate mustering. They remember being told by station owners that they had 'always got a home' there and could come to live there at any time. A further boast is that an individual could (and in some cases still can) always obtain beef from certain stations. Many bosses are now described as having been 'good old fellas'. Indeed, to say of an individual: 'poor fella he got no boss', is still understood by old people to mean he lacks the kind of material support and status that this kind of employment is seen to have entailed.[7]

When hostility arose between Aboriginal people and their bosses, the relationships appear to have ended fairly abruptly, sometimes with the assistance of the local policeman. One man explained how he and other workers simply 'pulled out' from a bush mustering camp, because of a dispute over food (*circa* 1935). They walked back to Wollogorang Station where their wives joined them, and they moved casually through the bush for several months. Much later (1961) this man was sacked from Riversleigh Station 'over a row', and in 1970 he 'pulled out' with his two working sons from Escott Station over similarly disputed working conditions (T79).

The White employers' perspective is available from written sources. During Wild Time there was little official supervision of Aboriginal labour on cattle stations. Turnbull (1911: 40), a pastoralist east of Burketown, was writing in 1896:

> The early settlers usually, and even now . . . try and get blacks out of the camps, say 8 or 10 years old, sometimes younger, and break them in to station work. These get their clothes, tobacco, some few presents at times (but no money), and with a strict boss who knows how to work them, prove valuable servants in a country where wages are very high and produce very low in price. In fact, inasmuch as they are good bushmen, good horsemen, and when well treated take an interest in the station, and are not so flighty as the somewhat independent white man, we are otherwise dependent on for stockmen up here, I prefer them to the whites. I cannot, however, say that one could do altogether with blacks; one must have a white out with them to steady and boss them.

As the Gulf pastoral industry developed, Aboriginal labour became central to the operation of many of the successful stations. In his reminiscences of the region as it was in the 1920s and 1930s, Carrington (1977: 17) comments:

> I think it is only fair to mention the part played by the aboriginal stockman over the years. They were mostly excellent horse and cattlemen and were the backbone of most mustering camps in the Gulf.

Gradually, the early White attitudes prevalent during Wild Time had to adapt to much greater regulation of labour relations, enforced by police and protectors. However, these attitudes appear to have changed slowly. Aboriginal accounts suggest that arguments between station Whites and protectors were not uncommon, and this is also evident from archival sources.

An example from the Gregory Downs protectorate is instructive. In 1943, an elderly station lessee who had in his own words (Murnane 2.4.1943) 'battled' alone in his remote bush setting since 1918 complained bitterly to a Queensland parliamentarian about the treatment of him and his Aboriginal 'boys' by the protector at Gregory Downs police station. The complaint referred to, among other things, inferior quality work clothes and other goods being provided to the station's employees, and his being given fewer Aboriginal workers than other station employers. The protector's reply (Hagarty 26.5.1943) argued that a shortage of goods due to 'War conditions' could not be blamed on him, that those items provided were always good quality and that in any case the lessee was a bad employer:

> Few, if any Protectors, in my opinion would have put up with . . . [the lessee] as I have done over the last five years. He writes down here and wants certain boys, and if they are not available and are substituted by others, he takes a dislike to them, and nothing they can do for him in their work is right. He, with each and every boy, from what Aboriginals say, is continually growling at them regarding their work. This is evidently why none of the boys like going there, and never want to go back . . . [The lessee] has always been an uncertain proposition regarding payment of wages . . . As the Department knows the demand for Aboriginal labour exceeds the supply.

This reply was supported by the protector's superior (Calligan 9.6.1943), the inspector of police at Cloncurry, who added details of the protector's work for the benefit of Aboriginal people at the Gregory Downs camp:

> For years past he has worked a vegetable garden to provide vegetables for the Aboriginals, and has also pit sawn bush timber and erected huts on the camp site, he has also sunk a well on the river bank . . .

Other correspondence (e.g. Murnane 7.3.1944) indicates that this dispute carried on for some time, with each side claiming that the other treated Aboriginal workers unjustly.

While supply of labour to this station was particularly difficult because the White lessee was known as a hard employer, other stations also complained about the shortage of Aboriginal labour, prompting the protector to write with some annoyance (Hagarty 15.6.1944):

> Do these people who write to Head Office imagine they are being penalised? I have a totally insufficient [number of] boys and gins [Aboriginal women workers] to satisfy all demands. Someone must go short, as they cannot be manufactured at a minute's notice and put to work.

And again, five years later (Hagarty 8.5.1949), when the protector gives his opinion on the arrangements necessary to maintain appropriate labour relations:

> As the Dept knows all the able bodies blacks [*sic*] in this Protectorate are in constant employment, and the demand for Gregory Downs Aboriginals has always totally outweighed the supply.
>
> I have found that an Aboriginal, in 99 cases out of 100, if worked and treated properly is always willing to return to his job after a spell, except of course in very isolated cases where a boy is a bit of a 'head' or a 'pointer'.[8] It will be found that in many cases where a boy is reluctant to return to a job, that it is bossed by some incapable jackeroo, who understands nothing of working blacks, and less of the work in hand, and consequently cannot command obedience or respect. Interference with boys' gins, bullying, liquor, and familiarity generally are some of the many causes that result in walking off jobs, or failing to return after a spell, and the origin of station labour problems.
>
> [A certain station manager] . . . gives the impression that he believes that the black is merely a chattel, and whether he likes it or not, or regardless of circumstances should be forced to return to a job. He evidently has much to learn in this line.

The available correspondence involving the Gregory Downs protector indicates continuing tension over such matters.

A further example during the early 1940s involved a dispute between Westmoreland Station and the protectors at Burketown and Doomadgee. Here the disagreement was over which rates of pay should apply to the large number of Aboriginal workers coming across the border from the Northern Territory and working on stations such as Westmoreland. Queensland authorities made enquiries regarding the station's Aboriginal labour in 1943 (Director of Native Affairs 29.1.1943), and were informed by the protector at Borroloola in the Northern Territory (McKinnon 9.4.1943) that regardless of whether their place of birth or usual residence was in the Territory, when working across the border workers would be entitled to Queensland conditions and rates of pay. He pointed out that it would no doubt suit the station lessee at Westmoreland to dodge Queensland conditions, as Territory wage rates were only five shillings per week or nothing at all if Aboriginal workers' dependants were maintained. The wage in Queensland then was twelve shillings and six pence to thirty shillings weekly (depending on age), plus keep but without clothing. The two sets of authorities agreed that Queensland conditions should apply at Westmoreland, but the station apparently continued to dispute the matter from time to time.

The attraction of work in Queensland is understandable. None of the thirty-nine Aboriginal men employed at eight Territory stations near the border in 1948 received wages (Kyle-Little 16.12.1948). At all of these stations, workers and some dependants were provided with varying amounts of food, clothing and shelter.[9] Only at Wollogorang (where the manager falsely claimed to be paying five shillings per week) does the visiting officer recommend wages 'of at least 15/- to 1 pound a week' plus certain improved conditions. This appears to be because of his judgement that, unlike the other stations, Wollogorang was doing very well economically, due largely to Aboriginal labour.

Only people of mixed race seemed to have a chance of receiving better wages on these Territory stations. The visiting patrol officer's comments (Kyle-Little 16.12.1948) concerning 'half-caste' employees reflect his belief that such individuals had the capacity to develop broader skills and possibly become owners of capital rather than remaining as wage labourers:

> [The head stockman at Seven Emus Station, 'an exempt half-caste'] is . . . a good type of man with a reputation throughout the district as far as Burketown as being an exceptionally good cattleman and shrewd businessman. He has a Savings Bank Account and a [large] credit . . . He expressed to me his ambition was to own his own property. (p. 3)
>
> [At Pungalina Station, a 'half-caste' stockman and the White lessee's two 'half-caste' sons] . . . were a good class of lad and were all recognised as smart stockmen. (p. 4)
>
> [At Wollogorang, three 'half-castes'] . . . are all classified as stockmen and carry out their duties as such. They work hard and long hours and no attempt has been made to educate them in any way. They live and eat in the native camp and in general are treated as an average Aboriginal stockman. I can see no reason why . . . [the White manager] should not be made to employ these half-castes as apprentices and provide quarters and better class of food. Each boy should have a bank account and their weekly wages paid directly into same. (p. 7)

No such comments are made regarding the prospects of people of solely Aboriginal descent.

'Kings' as brokers

During the period following Wild Time, station Whites and policemen introduced the practice of designating certain men as 'kings' of stations or areas encompassing them. This occurred particularly in the first decade of this century and possibly earlier, and the kings lived on through the 1920s, 1930s and 1940s. Aboriginal people now name kings whose 'runs' focused on various stations. A number of individuals who became kings at stations in Queensland were among those who had moved eastwards from their countries across the border. At least one man from coastal Ganggalida country left the region to become king of a station on the Barkly Tableland to the southwest.

From oral accounts it is clear that the kings were middlemen between camp populations and local Whites with authority, especially policemen and station managers. They would obtain commodities for 'their mobs' — any Aboriginal people within what was known to be their 'run', which encompassed their normal field of influence. The following man's comments begin with reference to a 'Burketown king', then deal more generally with kings elsewhere throughout the region:

> He can go to the police station in Burketown [and say]: 'I wanna get so much ration, I got about big mob down here [to] look after'. Well he buy the tucker . . . you [will] see load of tucker come out . . . no matter where they [Aborigines he is looking after] come from he still findim 'em tucker, because he's the leader in Burketown. If we go'n ask, me'n you come from somewhere else: 'We got no tucker'. He put his plate on, two of them, small one on the side and the big one in the front . . . and . . . police see him [and will say]: 'Oh yeh . . . what the trouble?' [and the king would answer]: 'Oh I got a big mob out here at the lake [near Burketown] — big camp there, I wanna get so much tucker for 'em'. He might get four or five bag of flour or might be more, two bag of sugar, tobacco might be . . .
>
> He [the king] just like the, y'know . . . owner of the station — he can go to that manager there and tell him: 'Oh you better kill a bullock, I got a big mob down here'. He [manager] say: 'Oh right, away you go, bring the killer [beast to be slaughtered] in', or might be out in the bush, just killim themselves. (T45)

In the Aboriginal view, such provision of material commodities was evidence of the way 'the government' would 'look after' kings.

To some extent, kings were viewed as carrying the authority of 'the government' in that they were seen as being able to mobilise White support:

> I seen that king mix in [fight] amongst 'em, no matter how serious — he spear fight, boomerang fight, he gotta be there no matter how he goes if you knock the king over, well you gone good-bye [you have committed an offence against the White system of authority] . . . well the king was the leader for everybody. (T45)

The king plate, usually an engraved crescent-shaped metal ornament that was hung around the neck, was regarded as the extremely important emblem of office, which empowered the wearer: 'you can't break that plate off him [in a fight] . . . if that chain come out of them two little holes, you gone now' (T45). The king's status was seen as ultimately backed up by the White police.

It was apparently regarded as appropriate that a child of the king inherit his plate and its attendant office. The oldest sons of the Escott Station and Turn Off Lagoon kings were known in English by the name 'Prince', the former as a first name and the latter as a surname. In the case of the Escott king it was also considered possible that a daughter inherit the plate and office: 'like Elizabeth Queen y'know, they can take over them things blangta their father, hey?' (T45). The Aboriginal conception of kingship was borrowed from the local White understanding of the European system of royalty. However, I recorded only one possible case of a child actually inheriting the plate, as the role of kings gradually became anachronistic.

While their children (and others) now describe kings as having had influence over large numbers of people (e.g. 'my father been king of all the Garawa'), their influence appears to have been most commonly confined to contexts involving their dealing as middlemen with local White police, employers and other officials. Contemporary discussion normally attributes to each of them one or more admired qualities (e.g. great knowledge, or skills as a fighter, dancer or singer). The kings at Westmoreland and Turn Off Lagoon are attributed particularly high status (at least among Aboriginal men) on the basis of the large number of wives they obtained throughout their lives. These two kings therefore have much larger numbers of descendants than the others, and it is primarily among their descendants that they are remembered as having been 'leaders'. Nevertheless, there is general agreement that the various kings appropriately negotiated with White authority figures for the supply of commodities throughout the periods spent living on stations and in fringe-camps.

Pastoralism and the consolidation of economic power

With sedentarisation, Aboriginal people became vitally dependent on 'rations' and other commodities, and incorporated within the pastoral economy. Colonial social relations were largely constituted by Aboriginal relationships to non-Aboriginal employers and government officials. The former desired Aboriginal labour as cheaply as possible, while the latter attempted to regulate labour relations according to the official ideology and law of the state, which was committed to the 'protection' of Aborigines through paternalist supervision and control of their movements and their labour. White Australian society exercised economic power over Aborigines, in that a constellation of the latter's material interests in sedentary (and semi-sedentary) camp circumstances necessitated their becoming wage labourers. While bush resources continued to be obtained (to varying degrees at different places), the hunter-gatherer mode of production was gradually diminished as access to those resources was constrained by pastoral land use. Furthermore, Aborigines became increasingly dependent on and attracted to certain material goods available from White employers and officials, particularly tobacco, flour, tea, sugar and beef. The desire for these and other goods necessitated working for non-Aboriginal people. Thus, the structural domination of Aboriginal society had strong foundations both in the region's economic life and in police enforcement of the laws of the state.

As wage labourers, Aborigines had little control over their working conditions and income, although a fine-grained analysis must also recognise an Aboriginal repertoire of manoeuvres designed to avoid blatantly exploitative labour relations with non-Aborigines. Some tactics involved enlisting the support of local White police. Moreover, the mutually supportive dimensions of many Aboriginal-worker/White-boss relationships must be recognised. Hence, the pattern of Aboriginal compliance was complex. It cannot be characterised as solely the product of structural domination via physical force or the threat of it, though the laws enabling the removal of Aborigines, particularly those who were violent, disobedient or threatened White interests, represent continuing domination by physical force. Furthermore, while economic domination of Aborigines is clear, some aspects of labour relations were accorded legitimacy by Aboriginal employees, particularly where close supportive relationships with non-Aboriginal bosses continued over lengthy periods (at times, well after the actual employment relationship had ceased). Moreover, Aborigines might align themselves with White authority in order to win out in disputes with both Aborigines and non-Aborigines, as is evident from the example of a man getting support from the White police in his dispute with his Afghan employer. After getting the Burketown police sergeant to legalise his marriage, the same man was able to effectively counter the opposition to it among his Aboriginal relatives. By all accounts, it was not uncommon for White authority to be regarded as a highly useful ally in disputes within Aboriginal society, and to the extent that White authority was perceived as potentially useful, it can be viewed as engendering some legitimacy.

However, neither economic domination nor the power exercised by the state relied on legitimations by Whites. Certain Whites appear to have claimed that they were working for Aborigines' best interests, as in the example given of a dispute between the Gregory Downs police protector and a pastoralist in his district. Yet both pastoralists and government employees regarded Aboriginal labour as a commodity to be used in the interests of the pastoral industry, quite apart from whether Aboriginal people shared this view, and indeed, apart from any attempt to convince them that this should be so. The notion of 'blacks being taught to obey' which was prevalent during Wild Time was, by the 1940s, transformed into the notion that 'if worked and treated properly' Aborigines would give no trouble. However, there is little evidence, from either oral or written sources, that the thinking of Aboriginal people was constrained to the point where they embraced the ideological preoccupations of non-Aboriginal society. There is no evidence that Aboriginal people intellectually embraced capitalist work values; and while workers accepted supervision from bosses while they remained relatively benevolent, it is not at all clear that White tutelage was thought necessary or appropriate.

The imposed office of kingship was conceived of as a form of leadership by Whites, and seen as contextually confined brokerage by Aborigines. From the perspectives of both employers and bureaucrats, establishing kings was an attempt to systematise necessary dealings with Aboriginal people. It cannot be regarded as any real attempt at incorporating certain individuals into the ruling colonial apparatus, and thereby legitimating White rule. Kings did achieve influence among other Aborigines through regulating their access to desired commodities, and through associated high status. However, while kings were perceived as being able to draw on powerful Whites for support, they were not seen to be part of the ruling colonial apparatus. They did not engender broad Aboriginal attribution of legitimacy to the structures and processes of White domination.

Thus, until they came to Doomadgee Mission, Aboriginal people of this region were dominated structurally by both the economic and political forces of the colonising society. With the establishment of

Doomadgee, economic and political domination was consolidated but another form of struggle within the colonial social relationship ensued — this was the ideological struggle by which Aboriginal thinking itself was targeted for reshaping. In addressing the history of Aboriginal institutionalisation at Doomadgee, the next chapter examines the process through which the colonised have been historically subjected to the forces of hegemonic domination.

Notes

[1] Note the comment by Schaffert (1981: 4), who was the manager at Gregory Downs Station from 1931 to 1944:

> It was the usual thing for our Aborigines to go on a walkabout towards the end of the year. Once the end of September came it was near impossible to hold any of them back. I remember the time when the Aborigines were ready to walkabout from Gregory Downs Station. From 100 to 150 were headed for Accident Creek where they would put all the young bucks through their initiation and so forth.

[2] In Queensland, *The Aboriginals Protection and Restriction of the Sale of Opium Act* (1901) required Ministerial approval for any marriage between an Aboriginal woman and a non-Aboriginal man, and prohibited any unauthorised non-Aboriginal person from being in an Aboriginal camp. Following an amending Act in 1934, *The Aboriginals Preservation and Protection Acts* 1939 to 1946 prohibited 'carnal knowledge' of female Aborigines by non-Aboriginal men. In the Northern Territory, the *Aboriginals Ordinance* of 1918 contained similar stipulations (sections 28, 45, 51, but particularly 53, which prohibited non-Aborigines 'consorting with' Aboriginal women). These legal provisions continued in Queensland until 1965, and in the Northern Territory until 1962 (Stevens 1980: 67). Both the Queensland and Northern Territory legislation provided that non-Aboriginal fathers of 'half-caste' children were in certain circumstances liable to contribute to the support of such children. This provision appears to have continued in Queensland from the 1901 Act until 1939, and in the Northern Territory from the 1918 Ordinance until 1953.

[3] In *Gulf Country History File* (Australian Institute of Aboriginal Studies library).

[4] Barker's (1964: 88–101) discussion of 'Afghans' in outback Australia notes that most such people really came from Karachi (in present day Pakistan), though Stevens (1989: viii) finds that they were indeed Afghans. They were nomadic, and many drove camel teams transporting various commodities.

[5] On some Northern Territory stations Aboriginal youths were simply abducted right up until the 1930s. Kyle-Little (16.12.1948: 2) reports that Aborigines at Manangoora claimed that '8 to 10 years ago [i.e. *circa* 1938–1940, police] had always taken young men away in handcuffs for no apparent reason', and the White owner told him that these 'boys' were then 'forwarded. . . on to drovers or cattle stations on the Barkly Tablelands

for work'. Consequently, 'the natives in the area are still very frightened of the Police'.

[6] Before 1919: the 1899 Regulations (QGG 1899: 746–7) did not stipulate any wage rate, but stated that the employer shall provide 'suitable shelter, blankets, rations (including tobacco), clothing, and maintenance during sickness' and shall return the employee to his 'native place' when the job is finished. In the Act of 1901, the minimum wage is set at five shillings per month ('exclusive of food, accommodation, and other necessaries'); and in the 1904 Regulations (QGG 1904: 1187–9) a lower scale for female employees (variable 'at the discretion of the Protector') is provided, with the stipulation that small amounts are to be paid weekly as 'pocket-money'.

[7] Cf. Anderson's (1983: 490–1) similar comments on relationships between Aboriginal workers and their bosses in small-scale tin mining enterprises in southeast Cape York Peninsula.

[8] Hagarty (personal communication 15.12.1984) explained in correspondence that:

> The term 'head' or 'pointer', 'Stirrer', 'Big mouth', 'too much yabber', 'Tongue to the arsehole' were labels that indicated an agitator or trouble maker among other blacks. He was the . . . type who knew it all, and invariably had it badly twisted, and after leading others into strife left them to foot the bill and denied any connection. He was the bad apple to be avoided if you desired harmony in the camps . . .

[9] Most of the 39 men had wives (and some had children). Some or all of these may also have been employed, though this is unclear from Kyle-Little's report.

CHAPTER FOUR

Doomadgee Mission: institutionalisation and a new form of colonial struggle

In 1930, a missionary couple who had recently severed connections with the Australian Inland Mission was directed to Burketown by the Brisbane office of the Department of Native Affairs. The couple had called there 'seeking a place where the Lord was not known among the dark folk of our land' (D. Akehurst n.d.: 1). They received 'commendation' (i.e. religious authorisation) from Open Brethren Assemblies in Sydney and, together with another young man from Sydney, had established a base at Burketown by early 1931. They cared for young children in their mission home in Burketown, and by 1933 had been joined by several others of similar religious background and had established a mission on the Bayley Point Reserve at Dumaji (a site on a long sand ridge 3 km from the beach, see map 1). This mission subsequently became known as 'Old Doomadgee'.[1] By late 1935 the site had been 'condemned as unsuitable for an expanding work by the visiting Director of Native Affairs' (D. Read n.d.). Early in 1936 a cyclone destroyed many of the buildings, and later that year the mission was shifted to its present site on the Nicholson River.

Correspondence from the Chief Protector of Aboriginals (n.d., but almost certainly written in early 1936, p. 3) indicates the reasons underlying official government support for the move to the Nicholson River site. The coastal site was regarded as too far from existing 'Aboriginal camps', with access difficult and little land suitable for agriculture. Whereas the site on the Nicholson River is described as 'centrally situated', being 'only 10 to 15 miles from Turn Off Lagoons' to the west and 'about 50 miles to Burketown' to the east. Thus, it would allow for 'better control of the natives, and improved facilities for the employment of Aboriginal labour by land holders of the district'. The chief protector anticipated that the population at the coastal site (fifty or sixty children plus about twenty adults) would, once relocated to the new site, 'more than double in respect of children, and also become the recognized permanent home of the various adult Aboriginals of the district'. This projected population increase certainly occurred:

> The first large group of Aborigines removed to the new mission was reported in 1938 when forty-eight destitute and old people from Burketown and the cattle station camps were taken there. These removals increased the mission population to 138 for that year but evidently the population remained less than 200 until 1947. After that the numbers increased rapidly from 152 in 1946, to 357 in 1956 and 519 in 1965. (Long 1970:49)

The founding missionary attitude

Written missionary accounts often refer to the rate of success in persuading Aborigines to embrace Christian Brethren faith and beliefs. One manuscript (D. Akehurst n.d.: 11) describes one of the earliest 'meetings' (the Brethren term for a collective prayer service) at Old Doomadgee:

> On the Sunday night we had a meeting at Hussien's [*sic*] camp[2] at which King Jimmy Dow Dow[3] and his gin were present. I count it a great privilege to tell these people the wonderful story of Jesus and his love.

On consecutive dates the manuscript refers to: the work being encouraging 'from a spiritual standpoint' and Aborigines 'beginning to understand' (p. 16, 31.10.1931); people gripping the truth of the Gospel and growing in knowledge (p. 28, 20.10.1932); the routine of Bible reading and teaching and prayer with 'our working boys' after breakfast and dinner, and the associated cleanliness, lack of swearing, truthfulness and good work of the latter (p. 38, 14.4.1933); the baptism of two 'boys' (adult men) (p. 48, 26.11.1933), four 'boys' and then 'one boy and three women' (p. 52, 11.2.1934), later two girls (p. 54, 1.4.1934) and a reference to 'seven of our baptised believers' (p. 58, 25.4.1934); and, in the absence of the White men on a Sunday, several Aboriginal men for the first time taking an active part by praying aloud in a Service (p. 72, 19.5.1935).[4]

The manuscript also refers to periods of opposition to the missionaries' work in 'spiritual' terms. In October 1932, Akehurst writes (p. 26) of 'Satan . . . strongly contending us', and in December of that year (p. 31):

> We are sure by now that Satan and the powers of darkness don't want us to establish a work for the Lord at Doomadgee or anywhere else up here as hindrance after hindrance has come as we make any advance.

By June 1934, she was able to speak of the previous six months as 'a time of great spiritual blessing', but also of how 'the devil . . . has been contesting every step forward, attacking us in unforeseen ways from unforeseen quarters and he is still at it' (p. 60). Despite a certain amount of initial Aboriginal opposition to embracing Christianity, these early missionaries continued to preach the Gospel (D. Akehurst 1933: 175).

However, possibly the more significant role in which Doomadgee residents remember the early missionaries is in compassionate work, which was an attempt to meet the severe medical needs of those who were suffering the obvious and immediate effects of dwelling on the fringe of White society. The material conditions of the Aborigines at Burketown are described in D. Akehurst's (n.d.) manuscript: the 'town camp' was about 1½ km from the town across a plain that was 'a sea of mud in the wet and a barren, cracked earth place in the dry' (pp. 3, 8); colds were very prevalent (p. 19), as was venereal disease (pp. 37, 71), and there were cases of leprosy (p. 71). From another source (D. Akehurst, personal communication n.d.*a*):

> When we came to Burketown . . . there was no one to care for the physical well being of the poor wretched Aborigines we found. True the local protector was kindly disposed toward them and faithfully dispensed Government rations and saw that they went to hospital if they were ill but that did nothing for the state in which they lived poor in every way, smothered in dirt, sores and flies in the heat and no one to care in any way. What else could we do but care for their bodies as well as their souls. [Then follow two relevant biblical quotations.]

The town camp residents are described as:

> that sad and sorry remnant . . . Filthy, smothered in flies when Trachoma was bad and often hungry . . . They were without hope and without God in this world and He directed us to help meet both needs. (D. Akehurst, personal communication 16.10.1979)

The missionaries made clear their commitment to provide material assistance in their correspondence to the chief protector in Brisbane:

> The people in these parts are of nomadic habit, and very much diseased, and whilst it is our chief desire to gather them together for religious teaching we would also be able to minister to and relieve the diseased bodies by treatment. (L. Akehurst 25.4.1931).

They had to justify this side of their work to their supporters in the Brethren Assemblies:

> Some do not hold with us touching the temporal side of things, saying that it should be left to the Government. It is very difficult to make them

> see the state in which the people live and how impossible it would be to make them feel a spiritual need while their bodily need is so great. We believe the Lord, seeing their need, would have us meet it. (D. Akehurst n.d.: 25)

Apart from medical attention, the missionaries provided food and clothing to certain Aborigines in return for their labour (e.g. D. Akehurst n.d.: 25), and also paid at least one man wages at Old Doomadgee (D. Akehurst 1933: 176).

While the poor physical conditions were an important factor in the missionary justification for gathering Aboriginal children under their care away from the parents (both in Burketown and at Old Doomadgee), they also stressed the 'moral danger' to the children in the camps:

> no little girl is really safe, such is the depraved condition of the people here. From the very earliest years, the children are conversant with the evil that goes on round them. You will understand what it means to get the children from such a place into the pure, clean atmosphere of a Christian home and daily being taught of the cleansing power of the Blood. (D. Akehurst 1933: 176)

Some Aboriginal parents are described as wanting their children in the Burketown home because of the better food and other material resources there (e.g. D. Akehurst 1933: 176), and because the children (at least the girls, especially the 'half-castes') would otherwise be sent away from 'moral danger' to Mornington Island, according to government policy (D. Akehurst n.d.: 9; Cantle 1980: 55). After the first missionaries' arrival at Burketown, apparently no further children were sent to Mornington Island for this reason (D. Akehurst personal communication 17.9.1981).

The early missionaries appear to have distinguished between acceptable and unacceptable aspects of what they perceived as Aboriginal culture. For example, they greatly enjoyed some dancing put on for them at Burketown in mid October 1931, although D. Akehurst notes (n.d.: 14) that other corroborees 'were very crude and we could not sanction them'. The 'pull of the old time way' was seen to provide 'trials and temptations' for the Aboriginal Christians (D. Akehurst n.d.: 70). Yet the 'evil' that they had to 'unlearn', and the 'old life' to which the children did not wish to return (D. Akehurst n.d.: 43–4) was not really regarded as Aboriginal culture but rather as the product of squalid camp life and the influence of 'ungodly' Whites (D. Akehurst n.d.: 26, 52). The missionaries did not learn much of any Aboriginal language or understand much of the traditions:

> in my day they did not show any special interest in tribal ways. I know they kept certain customs especially among those that came from West-

> moreland way as they tended to live away from ... homesteads. (D. Akehurst personal communication 17.9.1982)

And again (M. Read T91):

> I don't know whether there would have been many, if any, ... living tribally ... And I wasn't worrying much about old time stuff, excepting that I got to know enough about their beliefs to use it to help them try to understand what I was trying to teach them.

There was a certain closeness in the founding missionary-Aboriginal relationship. D. Akehurst's (n.d.) manuscript refers to the missionary couple's children: learning a song in an Aboriginal language (p. 13); being assigned fictive kin relationships with the Aborigines (p. 21); growing used to the Aboriginal people around them so that one asked if his mother had a baby would it be black (p. 44); and one of them believing he would grow into 'a black boy' some day (p. 80). This was despite the fact that the missionaries would not let their own children 'play with the native children except under supervision as they aren't very clean in their habits' (p. 17). At one point the White woman at Old Doomadgee was cooking for five 'boys' (p. 38), and the Whites were eating substantial amounts of bush food, much of it procured by the Aborigines (pp. 53, 57–8). This woman remembers that: 'We lived very close to them and our lives were open before them' (D. Akehurst personal communication n.d.*b*); and says:

> I would like to return not as things are now [1980] but as they were, when we loved and were loved in return by the dark folk and were trusted. (D. Akehurst personal communication n.d.*c*)

When this woman did return in 1969 (D. Akehurst n.d.: 77): 'what hugs and kisses, black arms coming from all directions "my old boss" "my old missus", we were patted and stroked'. She summarises the situation of the early missionary endeavour (D. Akehurst n.d.: 74):

> We believe we had a good relationship with the natives as they found we did not live on any luxuries but lived on the very plainest of food, that often we were hungry and were glad to get a wallaby for meat, and often they would bring something they had caught for us. In many ways we sat where they sat and our lack of money was noticeable. Never at any time were we in danger by any hostility and I was completely safe even when left alone [without her husband] ... and never at any time did I carry a firearm as most White women did, neither for that matter did my husband, except for shooting wallabies. The Lord gave us favour with all the natives and we thanked Him.

D. Akehurst's manuscript indicates that the missionaries were ostracised by other Whites in Burketown and the general district:

> We are finding great acceptance with the dark folk . . . However, we don't have much acceptance from the white folk, especially the women who seem to have decided as we devote ourselves to the care of the natives that we are very much beneath them — or perhaps it is that they don't understand us. (pp. 9–10)

And elsewhere:

> I suppose our stay here has been one of the biggest trials so far owing to the open hostility from white folk. You do not realise how hostile they are . . . We believe their consciences are pricked over their treatment of the Aborigines over the years and we have disturbed their way of life by caring and trying to lift them from their degradation. (p. 21)

The missionaries did not drink alcohol or gamble at the annual races, and they were branded 'ascetics' (p. 25). The White women in Burketown did not visit the missionary women (p. 28). Another source (D. Read n.d.: 1) states that the thirty or so Burketown Whites 'completely ostracized the missionaries', and D. Akehurst (1933: 176) believed that the Aborigines 'had been prejudiced against us by evil White men' before gathering at Old Doomadgee. A more recent document (A. Hockey 1970: 1) notes the report of a time of six months when the Burketown Whites would not talk to the missionaries. The opposition from certain Whites appears to have mellowed (e.g. in the case of some station men who were assisted by the missionaries when cut off from their homestead by floodwaters [D. Akehurst n.d.: 67]). There is also a report (n.d.: 64) of 'opportunities for personal work [i.e. of a religious nature] among the White folk' on one trip.

As already indicated, the missionaries had official governmental support, particularly for the establishment of the new mission at the Nicholson River site, although the Department of Native Affairs appears to have had to argue strongly for this in the face of opposition from the Lands Department 'to any Aboriginal institution in the midst of pastoral holdings' (Chief Protector of Aboriginals 29.6.1936). The Department of Native Affairs stated that the objection was groundless as surrounding land was not occupied, and that in any case the mission would enable better control over 'nomadic and other natives', thereby 'removing risk of disturbance to stock'. According to the Department of Native Affairs, the Aboriginal population of the district was 200, including forty under agreement in employment, and it pointed out that if the Department (rather than the mission) had to 'undertake relief of the indigent ones' it would cost from 500 to 1,000 pounds annually.

However, support was not always forthcoming from the local officialdom. The protector at Burketown expressed some reservations when the mission was first being established at Old Doomadgee. He was particularly concerned that 'active males' would be:

> induced to go to the settlement instead of taking up employment, where they do good and useful work, and get paid for same. To my way of thinking the taking of active males to the Settlement would be a mistake, for many of them are first class stockmen, and they would be a far greater asset to the country employed at station work, than roaming about the settlement. (Hosier 19.9.1931)

He also doubted whether many Aborigines, apart from those 'few that always live on the Reserve' could be induced to live there permanently:

> The old natives have what they term their own country, and would rather die there in poverty (if necessary) than leave it for any Promised Land. The young and active males when their term of employment is over are in the habit of drawing on their accounts for provisions, with the old people, and go on the walkabout, and apparently enjoy their freedom, until such times the stock season opens again, when they gather round the different Stations and are ready and will [*sic*] to go to work again. (Hosier 19.9.1931)

The protector may not have understood that the general vicinity of the Bayley Point Reserve was the 'country' of many of the Burketown residents, although his sentiments were correct with reference to the Waanyi people at Turn Off Lagoon who were certainly not prepared to settle at Old Doomadgee.

In 1931 the Burketown protector also stated that while they appeared to be 'very respectable people' he did not consider the missionaries 'suitable persons to control and train natives'. He does not elaborate, but his conclusion seems partly due to the missionaries' apparent lack of substantial financial support and practical achievement during the nine or ten months they had been there. However, the protector seems to have later changed his mind, writing in April 1936 to the founding missionaries (who had by then left the area):

> although you had many difficulties to contend with, I say without fear of contradiction that the success attained . . . was due to your personal efforts and supervision. (quoted in D. Akehurst personal communication 26.11.1980)

The final issue to emerge from source documents concerning the founding of the mission is the effects on the health of the missionaries. D. Akehurst's manuscript (n.d.) constantly notes their 'trials, difficulties, problems, disappointments troubles' (p. 6), with individual missionaries: getting trachoma badly (p. 9); being physically exhausted (p. 12); and contracting malaria or 'Gulf Fever' (pp. 19, 69), boils (pp. 24, 48) and diarrhoea 'brought on through bad water and nervous strain' during a trip from Burketown to Old Doomadgee, when they became bogged and stranded for nearly three months in the wet season (pp. 32–4). Moreover, the Akehursts' third child was stillborn during the trip by boat from Old Doomadgee to the Burketown Hospital (p. 39). While made 'tired and weary with the continuous strain' of all this (p. 60), and while having had to 'retire from the field broken in health after five years' these missionaries (as did others) maintained their faith and regarded their work as 'abundantly worthwhile' (L. Akehurst n.d.).

Mission management of labour relations

There are a few references by the early missionaries to Aboriginal people being well treated on certain cattle stations, but at others they perceived a range of problems. Aborigines are said to have been illegally given alcohol on some stations, and there are other descriptions of very bad conditions:

> One well known station used to throw the meat ration on to the ground for them. I could tell you of at least one boy who was chained and beaten. (D. Akehurst personal communication 17.9.1982)

There are also missionary references (M. and D. Read T79) to inadequate wages for Aboriginal labour on stations ('paying them just a few bob a week and then working their wives for nothing') and in Burketown ('get them to come and scrub or wash for them for a little bit of sugar').

M. Read was the superintendent and protector at Doomadgee from its establishment at the Nicholson site (1936) until 1951. He describes (T91) how wages were an arrangement between the protector and station employer, and how he constantly tried to raise them each time the agreement had to be renewed. It is unclear whether he was aiming for the legally stipulated minimum rates or just trying to get as much as he could for the Aboriginal workers. In any case, the desire for higher wage rates plus other incentives, including having relatives at the mission, led increasing numbers of Aborigines to request transfer of the handling of their agreements from other protectors (Burketown, Gregory Downs) to Doomadgee. The Reads explain (T91) that such events made the missionaries unpopular with many station people: 'They set themselves against us actually but over the years we won their respect'. Some station people were also apparently unimpressed with and embarrassed by the missionaries' moral disapproval of the circumstances that had led to the presence of the mixed-race children on the stations.

Nor was there always support from police and other government officials. Successive Burketown protectors mostly opposed transfers of Aboriginal workers' agreements to Doomadgee. The Doomadgee protector was accused of inducing good workers to transfer so their services could be used at the mission where an otherwise 'mostly ... lazy useless crowd' resided; and it was asserted that workers under Burketown supervision were better off by being in constant better-paid employment (Chambers 28.10.1948). The latter claim was (as discussed in chapter 3) disproved by a Department of Native Affairs investigation (Davis 19.9.1949), which found that nearly all Doomadgee males between the ages of sixteen and sixty were out at station employment, and that Aborigines from Doomadgee 'in most cases obtain higher wages than those signed on from Burketown'. Davis's report concluded that families were better off at the mission because of the schooling (not available on stations), hospital (at that point apparently better staffed than the Burketown Hospital), better diet and accommodation than on stations and the 'habits of cleanliness and discipline inculcated in the children' at the mission. The report found that the only disadvantage of transfer for married men with dependants was that, in accordance with the 1945 Regulations (No. 6), those resident at the mission had to contribute 10 per cent of their wages to the Department of Native Affairs' welfare fund, while those resident elsewhere contributed at the rate of 2.5 per cent. Moreover, families at the mission had to pay 'for rations not locally produced, such as tea, sugar, and flour' supplied to their dependants, except for dormitory children 'for whom the Mission receives Institution Child Endowment'. Davis recommended that such missions provide all standard rations free of charge to the dependants of working Aborigines and to the workers themselves when holidaying at the mission, providing that the Regulations were amended so that the compulsory wage deductions were paid direct to the mission rather than to the welfare fund. Following Davis's report, the mission was also instructed (Director of Native Affairs 14.11.1949, 5.4.1950) to cease charging the accounts of Aborigines not attached to the mission (at the rate of 7 shillings and 6 pence per day) for treatment at the mission hospital, for Aboriginal people were entitled to free treatment at any hospital in the state.

A subsequent Burketown protector accused the Doomadgee protector of issuing to visiting Aborigines (i.e. through funds in their Burketown-based accounts) goods and 'Pocket Money', 'prior to persuading them to transfer their accounts' to Doomadgee (Champney 2.2.1950). The latter also argued (Champney 1.2.1950) that all Burketown-based Aborigines were 'happy and contented in employment, until after a visit to the mission', where they were persuaded that mission life was much better than elsewhere. His opinion was that mission life was best only for old people and school-age children. His telegram to the Doomadgee superintendent (Champney 31.1.1950) requested the latter to 'cease immediately underhand persuasive tactics' in the matter of transfers, otherwise he would not allow Aborigines in the Burketown protectorate to visit the mission. Champney (1.3.1950) also claimed that despite the great demand by stations for Aboriginal labour, a large number of people were living in idleness at Doomadgee (and Mornington Island) until their previously earned money was used up, and that such individuals should be directed 'to suitable employment, as was done in the distant past'.

The problem of regulating Aboriginal employment at Westmoreland was also a focus for argument between successive protectors at Doomadgee and Burketown. Apart from the allegations that the station had constantly attempted to avoid paying either Queensland or Northern Territory wage rates for 'years past' (M. Read 21.4.1949), an associated issue was the alleged illegal employment (without wages) of Aboriginal children at Westmoreland. A Burketown protector (Nuss 12.11.1942) claimed that the Doomadgee protector was not cooperating in efforts to rectify this situation, and the protectors continued over some time to accuse each other of avoiding their responsibilities in these matters (M. Read 7.6.1948; Chambers 3.9.1948). Eventually, the families at Westmoreland gradually moved to Doomadgee.

Various station managements appear to have been opposed to the mission. In 1962 the director of the owning company at Westmoreland claimed that from previous experience he 'had found that mission controlled labour' was unreliable, that the Aborigines at Westmoreland had 'little in common with the Doomadgee natives', and that 'recognized rates of pay' and conditions were to operate at the station (Cunneen 8.2.1962). The company received some support from the Burketown protector, concerning the alleged desire of Aborigines to remain resident at the station in familiar surroundings and conditions (Jessen 6.2.1962, 16.5.1962, 2.7.1962), but the protector finally decided that they would be better off at the mission (15.12.1962), and that while the station director was 'making out he is kindly disposed towards the natives, [he] desires their labour on the cheap' (15.6.1963). Disputes between Doomadgee and Westmoreland over employment matters continued until the early 1970s.

From the beginning a major task of the Doomadgee administration had been the management of continuous large-scale Aboriginal employment on stations. According to Long (1970: 153), such employment was still occurring in 1965. By 1975–6, however, only approximately 20 per cent of the workforce were employed in the pastoral industry, and those were on short-term contracts (DAIA 1976: 15). Annual DAIA reports for 1978 to 1983 show that only small numbers were employed on stations, mostly on short-term contracts, although the mission administration also managed some employment of people with the Burke Shire Council. Lately, the main sources of employment at Doomadgee have been the provision of essential services for the mission itself, and some local industries. Large numbers of people have been unemployed, and the mission has managed the provision of various social security benefits to the population.

Continued missionary commitment to evangelism

According to the missionary M. Read, while the old law kept up a reasonably high level of moral conduct, the 'true Myall or Nomadic Tribal' people's knowledge of the spirit of man and of other spirits led only to fear (7.7.1946: 2): 'Truely [*sic*], apart from the Gospel they are a spiritually hopeless and helpless people, few having even a false hope to cling to'. The 'Detribalised' people were at a very low moral level, and (7.7.1946: 3) 'outside the effective influence of the law and moral ethics of both the old and new codes'. Ungodly White and 'asiatic folk' had introduced such moral degeneracy. The 'ideal environment' for Aborigines was (7.7.1946: 3) 'a native community centre under direct christian control and influence':

> The moral ethics of the scriptures are clear, plain, and profitable to follow. The moral tone of those on the reserve is far above that of their less fortunate peoples. (7.7.1946: 4)

M. Read points out that while there may have been some cause for doubt as to the effectiveness of spiritual work among Aborigines:

> there are others who bring joy and satisfaction, and it must be remembered that few of the natives of the present generation have anything in their background which will help them in their christian walk, and much that is against them because of their hereditary tendencies inherited from their forebears. (7.7.1946:4)

Elsewhere (T71), he describes how he never belittled Aborigines' beliefs, but constantly argued that belief in the greater spirit, God, would allow them to overcome their fear of evil spirits. Read claims there was 'an assembly of [about 50] accepted believers' when he left in 1951.

A document written in 1953 (Doomadgee 1953) claims '85 natives in fellowship':

> some of whom can and do take an intelligent and valued part in the spiritual exercises of the Assembly, although, as yet, help is necessary from those who labour for and with them [i.e. White missionaries]. (1953: 3)

The number had doubled over the previous four years, and twenty-two had been added during the previous three months:

> Long had they been captive to the power of darkness, bound by superstitious fears, enslaved to vice, to uncleanness, to dishonour. Contact with White civilisation, apart from Christian influences, did nothing to emancipate them, but rather worsened their moral condition. Add to these practices which still persist amongst the non-Christians — such evils as fathers giving their young daughters for money or other considerations, the pull of tribal custom evidenced when old men urge and force young fellows to submit to initiation rites . . ., the pitiful wailing for the dead, and the cutting of themselves with knives, and the offering of food to appease the spirits of the departed. (1953: 4)

Thus the Christian revival was regarded as a 'wave of spiritual blessing'; however:

> There has appeared a smouldering resentment on the part of some of the old-time native men and women — this may develop to test severely the new Christians. (1953: 5)

This document concludes with a request for more 'consecrated personnel' from the Assemblies around Australia. At that point Doomadgee apparently drew comparatively little financial support from the Assemblies, and was dependent on government grants, child endowment payments, local sale of cattle and local store profits.

In annual reports of the Department of Native Affairs, successive mission superintendents report on the changing rates of success of the evangelistic endeavours of the staff: daily religious instruction with good attendance (Read 1947–48: 31); encouraging results (Talbot 1953–54: 40); men and women coming almost daily for spiritual help (Talbot 1956–57: 33); a falling off in attendance at meetings and a decline in spiritual tone due to 'increased amusements', particularly the possession of radios (Talbot 1958–59: 33); attendances at meetings fluctuating (Hockey 1961–62: 10), and daily scripture lessons in the school (DAIA 1968: 6).

Doomadgee school children were said to receive 'far more Biblical instruction and training than the majority of children brought up in [White] Christian homes' (Dempsey 1948, quoted in G. Hockey 1969: 2) and, in general:

> No human policy has been sought as an over-riding aim. The workers have sought only the wisdom and will of God as their guide. (G. Hockey 1969: B3)

In 1970, the missionary manager pointed out (A. Hockey 1970: 2) that, apart from the many government regulations in other areas of administration:

> we function autonomously and there has been absolute freedom in regard to the proclamation of the Gospel and the conduct of such meeting[s] as have been thought profitable.

The manager also commented on the long-term degree of effectiveness of the evangelical endeavour (1970: 3):

> The joys and disappointments of the spiritual side of the work have been many and varied over the years. As in every phase of their life, stability is lacking. From time to time there have been those who would appear subjects of becoming towers of strength in the Assembly, then, alas, the evil one comes in and they are set aside. However, there always seem to be the ones and twos to encourage and to these we commit the things that we have heard that they may teach others also (2 Tim. 2:2)... Approximately 150 have been baptised over the years, but few have maintained a consistent testimony. There are an average of 30–40 who gather to His Name each week to remember Him in the breaking of the bread and drinking of the cup.

It is clear from written sources that the missionary life involved hard work and considerable stress. Throughout assorted newsletter clippings (compiled by Talbot, a mission worker from 1949 to 1958 and variously after that) there are references to physical difficulties and periods of illness experienced by various staff. Ill health forced some to leave, either permanently or temporarily. A quite specific reference (Bedford and Rossow 1960: 5) is made to the overworked medical sister:

> it is rare for her to have a full night's rest without interruption. The natives are inconsiderate and restless with sickness, particularly with children, and if cured, well that's all right — but in the event of death Sister is to blame.

Prospective visitors and workers are warned of the strain of the climate, and advised that:

> unless you are adaptable to the native people, [you] may well have a conscience, which is affected over some things you may see them do — such as smoking — and may not understand that their conscience is not as tender as your own and must wait till they grow in moral grace. (Bedford and Rossow 1960:4)

A broad theme of the missionary perspective is that the evangelical and material efforts made by missionaries over the years involved considerable personal sacrifice on their part.

The development of administrative authoritarianism

The missionary evangelical strategy included a high degree of routinisation of Aboriginal lives:

> Even under the more primitive conditions earlier [the early stage at the Nicholson site], a regular routine was followed — daily baths and clean

> clothes to all dormitory children and five days a week school . . . daily infant welfare with mother and babes, a weekly women's meeting, a girls' sewing class, bible class for older dormitory children and camp adults, a workers' fellowship, then Sunday morning worship meeting and evening gospel meeting with camp visitation and open air meetings Sunday afternoon when possible. (D. Read n.d.)

In 1953 (Doomadgee 1953: 3–4), a time of revival:

> Each Lord's Day [Sunday] morning at 9.45 the Christians assemble . . . On the same day at dusk, a Gospel meeting . . . On Tuesday evenings, a meeting for the ministry of the Word is held. Besides all the dormitory inmates, quite a number from the village, Christian and non-Christian, are present. Native brethren are largely responsible for the Wednesday evening Gospel testimony in the village, whilst on other evenings the native Christians gather around their camp fires for fellowship . . . Usually on Friday night one or more of the missionaries joins them.
>
> The women folk are cared for by a meeting conducted by the missionary sisters on Wednesday afternoons, whilst on Saturday nights a class of some twenty-three senior native girls . . . meets in one of the [White] workers' cottages for fellowship and edification.
>
> For the dormitory girls and boys there are morning prayers at 8 o'clock, . . . whilst every week-day evening devotional gatherings are held in both dormitories. Needless to say there is ample opportunity for personal work.

A somewhat less constant, but still very intensive weekly routine is described for 1960 (Bedford and Rossow 1960: 16).

Given that there was also secular supervision of Aboriginal residents, the reasons for the following missionary view in 1953 are clear: 'It may be truly said that the Mission personnel becomes complete caretakers of the people from babyhood to old age' (Doomadgee 1953: 6). However, periodic accusations that this caretaking was, in fact, over-authoritarian control have been made against the mission. The 1949 Department of Native Affairs investigation (Davis 19.9.1949) reported that children remained in dormitories from school age until they went to station employment (boys) or were married (girls). While the Burketown protector alleged that the Doomadgee staff discouraged single girls from marrying, the Davis report supported the Doomadgee superintendent's denial of this accusation. Under *The Aboriginals Preservation . . . Act* 1939 (section 19), the local protector's permission was required before any Aboriginal person could marry. The application form required information on the 'character' of applicants, their health (whether they were 'free from disease') and their financial position. Apart from such formal considerations, the Doomadgee superintendent's only proviso was that he was satisfied that the couple were 'sufficiently acquainted with each other to be sure of their own feelings in the matter' (Davis 19.9.1949:3).

In 1950, a government report (Director of Tuberculosis 9.5.1950: 4) described the Doomadgee Aborigines as 'the cleanest, the best fed and the best housed' but also 'the most severely restrained' in north Queensland. It focused particularly on the dormitory, terming it a prison in the case of young women:

> Doomadgee is the worst example of the ills of the dormitory system. It is here indistinguishable from slavery. There are only a few men on the station, all males over 14 or 15 being away at work, and the whole of the work of the mission, including the construction of buildings, cultivation and irrigation of the gardens (about 60 acres), as well as the domestic work of the mission, is done by the dormitory girls, who include many of mixed blood *and who range up to 24 years of age*. Girls are forbidden to leave the mission compound unaccompanied during the day and are locked up overnight. No amusements, other than hymn singing are permitted [my emphasis].

The Doomadge superintendent justified these restrictions on 'young girls' in terms of the Aboriginal population's low moral level in the recent past:

> It takes time to overcome the influence of past years filled more completely with evil contacts than with good dinners. Our aim has been to lift the natives up morally and socially by all possible means, and to slacken off necessary restrictive control as it is found the folk can rightly use and not abuse freedom. (M. Read 14.6.1950)

He also argued that 'the vast majority of the natives', (apart from 'a bad element about, from western parts') supported the dormitory system; for 'practically all' parents were away at stations for much of the year. Some men are said to have requested that their wives get 'added care and protection' by being allowed to re-enter the girls' dormitory in their absence. Finally, M. Read argued that Doomadgee Aborigines were not 'noted for docility' and would not stand for too severe discipline.

Dormitories apparently continued to operate until the late 1960s. In 1965 Long (1970: 152) referred to:

> a girls' dormitory with thirty-five inmates and a boys' dormitory with twenty-three. Both served as means of imposing a relatively rigorous mission discipline on the children in substitution for upbringing by their parents. Formerly the girls remained in the dormitory until they were married and the main purpose of the girls' dormitory was to postpone the girls' marriage and sexual experience. Recently the older girls have left to return to their parents before marriages have been arranged.

In 1972 Senator Keefe (1972: 680–1) accused the Doomadgee administration of 'inhuman conduct'. He alleged that a girl was punished for wearing a mini-skirt and also referred to an incident in 1960 when twelve girls 'all around the age of 14 years' ran away from the dormitory because they 'could no longer suffer the discipline'. When the girls were caught:

> They were subjected to physical beating by their parents under the supervision of the superintendent and were told that if they struggled during the beating they would have their hair shaved off. Some of the girls struggled and one of them . . . was among those who had the whole of her hair shaved off . . . That was a disastrous and traumatic experience for a little girl of 14 years. Admittedly this happened several years ago, but the punishment has been repeated since then on more than one occasion. A number of girls were punished for talking to a white man employed on the mission. (Keefe 1972: 680–1)

A woman who had been one of these girls wrote to the editor of Brisbane's *Courier-Mail* newspaper (16.3.1972: 2), confirming certain of the senator's allegations and adding various others: bad meals in the dormitory (including having to restew tea leaves already thrown out by the management); and the allegation that when she had visited the mission with a White husband she and her children had been expected to 'sleep at the camp' while the husband slept in the acting manager's house:

> Apartheid is the policy of the missionaries. Any contact with outsiders is strictly supervised by the management. All dancing . . . is forbidden . . . If I was asked to choose a word to sum up the feelings of my life the word would be fear. I was frightened for 20 years at Doomadgee . . . If I was married to an Aboriginal I don't think I would write this letter because we would be too frightened of what White authority could do to us . . . If I was asked to say what was wrong with Aboriginals I would say they have been too frightened for too long.

While there was apparently some argument over who actually composed the letter (its style indicating perhaps substantial involvement by the woman's White husband), many aspects of this account are confirmed by contemporary Aboriginal residents of Doomadgee.

Extracts from Doomadgee administration records known as the 'Punishment Book',[5] seemingly written in 1962 by the superintendent, further indicate aspects of disciplinary control:

> 4.2.'62
> Advised . . . that two girls missing from Dormitory approximately 4 a.m. Two girls . . . approached Miss [a staff member] . . . as she returned to Dormitory and said they had been with boys under the Dormitory. Found tracks early in the morning that led to the camp to different boys sleeping

> tents etc. Got all suspects to give a footprint to satisfy and confirm our decision (P[olice]/Boys and Councillors) that they coincided with those found.[6]
> 5.2.'62
> Had an inquiry into the above those who confessed as to having visited the Dormitory in past weeks were . . . [names given] Girls who admitted they had been out of the Dormitory at night over past weeks [were] . . . [names given] All Camp boys given 3 weeks punishment. First job to do is clean out septic tank. They are to pay for all rations out of 2 pounds per week.[7] Only receive beef on Fridays . . . not allowed to visit Mission Centre. No washing to be given to girls.[8] Not to resume talking to girls after work at night when punishment finished until speaking with the Superintendent and obtaining his permission [. . .] not allowed to choose place of employment . . . [two boys] . . . who had been allowed down the camp from B[oys]/Dorm on condition that they behaved themselves to forfeit their payment of 2 pounds per week. All girls involved to have hair cut as sign of being in disgrace and be dealt with [hit, smacked?] before other girls in Dormitory at night. [A particular girl] became abusive after her hair was cut. Was put in Detention overnight.[9]

Many of the 1945 Regulations (QGG 1945: 1063–74) were relevant to the operation of the Doomadgee superintendent's authority (and that of his staff): every Aboriginal person had to obey all his lawful orders (No. 18), and observe habits of orderliness and cleanliness to his satisfaction (No. 19); he could permit, in writing, dancing and/or other native practices providing such practices did not continue after midnight or commence before the specified time (No. 21); he could prohibit any game and take any money or articles used in it (No. 22); no Aboriginal person could leave the reserve without his permission (No. 25); he could, through force if necessary, confiscate anything which in his opinion was likely to be the subject or cause of a disturbance of the harmony, good order or discipline of the reserve (No. 24); he could direct Aborigines to work up to thirty-two hours per week without pay at tasks deemed by him necessary for the reserve's maintenance and development (No. 28); he could control the movements of Aborigines on reserves (No. 30); he could, with the approval of the Director of Native Affairs, open and peruse any letters or mail matter addressed to or written by Aboriginal residents of the reserve (No. 32). The Doomadgee superintendent could also constitute an Aboriginal court to deal with various offences (Regulations Nos. 35–44); there were gaols on reserves (No. 51); and he could appoint and control Aboriginal police (No. 52). An Aboriginal Court or the Director could order that any child under sixteen years be detained in a dormitory. Certain of these Regulations were modified in, or absent from, the Regulations of 1966 (QGG 1966: 2105–34) and/or 1972 (QGG 1972: 1457–79), but others were retained.

A number of restrictions appear to have caused further controversy among Aboriginal residents in the early 1970s, in particular the requirement that people wishing to marry had to inform the manager and, most importantly, the ban against Aboriginal people having motor vehicles. Senator Keefe's accusations (noted above) also include a reference to a person not being allowed to bring a car onto the reserve, and archival records[10] indicate that a petition complaining about the mission's policy against motor vehicles was sent to the Director of the DAIA in 1971. A letter to the editor of *The Australian* newspaper (1.3.1973: 6), from an Aboriginal man normally resident at Doomadgee but then at a station, complained bitterly about a 'long list of wrongs done to me by the missionaries of Doomadgee' and in particular about allegedly having his nomination as a candidate in an Aboriginal council election not accepted 'because I have always been an independent voice'.

Some individuals attempted independent action in the face of opposition from the local mission authorities. For example, in isolated cases parents kept their children out of the dormitories for periods. In 1952, one couple took their two school-age children back to the station where the father was employed. When the Doomadgee superintendent enquired about his right to compel the parents to leave the children (Talbot 9.4.1952) the Deputy Director of the Department of Native Affairs replied that 'it is not Departmental practice to forcibly separate children from their parents' even for such a desirable objective as their education, and that 'all moral suasion' should be used instead (13.5.1952). A more common tactic to avoid the Doomadgee dormitories was to move to Mornington Island. Belcher, the ex-manager at Mornington, reports that dormitories were discontinued there in 1954 and that 'around 1958 there seemed to be a flow from Doomadgee to Mornington Island'. He also claims that other attractions at Mornington Island included the environment being 'largely controlled by Aboriginal people themselves' and the administration's encouragement of 'traditional and cultural factors' (personal communication 20.1.1980).

Some older Aboriginal people certainly make clear that they avoided Doomadgee because of the dormitories ('We been mad for [i.e. emotionally attached to] kid — like to see them sleep with us'). Aboriginal accounts indicate that it was constant complaint from mothers throughout the 1960s, with at least one woman putting her complaint in writing to certain government officials and politicians, which finally resulted in the mission closing the dormitories (apparently after some pressure from the DAIA). Some people express positive feelings about the dormitories (e.g. 'hard days but good old days'; 'hard life for us — but children better behaved then ... straightened them up'). Consider also the following quote from a man who spent many years in the dormitory. After referring to the uncontrollable children of today, and to the physical punishment ('beltings') that used to be meted out to rule-breakers in the dormitory, he went on:

> and that's why we're civilised, most of us been in the dormitory. We might say that's been a hard and a tough time. I can appreciate it on the other side of things. (T55)

Various old people cite the dormitories as one of the reasons for a lack of continuity in traditional ritual life: 'this young generation, they been 'long dormitory — that's why they got lost' (T16). The missionaries were known to be largely ignorant of, and opposed to, many 'Blackfella ways'. Most were not happy for children to speak their own language, for marriage and other affairs to be organised according to kin obligations, or for 'Blackfella medicine' to be used in healing. They were against all forms of sorcery, and their antagonism to traditional ritual life was most evident on the issue of ceremonies, which have never been allowed in or near the mission.

The last time some men held an initiation ceremony a few kilometres west of the settlement (around 1953) is well-remembered by both the Aborigines and missionaries involved. Aboriginal people say that the superintendent threatened to call the Burketown police sergeant in an attempt to stop them, then did so. (The sergeant replied that it was not his province to stop Aboriginal ceremonies). The superintendent's own account illustrates the missionary strategy, which was to insist that such ceremonies could not be carried out on the Doomadgee reserve, while knowing that historical reasons, material necessity and ties to children in the dormitories would keep the people there:

> I wondered when I discovered that quite a lot of young men were missing and elders . . . and I found that they were at a gathering up the river . . . having some old time things . . . I confronted them: [A particular man] was spokesman, he'd just come to the mission. He confronted me and said: 'We're going to do what we like, that's why I've come here, that's the Aboriginal way and we're going to do it'. I said: 'There's plenty of room in Australia, and I won't bar you from doing exactly what you want — but not here'. He said: 'Well I'll be leaving. . .', but he stayed . . . He knew it was better on the mission, better conditions altogether, they were sure if things went wrong they got their food.(T51)

No further initiation (or other large-scale) ceremonies have been held at Doomadgee since then, although certain rituals associated with death have been practised at times. Over the years, a comparatively small number of (mostly Garawa) people have sent their young men to Borroloola to be initiated.

Mission institutionalisation and colonial struggle

The founding missionary attitude was to cater for the perceived spiritual and material needs of Aborigines. While remaining largely ignorant of local Aboriginal culture, the early missionaries lived closely with Aboriginal people, partly because of their own material poverty, and partly through their social and intellectual distance from prevailing patterns of local White social life. Particularly during the early stages of the establishment of the mission, in the 1930s, the missionaries were without much power in their own society. They received official support for largely economic reasons, and local station people opposed them partly for similar reasons, as they increasingly came to regulate Aboriginal employment. The missionaries thus came to constitute a third major White interest group dealing constantly with Aboriginal people in the region. For a time, missionaries appear to have been competing with local bureaucrats as agents of the state administrative apparatus, for control over the Aboriginal population. The basis of the pastoralists' power lay in their *de facto* control of the settings in which Aboriginal people found employment.

As the mission community became firmly institutionalised from the 1940s onwards, the mission endeavour became inextricably entwined with secular administration and firm control of an increasing population. The legal framework facilitated the process of authoritarian control by mission staff becoming a key feature of Doomadgee life. Particular aspects of such control were the routinisation of Aboriginal daily life, the institutionalisation of children and young adults in dormitories, and the opposition to significant parts of Aboriginal tradition. The written discourse of both missionaries and police protectors indicates this bureaucratic authoritarian practice. Each person was referred to in all correspondence by a label consisting of the first letter in his or her first name followed by a number. In this discourse, Aboriginal men are always referred to as 'boy'. The latter could be 'loaned' for employment by one protector to another (M. Read 5.2.1949), or 'withdrawn' from employment when considered necessary (e.g. Talbot 9.7.1958); the arrival of Aborigines 'without covering letters' was regarded as improper by protectors (e.g. Talbot January 1950 and 11.2.1950); and 'pocket money' was distributed selectively to Aboriginal workers and mothers receiving child endowment benefits.

Throughout social life within the institutionalised mission setting, the staff commitment to Christian evangelism was strong. From the missionary perspective, their secular restriction of Aboriginal lives was justified in terms of the latter's great need for moral leadership and tutelage. Restrictive controls could be slackened off 'as it is found folk can use and not abuse freedom', to use the words of the superintendent in 1950. Hence, it was considered appropriate to severely punish Aboriginal children when they sought to thwart what the staff regarded as controls over their behaviour that were imposed for their own long-term benefit.

The extent to which Aboriginal residents of Doomadgee have embraced the worldview and practices promoted by the staff is a complex question that remains to be addressed in the following chapters. What have been the effects of the historical attempts to control Aboriginal thinking and practices in the institutionalised setting at Doomadgee? Some data already suggest that the 'moral suasion' recommended by the state bureaucrats has worked to consolidate hegemonic domination of Aboriginal consciousness. For it was Aboriginal parents who, under the supervision of senior mission staff, physically punished their children when they ran away from the dormitory in 1960. It was Aboriginal police and councillors who in 1962 identified the foot tracks of the boys who had been meeting dormitory girls, so that the superintendent could see that they were punished. Thus, there was a degree to which some Aboriginal residents became incorporated into the structure of the authoritarian administrative aparatus. Furthermore, some adults have explained how the severe constraints of the dormitories had some positive consequences. These data constitute tantalising snippets of the nature of Aboriginal social life. The following chapters give a much fuller ethnographic account of the nature of Aboriginal responses to missionary administrative practices, as well as to the broader economic and political structures of the colonising society.

Notes

1 Missionaries could be appointed protectors and/or superintendents of reserves under sections 6 and 7 of the 1897 Act, and under *The Aboriginals Preservation . . . Acts*, 1939 to 1946 (section 9), reserves could be placed under the management and control of a religious organisation.

2 After his marriage to a woman of Aboriginal/European descent in 1909, an Afghan (or 'Arab') stockman by this name lived at a camp at what subsequently became the Old Doomadgee site (Dymock 1982: 109). Local Aboriginal people intermittently camped nearby.

3 According to Doomadgee residents, 'King Jimmy Dawudawu' was a man of much influence among Ganggalida people (see Plate 2).

4 At least one White woman was present, but Brethren doctrine does not allow women to speak at meetings for worship (Van Sommers 1966: 30).

5 Copy in author's possession.

[6] Aboriginal people at Doomadgee are usually able to identify individual members of the community from their footprints.

[7] This was clearly an amount received by the boys, however I have not been able to establish precisely on what basis they received it.

[8] I am unsure what the basis of the girls receiving washing was. However, the punishment may have been that they did not receive a small amount of money for washing clothes, and/or that the boys thus did not receive clean clothes which would have normally been washed by the girls.

[9] Contemporary Aboriginal accounts describe a 'detention centre' in which teenage children were detained, sometimes for lengthy periods.

[10] Held in 'Gulf Country History File' (Australian Institute of Aboriginal Studies library).

CHAPTER FIVE

Whitefella comin': power relations and the different domains

In the late 1970s and early 1980s there were two distinctive arenas of social life at Doomadgee which, to use local Aboriginal parlance, may be characterised as the 'Blackfella' and 'Whitefella' domains. These were arenas of material, intellectual and social activity which indexed a high degree of social distance between Aborigines and Whites. To some extent this distance derives from social closure among Aboriginal residents of the settlement, thereby entailing some resistance to colonial domination. In this sense, social closure is constituted through exclusionary practices on the part of subordinate Aboriginal people, and is reciprocal to the form of closure achieved by the dominant society through its control over essential material resources.

Two spatial domains

In local parlance, Doomadgee was divided[1] into the 'mission', the Whitefella domain, and the 'village', the Blackfella domain. An open strip of bare ground, 100–200 metres wide, separated the two areas (see plates 5 and 6). The main roads in the settlement ran between (and through) the village and the mission parallel to the river, roughly along an east-west axis. The roads crossed the open median strip to proceed through two gate-sized openings in a somewhat dilapidated fence, which ran along the western (mission) side of the strip. At the northern end of the strip, farthest from the river a large well-fenced rodeo ground separated the two domains (see figure 1).

The Whitefella domain consisted of the residences of the White staff,[2] plus the buildings and fittings housing the institutions and enterprises that serviced the settlement. The latter consisted of: medical facilities including the hospital and base for the government

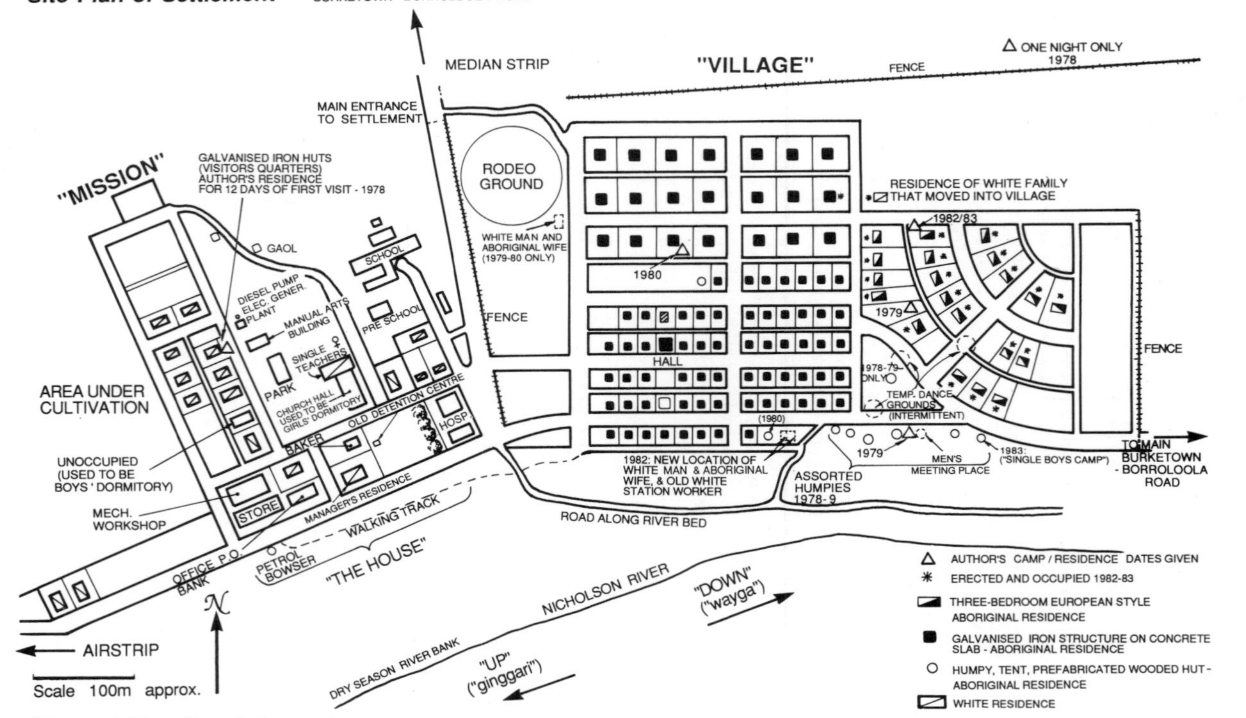

Figure 1 Site plan of the settlement

Aboriginal health program mobile team; education facilities including the school and pre-school; the store; the administration area, including the post office, banking and air transport booking facilities; the gaol; petrol and diesel pumps; the electricity generating plant; the airstrip and refueling facility for aircraft; a mechanical workshop; and an area sometimes under cultivation. The large hall used (up until 1983) as the church was also situated here.[3] The majority of White residences were located with the service buildings between them and the village. Until 1983 there were no Aboriginal residences in the Whitefella domain. Following the appointment of a Queensland government (DAIA) manager, and other associated administrative changes in 1983, two Aboriginal men (of mixed racial descent) and their families established residences in the White domain. One had spent much of his life away from Doomadgee, and returned in 1983 as a Christian evangelist; the other was provided with accommodation after becoming a Commonwealth Department of Aboriginal Affairs (DAA) funded outstation coordinator.[4]

The Blackfella domain contained the Aboriginal residences, which varied between European-style three-bedroom houses and small galvanised iron structures on concrete slabs, with a smaller number of humpies and tents in one area. While the number of Aboriginal houses in the village increased over the years, all were situated according to a basic grid system. There were no service facilities in the Blackfella domain.

Aboriginal residents moved to the Whitefella domain for specific purposes, commonly during Monday to Friday: to go to work (or school in the case of children); to go to the hospital as outpatients or visitors; to go to the airstrip to send off travellers or welcome those returning; to see films (screened on one or two nights a week); and so on. The largest number of people spent long periods of time there when Department of Social Security cheques arrived, were obtained from the office counter and then partially spent at the store. When cheques arrived, large numbers of people would congregate outside the office and store at the appropriate times, with men and women using two separate mango trees for shade. The area and its facilities were collectively referred to as 'the house', the phrase probably deriving from a primary reference to the 'mission house' (i.e. the nearby manager's residence), which has historically been regarded as the point from which all facilities were ultimately controlled.

It was rare for Aboriginal people to spend time in the Whitefella domain for reasons other than those I have stated. On weekends, when no service facilities operated (other than the hospital in special cases), very few Aboriginal people moved through the White domain; the exception was the group attending the Sunday morning church service. It was rare for people from the village to casually visit Whites' residences, or to spend leisure time in the White domain. Aboriginal children rarely played after school or on weekends in the White domain, either with the White children or among themselves.

Different Whites visited the village for administrative and work-related reasons: some attended Christian meetings at the 'hall' early in the morning on Monday to Friday,[5] or open air meetings on Sunday evenings. Manual workers worked on building and maintenance jobs; medical personnel came regularly as part of the mobile Aboriginal health program team (which at times provided midday meals for old people), and occasionally came from the hospital to attend emergency cases. Most Whites hardly ever visited Aboriginal dwellings casually. At most, a few White women, particularly school teachers, occasionally paid visits to the homes of Aboriginal women (usually those in European-style houses) with whom they may have established friendships. A number of committed Aboriginal and White Christian women sometimes met for such purposes as Bible study at one of the homes of one of the Aboriginal women (again usually a three-bedroom style house). White male staff very rarely visited casually in the village. White children did not play in the village.

By late 1983, the most obvious evidence of behavioural change concerned children: the departure of the missionary manager's family, after administrative changes during that year, appeared to lessen restrictions on the movements of the Aboriginal children. They generally moved more freely in the vicinity of White residences, and through the streets of the White domain on weekends. Occasionally a few young Aboriginal children apparently went to certain White homes to play after school.

The extreme social distance between the two spatial domains is thus illustrated strikingly by the separate areas for Aboriginal and White residence. While we can note the fairly common presence of Aboriginal inpatients in the hospital, or Aboriginal people in gaol for the night, I know of no Doomadgee adult Aborigines spending the night at White residences during the research period. Apart from the staff family discussed below, I know of no White staff to have ever spent the night in the village. Also, to my knowledge, there have never been any marriages between Aboriginal residents and White staff at Doomadgee, nor during the research period any relationships such as courtships which were intended, or ever appeared, to lead to marriage. Indeed, the notion of White women establishing sexual relationships with Aboriginal men was considered almost unthinkable. Consider the following Aboriginal man's reaction when a Torres Strait Islander with a White wife stopped briefly at Doomadgee: 'He introduced me to her [and said]: "This is my wife mate". I got the biggest shock! I thought she was his boss! I never seen Blackfella get White woman in this country'. When a young Aboriginal man who had recently returned from Mount Isa showed his family a photograph of a White woman he said was his girlfriend when he was there, the young man's father asked me in a bewildered tone: 'How man get White girl like that?'. If his bewilderment was at all feigned, his question was nevertheless put in order to stress that his son's extremely unusual achievement was worthy of considerable status.

Only in comparatively recent years have occasional White men from outside Doomadgee who have established *de facto* or marriage relationships with Aboriginal women been able to live in the village. In the past, such men were stopped from doing so by the authority of the White manager, so such couples would invariably leave the settlement. During the research period an occasional White man lived with an Aboriginal woman in the village, but usually only for a short time. In the few cases with which I am familiar, the main base for the couple was Mt Isa or Mornington Island. Such relationships were often (accurately) perceived by both Aboriginal people and staff as fairly temporary. One exception was a long-standing relationship between a White man and an Aboriginal woman. After living in nearby towns, this couple negotiated with the Aboriginal council and White manager to establish their caravan on the edge of the median strip opposite the council chairman's house. After a few years, they moved their dwelling into the village proper, close to some of the woman's relatives. Following the woman's death, the man continued living in the same section of the village. A second White man came to reside immediately adjacent to him; this man had apparently moved there with council permission during 1982, after he became too old to work on stations any more. Both men were said to have 'spent all their lives with Blackfella', and people accepted them because they were seen as needing help in the face of the remote wider White society of which they were not really part. They were seen as exceptionally different Whitefellas and to a large extent as comfortable living in the kinds of material conditions Blackfellas live in.

While some Aboriginal residents said that it was 'time for us to mix up now' or that 'it's stupid — we should be living together', there was clearly solid sentiment across the Aboriginal community that it would provide too much social discomfort for Whites other than those who have 'spent all their lives with Blackfella' to live in the village. At one point, a missionary family moved into a new house on the outskirts of the village, amid much discussion. The man was a son of the manager and had spent a substantial part of his life at Doomadgee — living in the Whitefella domain up until this move. Prior to the move, while some village residents appeared to approve, others were against it; those close to where the family was going to live remained apprehensive. An Aboriginal elder of the church reflected on sentiment throughout the village:

> some people might accept it some people might not . . . some on account of the condition of their house . . . Blackfella 'shamed of their dirty home and he don't like Whitefella to come in . . . I know these old people, if they're sitting round in a group, if they ever see Mr . . ., Mrs . . . [the manager and his wife] they'll say: "[whispering] *Mandagi* [Whitefella], *Mandagi, Mandagi*", and get up and run away then . . . [and the young child] will know what to do when he see a White man — he'll learn that habit from an early age. (T75)

Opinion also appeared to be divided on the question among the Whites. The couple were themselves aware that village residents remained apprehensive, and they were concerned not to offend people by their change of residence.

The missionary family did live in the village for approximately nine to twelve months, after which they left the settlement altogether (at the time of the administrative takeover by the DAIA). To some extent, Aboriginal people appeared to get used to their presence, although one nearby resident suggested they may have been 'spying', as the manager (the man's father) seemed to 'know more about what's going on down here' after the move. While some people in the village visited them, much of this appeared to be in order to get administrative or technical advice, or goods of the kind typically obtained from Whitefellas (the woman was a qualified nurse, and the couple worked hard to provide goats' milk from their small herd for undernourished babies). The children of the family did not play outside the yard, although some Aboriginal children went inside the yard to play. In summary, village residents appeared to regard the family residence and yard as a transplanted piece of the Whitefella domain.

The other kind of Whitefella who has lived in the village during the research period has been myself. The process of my first attempts to establish residence in the village provides further evidence of the social gap between the two spatial domains. On the first two nights of my first visit to Doomadgee (in May 1978), I had rented accommodation in a small shed-type structure in the White domain. On the third night, I set up camp in the bush adjacent to the northern side of the village, but some 50 metres outside the fence along that side. A young man helped me to put up the tent at his mother's direction, partly because she felt sorry for me being alone. However, no visits from village residents that night, and a dust storm, had left me feeling quite lonely indeed the next morning, and I returned to the accommodation in the White domain. My unedited diary entries read:

> Residence is a real problem. Because the gulf between the staff and Aborigines is so wide, I have to either stay in the staff section or try to live in the village or find a 3'rd. independent place. The weather is bad. A very strong wind . . . Everything in my camp was covered in dust and all was chaos. As well, no-one had come over to my camp. I had misjudged the size of the barrier between all Whites (by definition) and Aborigines in the village. I have moved back to the quarters on the missionary side. I am currently viewed as the same as other Whites who come and go.

The diary entry for the fourth day documents what I saw as my options for residence: try to move directly into the village; stay in the White domain; camp in the riverbed (where I had been told by concerned Aboriginal people I would be 'in the way of the grog'); or camp in the median strip (which I decided was too public a position as far as both Aborigines and Whites were concerned). I stayed in the White domain.

Over the next few days the news filtered around that I was interested in 'Blackfella ways' and 'country'. I had made it known that I was looking for a place to camp, and on that fourth day an authoritative old man, separated from his wife, offered me a place in the area of his humpy. However, I now wanted to gauge the attitudes of more people; in particular, I did not want to be aligned so quickly with this particular old man and his 'mob'. I remained in the relative comfort of the quarters in the White domain, with the further thought that I might be able to 'interview' people there. On the fifth day a diary entry reads:

> Started by going down and bringing [a particular man] up to my quarters. He was not at ease [e.g. he asked me if it was alright to smoke there], and I will not try it again.

For the same day:

> My residence is certainly a vexing problem. When asked about where I should camp (in the village) many people say with a worried tone that I should be 'up the river' — i.e. away from direct observational access to the action. They talk about how I should be out of the way of the grog. Yet are they just using 'grog' as an excuse for a more fundamental difficulty they have in accepting a Whitefella living in the village at all?

By the twelfth day I had gone to the village to work each day, and had spent two nights away from the settlement on short trips to places in the bush where people had wanted to take me. On this day the diary reads:

> The issue of residence is still a difficult one. I have 'taken the plunge' and asked [the council chairman] 'what he thinks' about me setting up camp in the village. His response was that if the Councillors agree, it will be O.K. It will be interesting to see what part [the white manager] plays in the issue . . . [a certain Aboriginal man] has agreed (with the tiniest trace of uncertainty) to my using his toilet and bathroom facilities.

On the thirteenth day: 'Not much time for writing now due to a terrific "breakthrough". Camp is now down at the "village" '.

From that time on, I lived in the Blackfella domain on field trips to Doomadgee. Unlike the missionary family, I have not been regarded as a transplanted piece of the local Whitefella domain. Also, unlike the two White men referred to above, I was not thought to be in need of 'looking after' in the face of White society. I have been regarded as another kind of exceptional Whitefella; one whose work involves learning about 'Blackfella ways', and who can to some extent operate socially like a Blackfella and (for a time at least) appear not to be too uncomfortable living in similar material conditions to Blackfellas. Though I have not always enjoyed cordial relationships with all Aboriginal residents, it is relevant to my argument that I have on occasions been referred to as an example of the kind of Whitefella who is acceptable in the village. Consider this church elder's comment:

> You just like one of us in the village, sometimes I don't know who you are when you're talking, like listening to one of them old Blackfella from down the village [the speaker is blind] . . . I said to [a particular person] the other day: 'If those missionaries, any of these White men want to come in, mingle with the Aboriginal down here, get right into it, really commit themselves with us, all right — they [should] come about like old *ganggu* [reference to D. Trigger, using a kin term], old *ganggu* be accepted in any place, anybody's home, that's making himself to become one of us'. And it put me into a spiritual line — Jesus had to become one of us, from heaven, he couldn't come in his glorious form — he'd blind us; he had to become one of us. And if those White men up here [had] seen that in the first place, instead of putting a fence across up there. (T75)

The council chairman told me that in formal discussions on plans to relocate certain White staff into the village, he had pointed out that they would have to be able to operate in a way similar to me before the move would be acceptable. As he explained to me: 'I wouldn't class you as a Whitefella!', which I interpret as: 'You don't behave like a Whitefella'. The significance of my area of residence at Doomadgee, from the Aboriginal perspective, was also evident on the number of occasions where my introduction to Aborigines at places outside Doomadgee would include as a focal statement: 'He camp with Blackfellas all the time'. I regard these sorts of unelicited comments on my status as an unusual kind of Whitefella as a further indication of the entrenched, emically recognised, social distance between Aborigines and Whites.

Finally, to describe two spatial domains as I have done is not to suggest that either is necessarily the locus of a homogeneous group. Nevertheless, it is apposite to point out that it has not only been Aboriginal residents at Doomadgee who have been linked by kin and other close historical ties throughout the settlement's history. One staff member named seventeen of the 1980–81 adult staff who were linked through affinal and consanguineal ties. Five married couples then there had originally met at Doomadgee. There appears to be a strong preference for endogamy among the Brethren. The wider families of mission staff have typically taken interest in the settlement, with many visiting from time to time. Children and some grandchildren of earlier missionaries have come to work there over the years. Doomadgee has been a meeting place for people from certain Brethren Assemblies throughout Australia. During the research period the White domain, as well as the Black domain, contained individuals with considerable social commitment to one another.

Consciousness of the two domains

Aboriginal residents conceived of the White domain as containing White (Christian Brethren) values, and of the state of the material world there as manifesting those values. The White residences were more substantial structures and equipped with many more facilities than the Aboriginal dwellings. They were also patently used differently: Whites did not use the areas outside the house for cooking fires and domestic living in the way Aborigines did; and Whites were stricter than Aboriginal residents in controlling children's treatment of floors, cupboards and furniture. Parts of White houses were used only for certain purposes: Whites did not generally use the lounge-room and verandah for sleeping. White houses contained fewer people and it was known that Whites regarded Aboriginal homes as dirtier and containing more vermin than White homes, and as containing far too many badly controlled dogs and cats.

As well as perceiving the different domestic lifestyle in the White domain, Aboriginal people commonly conceived of the general conditions there as distinctly reflecting the material complexity and richness of White technology. When items broke down there they were repaired fairly promptly by Whites with trade skills. The White domain directly received essential commodities (e.g. spare parts for machinery, and food and medical supplies) from the wider Australian society; it, rather than the Blackfella domain, was the base for White technology and material culture.

An extreme (albeit unusual) example of the conceived power of White technology, and the lack of understanding of the mechanisms by which it works, was a widespread belief concerning the standard cameras used by White police at the scene of a crime. It was believed that, by photographing the scene of a crime after its occurrence, police could make a picture that recreated past events there, in particular the crime being committed by the offender(s). Traditional techniques were used historically in this area to identify a guilty person (particularly a sorcerer) after an offence. In earlier periods, Aborigines at Burketown would, it seems, under cover of darkness, sometimes exhume a relative's body, buried at the direction of White authorities, and by keeping watch over it and using certain ritual singing and other techniques, interpret through various signs the identity of the individual(s) who caused the death. The role of such 'inquests' in traditional practices has been discussed by other writers (e.g. Maddock 1972: 163–9). Thus, at Doomadgee, the White police were presumably seen as simply using their own techniques to achieve a logically familiar result. However, the potency of White technology, which could actually create a picture of the offender, was marvelled at. While most would admit that they had never actually seen such photographs, one member of the local Aboriginal police force produced in my presence a photograph showing himself looking at tracks at the scene of a crime, taken by the White police, he claimed, some five hours after he had been in the position shown. The comments of onlookers indicated that they regarded the White technique as very powerful and marvellous: 'must be powerful thing inside camera — sort of draw them [i.e. the image] back'; 'must be magic — *gurdugurdu* [term for secret-sacred phenomena]'; '*Mandagi* [Whitefella] clever bugger hey — *nugami* [footprint] holdim [the image of the body] there hey?'.

However, while the material complexity, wealth and sophistication of the White domain was recognised and sometimes marvelled at, White technology was not always valued highly. At times its clumsiness and typical heaviness drew open comments. Nor was the technology regarded as indicative of any general intellectual and cultural superiority within European traditions, as was the reported view among Aboriginal people at Hopevale settlement (in northeast Queensland) during the early 1970s (Terwiel-Powel 1975: 302–3).

Because it was the setting for perceived technological sophistication, there was a tendency for the White domain to be regarded as safer for important material items than the Blackfella domain, e.g. a person purchased an expensive present for a child at the store but left it there for 'safe-keeping' until the child returned from a visit to a nearby town. Similarly, a man entrusted with the temporary use of a Toyota vehicle from the local cattle station where he worked parked it for several days 'up at the house for safety', rather than at his own house in the village. Aboriginal people would commonly worry about the safety and security of my caravan and other gear in the village; this was so particularly when I was absent on bush trips, and at times somebody would be designated to camp there to protect it from unpredictable dangers such as children or drunk people. A few people suggested that I leave very valuable or important items 'up la mission', i.e. in the White domain.

That I left the caravan with a particular family over the research period, for them to look after and use, was regarded as further evidence of my being an unusual kind of Whitefella. The White staff very rarely lent valuable items to Aboriginal people. Indeed, my leaving my Toyota with a family in the village during a three-week absence and my entrusting it to two Aboriginal men for a day's driving over rugged bush roads, struck at least several Whites as foolhardy. From the Aboriginal perspective, Toyotas were extremely valuable and high-status commodities, and like most '*Mandagi* cars' the one in my possession was perceived to be in very good material condition, unlike 'Blackfella motorcars' which were known to be conspicuous for their poor condition. My willingness to entrust such a vehicle to the Blackfella domain was contrary to the normal tenor of race relations.

The relative material complexity and sophistication of technology in the White domain, as compared to the village, may well be the basis for the implication in local parlance that the former is 'higher' than the latter. In the speech of both Whitefellas and Blackfellas, you go 'down' (*wayga*) to the village, and 'up' (*ginggari*) to the 'house' or White domain (see figure 1). The village is indeed downstream from the White domain. However, the fact that the settlement was organised this way in the first place may well reflect a view on the relative positions of Aboriginal and White domains. It may have been deemed inappropriate, for example, for Whites to have taken water downstream from where Blackfellas were using it, and more generally, to have been located physically 'below' the Blackfella domain. This would have conflicted with the notion that the White domain was socially 'above' (i.e. more advanced, sophisticated and civilised than) the Blackfella domain.

People would commonly wash and 'dress up' to go to the White domain. It was viewed as a 'clean' place. One man (not without sarcasm) suggested that the manager did not want to 'get his shoes dirty', and that was why he at times drove slowly through the village without getting out of his car. Despite a badly infected leg that caused him intense pain during several days with me in the bush, one old man was most concerned that he 'get cleaned up' before being taken to the hospital for treatment. When returning from bush trips people generally did not like going to the White domain before getting 'cleaned up'. It was also known that in the towns in the region Blackfellas are regarded as 'dirty', and that indeed it is usually possible to determine whether, for example, a dwelling in Mt Isa is a '*Mandagi* house' or 'Blackfella house' according to its material state and the neatness of its yard. In the settlement, the fact that visiting Whites (such as public servants) rarely, if ever, met with people in the village did not go unnoticed. One such male liaison officer, concerned with social welfare matters, told me he would not go anywhere near Aboriginal dwellings at Doomadgee because of their smell.

The White domain was also recognised as containing extensive bodies of knowledge and opinion that were not derived from Aboriginal tradition. This was clear for such formalised knowledge as Christian religious belief and systems of jurisprudence that differ from 'Blackfella law'. However, the difference between certain kinds of more informal background knowledge held in the two domains was also evident. It would impinge on Aboriginal people whenever a particular situation required knowledge not routinely held in the Blackfella domain, such as people having to enumerate for administrative purposes the precise ages of their children or the number of weeks they worked for an outside employer; people trying to understand issues broadcast on ABC radio, but remaining baffled by complex English speech; people trying to understand, at election times, matters concerning levels of government, differing electoral boundaries and the existence of different political parties.

From 1983, a new source of information about White society were video cassettes, as an increasing number of families acquired the machines to play them. This information, including all kinds of fiction, was taken as further evidence of the great expanse of White society, as yet unfamiliar to most local Aboriginal people. The local White domain at Doomadgee was thus viewed as linked to the wider knowledge and resources of Australian society — to the towns and cities that are more remote White domains, where Blackfellas are expected to live and behave like Whites, yet usually cannot do so. Alternatively, the local Blackfella domain was linked to the bush, to 'country', from where 'Blackfella ways' were thought ultimately to derive and where many local Whites were thought to be less competent than Aborigines. Whites only rarely took Aboriginal people with them in their vehicles on weekend bush trips. To my knowledge, no White staff ever travelled during my fieldwork periods on bush trips in any vehicles owned by Aboriginal people. Groups of Whites (e.g. school teachers) sometimes themselves went on camping trips to waterholes in the bush. There was a feeling among certain older residents that the Whites should have consulted with key old people before visiting some areas. On one occasion a senior woman complained bitterly about how a younger Aboriginal man had shown a White family the way to a particular area without consulting her. Another old man complained that Whites had used available water inappropriately at a site. Generally, it was felt that Blackfellas have a much more intimate relationship with the bush; on several occasions, particular Whitefellas were said to 'have no country'.

The conception of the separate origin of Aboriginal and non-Aboriginal things in fact extended to the natural environment where '*Mandagi* [Whitefella] trees', i.e. apparently introduced species such as 'bean tree' (*Parkinsonia aculeata*) and 'mimosa' (*Acacia farnesiana*) were distinguished from the rest of the bush. Similarly, introduced trees such as the frangipani, poinciana, and mango that grow in yards and along streets in parts of Doomadgee (and other settlements and towns) were known to be '*Mandagi* trees'. Whites were known to be selective in their choice of bush foods (e.g. mullet but not catfish), so that exceptional individuals become well-known: 'he not *Mandagi* — he eat anything' (said about a White man from Mt Isa who often camped out in the bush in the Doomadgee area with his mixed-race *de facto* wife). Jokes were at times based on accentuating the common knowledge about differences in taste, custom and etiquette between Whitefellas and Blackfellas: 'I can't boil crab — I'm not *Mandagi*!' (the Blackfella style of preparation being to cook such food on coals); or '[jokingly] *Wayjbala! Wayjbala!* [Whitefella]', said when a person behaves in what is known to be a stereotypically Whitefella fashion (e.g. by cooking 'johnny cakes' or fish in a frying pan rather than in ashes or on coals, by 'hunting away' dogs from a sleeping area, or by making a point of sitting on a drum or chair near a fire, rather than on the ground).

From the Aboriginal perspective, Blackfellas and Whitefellas have always divided themselves into two domains for living. This was so on the cattle stations where there were separate Aboriginal camps, and in the mustering camps:

> One time ago, a White man, in the mustering camp, he'd dish his tucker out and the Blackfella couldn't go over there and get his tucker out from the saucepan into a plate — White man had to do that. He'd just ring the bell and one [Aboriginal] man would walk over, or two, one carry the billy, one carry the tray of stew or something, and we'd go and have a feed underneath the shady tree; [Blackfella and Whitefella] never sit together — [Whitefella] won't let him touch the saucepan, won't let him touch the bread, can't let him touch the syrup or jam. (T75)

This man went on to say that the young stockmen tell him that nowadays Aboriginal and White stockmen eat together, and generally live closer together. While this may be partly true, several stations I visited during fieldwork housed Aboriginal stockmen and their families in areas separate from the residences of non-Aboriginal people. The Aboriginal people living there did not voice open complaint about this separation. Indeed, on one occasion, after eating his meal outside at a station while I was entertained inside, an old man explained how he would have been 'too shamed' to eat inside even if this had been possible (which it was not).

There are some ways in which various Whites once on the stations are regarded as having lived closer to Blackfellas than do the Whites of the contemporary settlement. Many did not interfere with Aboriginal ritual life, most swore and smoked and some even chewed tobacco — sometimes 'bush tobacco' (i.e. leaves from various indigenous plants). The White children once at particular stations (and also those of a police sergeant in the area for many years) were described in affectionate terms: 'lovely kids — real Blackfella kids' or 'they eat anything [i.e. bush foods] — they really Blackfella kid'. The willingness of such White men to seek Aboriginal women as sexual partners appears also to be regarded (by Aboriginal men at least) as evidence of a previous closeness to Blackfellas that has not operated in the settlement; consider the following comment made with amused affection about a man once at a station in the area: 'real gin burglar too'.

Nevertheless, the Aboriginal perspective clearly recognises continuity in the separation of Blackfella and Whitefella domains from the earliest times at cattle stations and ration depots, through to the contemporary settlement. There is also continuity in the separation from the organisation of the coastal 'Old Doomadgee' mission. A plan (surveyed on site) of the spatial organisation of the old mission shows that 'the camp' residence of most adult Aborigines was located approximately 730 metres from the nearest parts of 'the mission' area. One old woman has given an account of how this spatial organisation began. In her words, the missionaries said:

> Oh, we've gotta have house here for the children's school-house, youse can go down and camp down there, stay there [eastwards down the sand ridge]. We been go down then. (T82)

She described how they would walk 'up' for rations and to sit with Aboriginal children who were being looked after by the missionaries. Missionary accounts concur in that they mention the different styles of behaviour in the two domains. For example, D. Akehurst (n.d.: 76) states that while the 'entirely unselfconscious' nakedness of

Aborigines was not offensive: 'in deference to the white folk, we had to insist that some kind of covering was used when coming up to the house'. Similarly:

> When the women came up the ridge to greet us, they came one at a time and each one had the same dress on, so it did not take us long to realise that they did not have proper clothes and each had to wait their turn for a loan of the one and only dress. (Cantle 1980:61)

Apart from their recognition of this historical continuity of social distance, Aboriginal residents at Doomadgee during my research knew that some of the local Whites were quite acutely aware of the current separation of Aboriginal and White lives. One man pointed this out to me as follows:

> I tell you one old [White] preacher come up here from [a southern city] and he said [to the White missionaries when preaching publicly]: 'I'm glad you've [done many good things here] but, you've lost your first love, you're not living with them, you're so busy in the office, store, garage, elsewhere, and your love for the Aboriginals that you said you've got — not even showing to anything'. (T75).

The speaker went on to say that he thought that many of the missionaries were aware of the separation between Blackfellas and Whitefellas, and that they were concerned about it. Indeed, such concern was a major reason for a White family's move into the village (described earlier in this chapter). After having lived there for some months the couple felt that they were much closer to village life; they were more comfortable walking and driving through the village, whereas prior to the move they had felt somewhat like intruding administrators. They were still aware of the gap between themselves and village residents, however, partly through the way it constrained their own behaviour. The woman explained that she could not put up the curtains of her choosing as she was apprehensive about being considered 'too flash', and the couple mentioned how they curtailed their habit of working under the house into what by White norms was the early hours of the night, using an electric light, as this was apparently disliked by some nearby Aboriginal residents.

Other Whites were generally also aware of the social distance between the two domains, and not all of them approved of it; at least two referred disapprovingly in my presence to the median strip as a 'no-man's-land'. However, most staff felt that ultimately Aboriginal people would have to change their lifestyle. The teachers, in particular, expressed the opinion that regardless of how different the lifestyle in the village might be, the role of the school was to prepare Aboriginal children for operating in the wider Australian society. Thus they considered it appropriate for the school domain to reflect a White Australian lifestyle. If anything, they were concerned that the school was failing to do this sufficiently, so that the 'learning environment' was not as 'good' as it should be. Indeed, this was an issue that caused much concern among those staff with their own children in the school. In 1980, these White families made it clear to the principal (himself a parent of school-age children) that they were worried that after some time at the Doomadgee school, their children would not be able to re-enter mainstream schools without suffering educational disadvantage. And the resulting action by the teachers illustrates one of the few arenas of social life in which the culture of the village was seen to be impinging intrusively upon the White domain.

As explained by Murray (1982: 31–3), the White parents felt that their children increasingly lacked motivation for learning because of a classroom atmosphere where group pressure was against individual children excelling above their peers. Because of this pressure, it was argued that some White children no longer contributed to discussions because of fear. The parents also pointed out that their children were exposed to a 'restricted' language variety both inside the classroom (as teachers generally used simplified English) and outside the classroom among the Aboriginal children. One or two parents claimed that they even had difficulty understanding what their children were saying at home, away from the school environment. The result was that the teaching staff decided to withdraw all White children, plus those Aboriginal students performing well above their peers, into one class known as the 'special program grade'. This class proceeded from 1980 with standard English as the medium of instruction and the aim that the group would reach mainstream educational standards. In that it drew all the White children together (albeit along with some Aboriginal pupils), the special program grade was a public expression of White parents' consciousness about the difference between the futures of their own children as compared with those of the Aboriginal children.

Admittedly, there were occasions on which Whites were able to point to a gradual decrease in the social distance between themselves and some Aboriginal residents. For example, one woman discussed how during the early 1970s 'it wasn't done' to go down to the village; as she put it: 'I was too frightened' (she knew the senior missionary management was opposed to such casual visiting). Yet by 1983 some Aboriginal people were coming to her house for meals and she was generally having much more social contact with certain people. Some Aborigines also conceived of the distance as decreasing, particularly after 1983, when the manager and his family moved out. Several made the point, though, that this had so far involved Aborigines going to the White domain, moreso than Whites coming into the village.

Thus, both Aboriginal and White consciousness recognised the fact of a sharp separation between the two domains, although neither perceived the other domain very accurately. For example, there was a tendency among many Aboriginal people to blame local White office (and other) staff for problems encountered in obtaining Department of Social Security welfare benefits or other services from government departments; whereas it was most often not the fault of the local staff, but rather of the wider bureaucratic system. Many Aboriginal people understood little of the way the banking system operates. A background hostility towards Whites generally was often framed in terms of the superior material conditions they certainly enjoyed. However, at times complaints about the alleged self-interest of the Whites appeared somewhat exaggerated: for instance complaints that 'those White missus [women] really boss for [i.e. dominate the purchase of] that fruit' when it became available in the store, or that White staff were generally making a lot of money in the course of working at Doomadgee. For their part, the Whites remained ignorant of all but a few trappings (about which they were nearly always misinformed) of the Aboriginal systems of kinship and social organisation, beliefs regarding country, illness, injury, good health, the causes and aftermath of death, and so on.

Social interaction between Blackfellas and Whitefellas

Most Whites hardly modified their behaviour at all in the Blackfella domain. The odd individual appeared to learn a few words from one of the Aboriginal languages or something of Aboriginal styles of interaction, but this was rare, and when it occurred was the subject of much Aboriginal comment. Indeed, it has historically been a matter of principle to many missionaries that they provide a (White Christian) model of behaviour and speech for the Aborigines to follow. The Whites rarely modified their use of standard English when conversing with Aboriginal people in either the Blackfella or the Whitefella spatial domain. This was particularly obvious when they preached publicly or spoke at public meetings. They did not become aware of general rules of Aboriginal communicative style, (e.g. the indirectness of forms of address and reference — they would address and refer to people directly by name rather than by pronoun or kin term — or nickname in the case of terms of reference[6]). Nor did Whites become familiar with the indirectness of Aboriginal general facial expression and gesture — they would point openly with the arms and hands rather than subtly with the eyes and lips. Whites would walk or pass things across the direction of someone's path of movement, vision or personal orientation, rather than proceeding behind such lines of personal social presentation; they would hardly ever sit on the ground, and would abruptly arrive at and leave social interaction rather than more slowly announcing arrivals and departures. That is, Whites understood and practised little, if any, of Aboriginal styles of etiquette.

Aboriginal people largely accepted that Whites have never and will never modify their behaviour. An example of this is an Aboriginal woman's response to a White staff member who asked her whether people should call the name of recently deceased persons. She said that while Blackfellas should not and generally would not do it, 'White is White' and therefore it was alright for Whites to do it. Such behaviour has reportedly been obvious for years at funerals where, as during the research period, White speakers have continually referred to the deceased's (usually first) name. Aboriginal people who preached at funerals would typically use a kin term or some other form of indirect reference, although some combined the kin term with the deceased's first name (e.g. 'uncle John'). Some said that in certain other places (such as Normanton), White 'preachers' at funerals have been asked not to use the deceased's name, but such a request appears never to have been made at Doomadgee. Rather, the operation of two sharply demarcated domains of styles of behaviour and speech has become the norm.

When Whites were in the village, their movements were monitored closely. This was particularly so if they were on foot or pushbike, rather than driving by quickly in a car or on a motor bike. There was nearly always an administrative reason for the White person's presence, and if this was not immediately evident it would be deduced from such evidence as the type of service with which the White was connected, the dwellings or people he or she was visiting, and the length of time spent there. As a White approached specific groups of people or a particular dwelling, certain preparations would be made to deal with him or her. These included notifying the person with whom it was thought the Whitefella wanted to converse where this was known, e.g. a nurse wanting to visit an old or sick person, or a tradesman wanting to see a man about work-related matters. The household would most commonly be notified of the impending visit by statements such as: '*Wayjbala* [Whitefella] comin', or '*Mandagi* [Whitefella] there, look!'. The presence of the general category of 'Whitefella' would usually be announced first in this way, because it is the most significant social fact of the situation. The particular individual might then be referred to specifically.

As long as the residents were ready for the White person's visit, the interaction provoked little social discomfort. I have observed women express great affection for a nurse after a visit: 'She just like *ngardanya* [mother], like a mother — she looks after people'. On the other hand, when the visit of the same nurse was unexpected, I have witnessed the women of another dwelling hastily covering meat and the contents of a cooking pot (knowing that uncovered food is strongly disapproved of by Whites). One of them exclaimed with great annoyance: 'What she want?'. In this sense, the presence of an approaching Whitefella in the village could be regarded as an uncomfortable intrusion; and this was particularly so if there had been insufficient time to modify the appearance of the dwelling, and/or the behaviour and general appearance of the children, in the direction of conceived White standards.

An instructive case of Aboriginal restraint over behaviour in the presence of Whites in the village concerns the occasion of death of a close relative. The White manager was usually informed by radio of the death of people who had been taken to Mt Isa hospital, or who may have been living temporarily or semipermanently at places such as Borroloola, Mornington Island, or Burketown. He (sometimes with his wife) would then drive to the village to tell the relatives of the deceased. At times he also did this when a person had died at the local mission hospital. If the death had been at all expected, people would sense the nature of the 'bad news' as the manager's vehicle slowly stopped outside the house of the deceased's closest relatives. While the manager related the details of the death, all would remain very quiet. Only after he got back into his car and drove off would loud mourning behaviour begin, and continue for a long time. The intensity of this wailing and shrieking indicated great restraint in remaining quiet in the presence of the manager. At the funeral, however, people would cry and mourn loudly in the presence of White people. Indeed, on a few occasions I witnessed, the White manager told mourners to 'stop crying now'. All present certainly wished to proceed with the preaching for the formal part of the funeral, but perhaps the Whites regarded too much intensely overt mourning as inappropriate.[7] Whites never joined with Aboriginal people in the village in the physically and socially intimate mourning following news of the death.

Most Aboriginal residents of Doomadgee can speak and understand a number of varieties of Aboriginal English. They typically speak as standard English as they can when conversing with Whites, for it is known that Whites will thereby understand more and that they value standard English highly. When an Aboriginal speaker did not wish to give Whites understanding of particular subjects, however, this was not normally achieved by speaking very non-standard English to them, or in their presence. Rather, it was achieved through silence, by briefly professing ignorance about the matter or by as briefly as possible agreeing with whatever the White person said. Information was generally not offered to Whites. Sometimes this happened when Aboriginal residents knew that certain information would incriminate an Aboriginal person to White authorities or employers, but in any case local Whites were known to view many aspects of village life with disdain (e.g. ritual life), or disgust (e.g. social grooming behaviour associated with head lice — see Trigger 1981). Nor was information concerning kinship relations given freely by Aborigines; in fact White misconceptions on this subject have at times been deliberately allowed to continue.

In interaction with Whites, behaviour was usually formal and Aboriginal people avoided practices known to be disapproved of by Whites. Some who openly smoked tobacco or chewed *bundija* (a mixture of tobacco, ash and water) in their homes or in the village generally, did so covertly or not at all in the presence of Whites. If fights or arguments broke out in the White domain, onlookers would usually call out to the protagonists to stop fighting and swearing, whereas such behaviour was simply observed keenly (and often with some enjoyment by those not involved) in the village. One man described the time, many years ago, when he first came as a young man to live at Doomadgee and discovered the rules there concerning behaviour:

> I didn't know nothing about Christian people, [I was] meeting me old mates, swearing away [in the presence of the White manager] and everybody looking guilty y'know, they been tell me: 'These fellas don't swear, this the mission and all this and that . . .'. I was 'shamed too; see I was so used to all the *Mandagi* [Whites outside Doomadgee] y'know. (T59)

During the research period, there were still differences between the behaviour of the local missionaries and that of some Whites from outside the settlement. A number of Aboriginal men were impressed, for example, by how a White man from a nearby station addressed the manager's wife by her first name. The other missionaries would always address, and usually refer to, her and her husband as 'Mr' and 'Mrs', followed by the surname. And it was unheard of for any Aboriginal person to use first names to address this senior missionary couple; in fact, it was unusual for them to do so for any White staff (much to the concern and embarrassment of some of the younger staff who indicated that they wished to establish more familiar relationships with individuals from the village). In my case, then, it became difficult if Aboriginal people had to address me in the presence of Whites: to behave as usual as if in the Blackfella domain and use the appropriate kin or subsection term would be breaking the rule of speaking as standard a form of English as possible, particularly in addressing a Whitefella. One man stuttered in addressing me in front of a nursing sister at the hospital: '. . . Mr Trigger, or . . . what's it your name . . . whatever you're called'.

Other Aboriginal behaviour towards me at times reflected the contrary usual style of behaviour for White staff, in that people would comment on how their behaviour towards me was an exception. This occurred when people offered to me, and requested from me, food, cash and a place to sleep, or when they requested me to take them somewhere in my Toyota, or asked to borrow or buy petrol. People commented continually that they could not request such favours from the local Whitefellas, and they would not usually offer any of these kinds of assistance to Whitefellas. There were complaints that Doomadgee Whites should, and did not, stop on the road to assist Blackfellas whose cars had broken down. One young Aboriginal man, when somewhat drunk, phrased his request to me for transport to the airstrip (in order to avoid the Aboriginal police) in a way that indicated both his perception of the kind of people you may ask such favours of, and the tactics he may have thought most likely to persuade me: 'Come on Blackfella, you gotta take me Blackfella, yeh, you, Blackfella'. Similarly, one man related a conversation as I approached a 'gambling school':

> Person A: 'Hey look! One *Mandagi* [Whitefella] coming!'
> Person B: 'No more [i.e. no], that'un countryman.'

It would be unthinkable for a group of people to continue gambling in the presence of a White Doomadgee staff member, as happened when I reached the group.

Aboriginal people occasionally disregarded the presence of Whites (e.g. in a major dispute, the White manager's presence would not stop the protagonists from fighting). Some individuals were less prepared than others to appear to accept White values in the presence of staff. On one occasion, I observed a man handing a can of soft drink to his son during school time, when the class visited the store (in the White spatial domain). The young teacher who was looking after the class was unsuccessful in his attempt to cloak his disapproval with a half-joke: 'Favouritism hey?'. The man's reply forcefully stated a strongly held Blackfella value which he considered to override the constraints of the White school-time domain: 'That's my son, mate, I gotta feed him!'. He then moved away angrily. At times there was approving talk of how certain 'old people', usually individuals now deceased, did not modify their behaviour for Whites. For example, one man apparently continued to wear a short bone through his nose even when working up at the mission: 'he didn't care about White man — nothing' (T83).

Finally, there is evidence that an increasing number of individuals believe that Aboriginal people should not always have to appear to Whites to conform to their values. One woman, talking about sharing with local Whites knowledge of obtaining and preparing bush resources, said 'we used to be quiet [i.e. reserved] about our *dandi* [earth oven — a reference to cooking bush resources], but now we're open, we're still hunters, no good saying we're not'. Another man explained how only after the departure of the missionary manager in 1983 did certain people (including himself) smoke in the area outside the store and administration office. Previously they were 'too frightened' of the manager's disapproval. Only after the administrative changes in 1983 were tobacco and cigarettes sold in the store.

Social closure, domination and the Blackfella domain

The ethnographic material in this chapter indicates that the imperative for Aboriginal residents is generally to insulate the domain of Blackfella space, thought and behaviour from the administrative White domain. While selective occupation and use of physical space has been the base for presentation of this ethnography, it is clear that the Blackfella and Whitefella domains of social life are by no means solely constituted by control over physical areas. Control of physical space stems from social conditions such as the people present, and the subject, style and context of social interaction. Thus, sites within what is usually the Blackfella domain of the village can become areas where Aboriginal residents temporarily restrict their behaviour because of such social conditions there as an open air Christian meeting, or a visiting Whitefella performing an administrative task.

The point is further illustrated by the case of the cemetery, located some 4 kilometres from both the village and the mission. On the one hand, Aborigines conceive of it as intimately linked to the Blackfella domain through the burial of relatives there; there are no Whites buried there. However, the social context of the operation of the cemetery overshadows this physical association. Our analysis must designate this area as more fundamentally conceived by Aborigines as within the White domain. For certification of death and burial is done by Whites via bureaucratic written means and sometimes involves White police and/or an autopsy performed by White medical personnel in Mt Isa or Brisbane, involving the transfer and receipt of the body by Whites using what Aborigines and Whites both view as serious official Whitefella means. These White-controlled operations culminate in the White-administered burial proceedings.[8] It is on such fundamental social processes that the analysis of separate domains must focus.

In this chapter, different domains have been identified according to cultural (and racial) diversity. Indeed, this kind of diversity in itself, is given as *the* reason for social separation by certain Whites, and as *a* reason by certain Aborigines. However, the broader analytical question is whether the imperative for the maintenance of a high degree of social closure between these two broad domains is indeed due solely to cultural difference. Cultural difference does not fully explain the facts of separation as described above. Why are Whites not impinged upon to take the Aboriginal domain into account in any way similar to the way Aborigines defer to White modes of behaviour? Indeed, why do Aboriginal people appear to be generally more committed than Whites to the maintenance of the separation of the two domains?

It is clear from the data that the answer must deal with the issue of power relations between the two domains. Earlier chapters have dealt with historical dimensions of the economic and political structures of domination of Aboriginal society in this region. However, a critical fact entailed in this chapter dealing with social life at Doomadgee in ethnographic detail, is that an analysis *solely* positing continual domination of Aboriginal society would be inadequate.

Through maintenance of the separate Blackfella domain, Aborigines effect a form of social closure. While they are clearly not the dominant group, this closure is nevertheless exclusionary rather than usurpatory. That is, it is designed to exclude, limit or subject to conditions, the access and participation of non-Aboriginal people (cf. Weber 1968 I: 43). As the subordinate group, Doomadgee Aborigines are certainly unable to usurp greater access to material resources and/or the means of producing them, through effecting closure. But the form of exclusionary closure by which the Blackfella domain is maintained is not oriented towards this goal. Doomadgee Aborigines exclude Whites as part of a defence against constant administrative intrusiveness and attitudinal ethnocentrism on the part of White Australian society. In this sense, social action by local White staff should be seen as having been oriented towards gaining intrusive administrative (and associated evangelical) access to the Blackfella domain. State policies have also sought such access, in sponsoring and formally regulating missionary administrative practice. The desire for this type of access on the part of the colonising society may be separated analytically from the exclusionary closure of the broader society concerning material resources.

To the extent that Aboriginal social action denies this form of access, social life within the Aboriginal domain can be regarded as at least in part an arena of resistance to the colonial imperative of assimilating the colonised to the beliefs and practices of the colonising society. Though the settlement has in many ways resembled a type of 'total institution', as described by Goffman (1961), Aboriginal residents have maintained more than just constricted 'free places' away from staff surveillance such as Goffman describes for institutions like prisons or hospitals. For the Blackfella domain is the norm in that it constitutes the setting for all of domestic life, quite apart from other knowledge and practices such as are associated with aspects of traditional relationships to country, religious ritual, folk-healing, gambling and drinking of alcohol.

Finally, social life within the Aboriginal domain derives in many important ways from Aboriginal tradition (as is discussed in the next chapter). Equally, life in that domain also incorporates many social and cultural forms derived from the traditions of the colonising society. In terms of my analysis here, the important feature of Aboriginal practices within the Blackfella domain is not whether they are 'traditional' or 'introduced', but that they constitute an arena of life in which the legal authority of the state and the derived powerfulness of its local representatives do not intrude routinely.

Notes

1 I have used the past tense here (and in subsequent chapters) in an attempt to represent most precisely the administrative setting from which the data are drawn (1978 to 1983). Some major administrative changes occurred during 1983, involving the Queensland government (DAIA) taking over the administration from the Brethren Church. When material is drawn from the period following this change, it will be made clear in the text.

2 For the sake of convenience, I use the term 'White' for all non-Aboriginal staff, although on several occasions during the fieldwork period there have been one or two staff of Asian ancestry.

3 During 1983, a new church was built in the median strip. A group of Aboriginal and White Christians selected this location, reportedly in the hope of reducing the social distance between Aborigines and Whites. Some people believed that the mission manager opposed the location, ostensibly on bureaucratic grounds concerning the existing town plan.

4 While the social position of mixed-race people was distinctive in some ways (see chapter 8), the apposite point here is that they were recognised as a separable social category *within* the Blackfella domain (see also Trigger 1989).

5 This 'hall' was an old building in the village, separate from the 'church'.

6 While Aboriginal discourse does include use of names to address people in certain contexts, this form of address is much less frequent than the pattern of use in White Australian society.

[7] White disapproval of Aboriginal mourning behaviour is evident from a mission document (written in 1953) already quoted in chapter 4, where 'the pitiful wailing for the dead' is included in a list of evil Aboriginal practices (Doomadgee 1953: 4).

[8] There were, at least initially, apparent increases in Aboriginal control of funerals after the administrative changes in 1983.

CHAPTER SIX

Politics and identity within the Aboriginal domain

Social life in the village produced its own internal politics during my fieldwork. In particular, several aspects of individuals' ascribed identities were critical to the politics of status among Aboriginal residents. A plurality of inherited identities entailed a diversity of local level political interests, at least as far as political life within the Aboriginal domain was concerned. If the pattern of village politics seemingly engenders a lack of Aboriginal political unity, it simultaneously entails the maintenance of criteria for the attribution of social status that differ greatly from those operating in non-Aboriginal society. Thus we arrive once again at the question of accommodation and resistance in Aboriginal social life.

Linguistic affiliation, social identity and status relations

People inherited affiliation(s) to one or more languages from their parents and grandparents; hence, this aspect of their identity was ascribed from birth. Because the rate of linguistic endogamy has apparently been decreasing over recent generations (Trigger 1987: 225–6), most residents could describe the way their linguistic identity was 'mixed' or 'half and half'. That is, most people inherited more than one linguistic affiliation, and historical factors determined which was used as a primary identity label. The choice between linguistic identity labels was usually made in terms of whether a person's past and present life circumstances were regarded as being closer to those of their mother or father. For example, whether there was a recognised greater personal social closeness between them and their mother or father; and, to the extent that perceived separate bodies of tradition (and areas of country) were glossed by using language names as descriptive labels, whether a person could be regarded as having been socialised more in the traditions of one parent than the other. Also relevant was whether he or she had remained in closer physical contact with the linguistic territory of one parent than that of the other.

However, such resolution of a primary linguistic identity was never absolutely complete, in that people would occasionally modify their usual affiliation according to social context. For example, a person usually identifying primarily with her mother's language might forcefully state her affiliation to the different language of her father in order temporarily to align herself with others of that affiliation over a particular issue. In this way, any ongoing unity of resultant 'language groups' was constantly weakened by the possibility of cross-cutting linguistic affiliations. Furthermore, there was no widespread residential discreteness of 'language groups' in the village (Trigger 1987: 227–9). Data from a census of the primary linguistic affiliations of the senior married couples in village households (in November 1980) are consistent with the emic notion that people resided in a 'mixed' fashion with respect to linguistic identity.

Nevertheless, participant observation in village social life made quite evident the situational currency of linguistic affiliation as an idiom for discourse about the shared social identities of individuals. While this affiliation was explicitly to a language name, and implicitly to both the language itself and an associated linguistic territory, it did not necessarily require competence in speaking or understanding the language, nor detailed knowledge of the linguistic territory. While Aboriginal people generally *spoke* about 'language groups' (i.e. people who shared a linguistic identity), rather than gave them collective behavioural expression, on one instructive occasion there was an attempt to mobilise collective action among 'Ganggalida people'. This case not only illustrates the political salience of the multiple linguistic labels in village life, but also indicates an important aspect of the influence of state bureaucratic practices on social relations among Aboriginal people.

The case involved an attempt to establish a 'Ganggalida Society' as a legally incorporated body. In August 1980, a meeting of 'all the Ganggalida' was called at the instigation of an old woman acknowledged by everyone to be one of the most knowledgeable Ganggalida people. She wished to spend periods of time away from the settlement in Ganggalida country, which includes her mother's father's estate. One of her daughters was to go with her, along with other kin, including her sick brother whom she wished to 'take away from this sick place' (the settlement), where she felt people could not get well because they were all 'boxed up', both socially and physically. She pressed her case through a male kinsman who was then the chairman of the Aboriginal council, and the meeting was held at night at the chairman's house. I was asked to attend and bring my documentation on Ganggalida country and the people affiliated with it.

The meeting was attended by about fifty adults, all of whom emphasised Ganggalida as their primary linguistic identity, and many of whom were related by consanguineal ties (though by no means all Ganggalida people were present). After considerable discussion, which included my being called on to give an opinion about how people could secure use of the Bayley Point ('Old Doomadgee') Reserve and other parts of coastal Ganggalida country, and during which the chairman continually emphasised how he would fight for what his people (i.e. in this context 'Ganggalida people') wanted, the decision was made to form a legally incorporated body known as 'Ganggalida Society'. However, it was thought appropriate for this body to have a Ganggalida name, which was provided by the authoritative old lady who had instigated the meeting: *mudara gangga Ganggalida* (a lot of Ganggalida language and people).

The meeting discussed how the society would elect formal representatives and apply for government grants for such items as vehicles and other desired commodities. The formation of the Ganggalida Society was framed primarily with respect to 'Ganggalida country', and this area was to be used for the following purposes: as a holiday place, particularly but not exclusively for Ganggalida people; to take the children there to be taught aspects of the culture and history of their people; to attempt to muster, use and possibly sell cattle and horses (and for this the Society needed its own brand); and to catch fish both for subsistence and for sale at the settlement. However, such economic activities were not envisaged as being carried on collectively; there was strong support for the idea of private businesses being established by individual families.

Following the meeting, much discussion of the decisions ensued. Nine days later, the council chairman called a public meeting in the normal place in the village. The White manager was present, after presumably being notified of the meeting by the chairman. As was common in such meetings, speakers used a microphone and loudspeaker so that a substantial number of people throughout the village could hear. Among other issues discussed in this long meeting, the chairman put the notion of a Ganggalida Society and called for people to speak their mind publicly on the matter. In doing so, he described it as primarily a means for getting more government funds for housing and other material improvements for the settlement, and as well some money for the use of the Old Doomadgee area. That is, he modified somewhat the earlier strong focus of the initiative towards Ganggalida people, which had been so forcefully resolved at the previous meeting. However, the notion of a 'Ganggalida

Society' expressed in concrete form the concept of discrete language groups within the village. Aware of this, the chairman made sure to stress that it would in fact benefit the whole community:

> There was a good meeting the other day with most of the people as Ganggalida people and we thought of . . . the idea was — Ganggalida Society. And not only just going to take up Ganggalida people but it might help Garawa, because we all mixed married now, you know Waanyi and so on. It's hard to split us up now really. (T55)

Of the eight speakers at the meeting (all male), five were publicly classified primarily as Ganggalida people through one or both of their parents. The fact that it was a specifically Ganggalida initiative was made:

> Now we've got a mob of what-a-you-callim countryman here, Munggabayi [name for the vicinity of Burketown] mob or Ganggalida mob, there's a mob of us here. Now we're the first mob been moved out hey? From Burketown over to the coast. I was only a piccaninny . . . yeh, don't you fella worry, come on . . . [calls names of six Ganggalida men]. (T55)

Soon after this speaker, a man of Garawa parentage registered some disapproval:

> Very good idea . . . we were going to form a body and going to call it 'Ganalanja [Waanyi name for Nicholson River] Land Council'. All you people agree with that or you sooner have the 'Ganggalida Land Council'? (T55)

While the introduction of the term 'land council' made an aspiration regarding land explicit, the point of major relevance here is this speaker's suggestion of a Waanyi name for the organisation, so that it would not be nominally a Ganggalida organisation. He was not so direct as to suggest one of the other main language names as the formal label of the body, but instead gave the Waanyi term for the river on which the settlement is located. The Ganggalida name for the river is very similar (Ganalanda), but there was no agreement about whether the section of the river adjacent to the settlement site is part of Waanyi country or Ganggalida country, and his suggested name was much more neutral politically than 'Ganggalida Society'.

The chairman moved immediately to maintain the original name, but also to reiterate his original point about 'benefit for all'. He referred to a similarly constituted body on Mornington Island and one in Burketown, said that they 'cover' all the 'tribes' in those places, and then went on:

> Little bit muddle up there on name . . . this Ganggalida, it's only just name, language y'know, because . . . early time, missionary took the Ganggalida. It doesn't leave anybody out. It doesn't leave any tribe out. It doesn't leave Waanyi out, it doesn't leave Yanyula out, it doesn't leave any other Garawa out y'see. Now we don't want to bring a division between people or us all. I know at times it can get like that. (T55)

In his final statement the chairman named nine people as possible representatives of the Society; all were defined as Ganggalida people in this context.

Following lack of support from the Commonwealth Department of Aboriginal Affairs, and argument against the idea by the local White manager, the Ganggalida Society was not formed. The attempt to form it represents one of the few occasions where the emic concept of shared linguistic identity was manifested in collective action. The discussion about a legally incorporated body which would be nominally Ganggalida was in part an aspect of the Aboriginal relationship with the bureaucracies of the state. Many village residents were aware of the importance in Australian bureaucratic procedure of corporate social units with formal office holders and representatives, and those most involved in Aboriginal dealings with the bureaucracy understandably concluded that conformity with the procedure leads most quickly and effectively to acquisition of the commodities and services at stake. Linguistic affiliation provides a suitably general feature of Aboriginal social identity to be used in the flexible social construction of such nominally corporate groups. However, at Doomadgee these 'language groups' had very little stable sociopolitical unity. The salience of linguistic identity was focused much more routinely on the politics of status relations among individuals.

The basis for the political currency of linguistic identity was that people generally attributed less social honour to languages other than their own. The latter were typically said to be 'too rough' and harder to speak than their own and this sentiment was expressed by people including those who were unable (or only partially able) to speak their own language. Languages were at times mocked, though not normally within hearing distance of people affiliated to those languages, for such behaviour would be regarded as highly offensive. Because of the broadness of cross-cutting linguistic affiliations, such mocking behaviour was usually reserved for geographically and socially remote languages (e.g. the speech of people from a Cape York settlement residing semipermanently at Mornington Island, and encountered when Doomadgee people visited there). The sound of one nearby island group's speech was particularly singled out for such ridicule, with some people mimicking it to suggest that the speakers appear to be choking on the sounds.

While the sound of speech was thus made the direct focus for the attribution of social status, the more basic factor was pride in language as a form of cultural property. Like certain other traditional property, a language is valued highly primarily because it is regarded as one's own. Other languages are assigned lower status because they are inappropriate to one's own social identity and that of one's children. This fact emerged clearly when the Doomadgee school began a 'culture program' (mentioned briefly in chapter 1), which included the teaching (by several mostly older 'culture teachers') of words and phrases from Aboriginal languages. From the outset the widespread opinion among village residents was that children should be taught their own language. When it appeared at one stage that Garawa was the only language being taught, Ganggalida and Waanyi people complained that this was a completely unacceptable situation. For their part, several Garawa people pointed out that Garawa was 'too strong', that it was most easily learned by the children, and that it might well 'take over' at Doomadgee.

My own tendency to learn more Garawa than Ganggalida or Waanyi was taken by Garawa people as further evidence of the strength and hence high status of their language. They thus overstated my limited competence in Garawa, which they saw as evidence of my social alignment with Garawa people. The fact that a personal name I was given is conceived to be a Garawa name was stressed publicly on several occasions, and some Garawa people told me: 'you Garawa all the time'. Several older Waanyi and Ganggalida people occasionally showed their disappointment at my seeming inability to learn their languages to the same extent.

Politicking using the idiom of linguistic identity also concerned the concept of linguistic territories. Broadly competitive comparisons were made between linguistic territories, and in the context of such discourse people would tend to posit the extent of their own language over the widest possible area, as indicative of its 'strength'. The evidence (or justification) drawn on when arguing for the expansiveness of one's own linguistic territory was normally the parallel historical movement of one's people (defined in terms of a language name). Indeed, when people state that their own language has 'taken over' an area, they appear to be referring primarily to the comparatively recent historical association with it by people of their own linguistic affiliation. While some also attempt to extend their linguistic identity to major totemic figures in the area over which their language group has expanded, these statements are not easily sustained.

Examples of such competitive discourse using the idiom of linguistic territories include suggestions by senior Garawa and Yanyula people that these languages would 'take over Ganggalida country' because too few of the younger and middle-aged Ganggalida people knew their country and because they were further 'behind the law' (i.e. alienated from ritual obligations) than others. These types of suggestions have little chance of being accepted; they directly attribute low status to Ganggalida people. Indeed, they would not be made in the presence of senior Ganggalida people (except perhaps as a deliberate insult during a dispute), and are made in other settings more as a form of jingoistic sarcastic speculation than as a description of an actual state of affairs.

Arguments for linguistic territory expansion more realistically represent actual claims when there are no longer Aboriginal people asserting original primary linguistic affiliation (or other affiliation similarly based on descent) with the territory being 'annexed'. For example, many Ganggalida people asserted that the Burketown area was part of Ganggalida country. Middle-aged people who were born there often referred to Ganggalida people as 'Burketown side' and to their language as 'Burketown language'. In fact, however, the few older people who had more detailed knowledge of the area stated that it was 'Min.ginda country' ('Min.ginda' being the name of another language) and this view is supported in the literature.[1] These old people also at times concurred with their children's generation that Ganggalida people 'took over' the Burketown area through historical association after Min.ginda people 'died out'.

A further example is an unresolved difference of opinion about whether the settlement site is within Ganggalida country, which hence extends that far southwards from the coast, or Waanyi country which hence extends that far eastwards down the Nicholson River[2]. Disagreement on this issue was infused with substantial sentiment, for what is at stake is not only the status of one's own linguistic identity, but also evidence of primary ties to the country in which the valuable material property of the settlement is located. Through such primary ties one could assert the strongest rights to reside in the settlement. Indeed, on two recorded occasions certain Ganggalida people used the idiom of linguistic identity to suggest that particular Garawa people should be told to 'go back to their own country' (i.e. to the west of the settlement in the Northern Territory). This occurred once in the course of discussing the dominance of Garawa in the school 'culture program', and once when those attempting to hold a male initiation ceremony were categorised as Garawa people. In the latter case, several Ganggalida people asserted that 'all the stranger people' (referring to those of Garawa social identity) should go back home.

In summary then, the linguistic affiliation of individuals is one of the features of their social identity that is entailed in their political relations with other Aboriginal people. It is one means by which status honour is attributed to social identity. Such honour may be tied to the sound of various languages being spoken, and to features of different linguistic territories, but above all, it is attributed on the basis of a profound chauvinism about one's own linguistic identity. When, for example, as I have observed, a person shouts in the course of an argument or fight: 'my father Yanyula!', the statement is immediately understood by all present as a political one. Through a forceful assertion of one's linguistic affiliation, the statement asserts, with great pride and resolve, an important aspect of one's status and identity.

The politics of 'country'

Affiliation to sites and tracts of land (or 'estates' as discussed in the literature, Stanner 1965b), both termed 'country', was also an important feature of individuals' social identities. Traditional land tenure enables people to be linked with country in a variety of ways, including links to the estates of one's four grandparents and to one's conception site (regarded as where individuals were spiritually conceived). People would state freely the similarities of their identities according to jointly held ties to country, e.g. 'We two got one granny country' (i.e. mother's mother's estate), or 'Me and her come from that same water' (i.e. have the same conception site). While people in this way manage the historical and genealogical aspects of their publicly known biographies in order to situationally claim a considerable array of ties to different areas, they are constrained by the prominence accorded ties to the estates of their own patrilineage and that of their mother, within the ideal system. In some cases, people would identify more with either the estate of their father (and father's father) or that of their mother's father, citing historical factors similar to those affecting primary ties to a linguistic territory. Nevertheless, in terms of salient groups of people forming on the basis of joint ties to a particular estate, these groups were cognatic (and reasonably labile).[3]

From about 1976 onwards, Doomadgee residents have been increasingly aware of the possibility of gaining legal title to tracts of land (on the Northern Territory side of the border), and associated commodities used for visiting and establishing bases on lands (in both the Northern Territory and Queensland). This has meant that politicking focused on just who has rights to various lands according to Blackfella law has been intensifying during this period. Factions within broad cognatic groupings have actively disputed questions of genealogical and historical detail, particularly as they can be brought to bear on the issue of which faction should control any valued goods and services provided by government bureaucracy to those recognised as having 'traditional' rights to country. In this process, the factions have sought and variously received support from different old knowledgeable people both within the village and in other places throughout the region.

The issues focused upon in these disputes have been wide ranging. They have included such accusations as that an individual's socially recognised father is not his or her actual genitor, and that therefore that individual has only weak rights to an area. A further contentious matter could be that a person's parents were married 'wrong' in terms of the subsection system, so that the progeny of the marriage do not unambiguously have the same subsection–couple (or semimoiety) affiliation as that of their patrilineage estate. Hence, it might be argued that their rights to the estate are diluted in comparison with those whose parents married 'straight', and who are regarded as having the 'full' subsection–couple affiliation of their father's estate.[4] Individuals have been accused of lacking substantial historical contact with an area of country, and as thereby having diminished rights to it. On some occasions, people have claimed rights to an estate (of the appropriate semimoiety, but not inherited directly from their own lineage ancestors) on the basis of one or more of their ancestors having lived there continuously during earlier times; as one man put such a case when visiting an area: 'my father been hold a spear la this place, he been look after this country'. The claim about diminished rights was also made with regard to adults lacking appropriately held knowledge of the totemic features of the estate they were claiming as part of their inherited cultural property. And as a final example, spouses of members of land 'owning' groups have been accused of inappropriately interfering in matters concerning the groups' claims to an area of country.

None of these matters was sufficient in itself to dislodge individuals' or groups' rights to country. However, the effect of such internal politicking was that there was no strong emphasis towards maintaining broad unity of purpose or aspiration throughout country-affiliated groups. Indeed, if anything, social relations operated according to a principle emphasising the discreteness of interests in and ties to country among individuals. Thus, while the wider 'mob' asserting ties to an estate was typically conceived as a broad cognatic group, the political strategies of singular parent–children factions within such groups were often evident in actual social behaviour. And predominant among such strategic behaviour were disputes that focused on control of material commodities and services provided by wider government bureaucracies.

A further important issue in considering the politics of country in settlement life is that, as with languages, areas of the landscape were attributed varying amounts of social honour in different ways by different individuals and groups. As with language, people would generally state the virtues of country to which they themselves asserted a close tie, and also (though less commonly) they would proclaim its superiority over other country. Speakers were aware that these kinds of comparisons could give offence to others closely affiliated to the country stated to be inferior. Nevertheless, comparisons were made on the basis of key attributes of country: desired resources (the nature and extent of available water, and plants and animals); dangerous or annoying features (such as mosquitoes, flies, or ticks); and preference for certain kinds of topography and climate. Great pride was taken in such material features of one's country, as was evident when I observed individuals visiting their country after a long absence (or in some cases, for the first time in their lives). People took containers of what is regarded as 'my water' back to the settlement to show and distribute to other members of the country-affiliated group (particularly children). Also taken back and presented with great pride were 'bushes' (leaves, twigs and branches), and stone tools found in the country. Similarly, some people requested that photographs be taken of them at their country, and these were subsequently viewed with great interest and pride by those affiliated with that area. The material evidence of earlier Aboriginal occupation was treated with pride, awe and nostalgia: stone tools, camp sites, rock art, marked trees, and so on were interpreted as evidence of previous habitation by one's own 'old people', and commonly led to people stating with great nostalgia about such places, that one of their grandparents 'must have been here'. Some grinding stones were said to have been the property of particular deceased women, and in several cases a daughter of those women took these back to the settlement. On another occasion, stone tools were placed carefully in crevices near where they were found, for safekeeping.

Apart from its material properties, the status of country is derived from its totemic features. Indeed, the environment is seen to be ultimately dependent on the totemic forces in the country. It is not only totemic forces productive of immediately beneficial resources which can be regarded as positive features of one's own country, for while a potentially malevolent force such as that at a 'sickness dreaming' place must be treated carefully and normally avoided, such a feature can also be regarded as evidence of the strength or perhaps potential power of one's country. Furthermore, a repertoire of songs and associated ritual that can be used in sorcery contexts for offence and defence is regarded as belonging to each of the four semimoieties. In the emic view, their power derives from certain of the major totems of each semimoiety, and hence these powers are intimately tied to various sections of country.

Thus, an aspect of the social identity and status of all individuals is entailed in their ascribed affiliation to country. To the extent that people engage in politicking in managing this affiliation, their status through publicly acknowledged links to country is also an achieved status. However, it is particularly in the case of those regarded as expertly knowledgeable about country, its features and the principles regulating human affiliation to it, that matters of country become a potential source of high status. As Hiatt (1984: 23) has put it in concluding a review of several recent studies of traditional land tenure (though without stipulating a settlement context): ties to country provide people with 'a potential springboard to fame'.

In fact, such a wide body of traditional knowledge entails matters concerning country that it was in relation to the general notion of 'Blackfella law' that certain individuals were considered to have the status of expert. Their high status knowledge thus also concerned life-cycle crises (particularly matters associated with death), and illness and health. They were usually aged in their fifties or over, and would always be regarded as an 'old man' (*malbu*) or 'old lady' (*bardibardi*). Both men and women were thus represented among them. With only a few exceptions the men had been initiated (during their youth) — most to what can be glossed as the 'first degree' (in ceremonies involving circumcision) — and a few had been initiated to the 'second degree' (which involves subincision).

During my fieldwork, some individuals were widely regarded as among the few remaining people (at times the only person) with detailed knowledge of certain areas of country. As a scarce, highly valued resource, this knowledge was not flaunted, nor usually given to others haphazardly. To be told detailed information about an area of country to which one may only know that he or she is affiliated through ties to ancestors can in fact occasionally entail being publicly ridiculed. More commonly, it simply involved being manoeuvred into the socially junior position of the pupil in the presence of the knowledgeable expert. For this reason, few people actively sought information about 'law' matters from the experts, and instead listened when they chose to speak.

The experts themselves engaged in competitive discourse focused on country (and other 'law') matters. They were not committed to one another in any enduring way, any more than they were to others in their own networks of wider alignments throughout the village population. However, their joint status was partly evident from the restriction of the arena of competition concerning important matters to the senior age category. There were also separate senior male and senior female arenas of competition. Senior women appeared not to compete over knowledge of restricted male ritual matters, and the healing skills of expert men and women most likely entailed some matters exclusive to males and females respectively. A number of senior women were regarded as expertly knowledgeable about the genealogical details concerning persons' affiliations to sites and estates, and the totemic significance of particular areas of the landscape. Thus, while I have certainly witnessed circumstances in which a senior woman would defer to her husband when such matters were being discussed, it would be overly simplistic to regard such behaviour as indicating actual lower status on the part of senior women in any general way agreed upon across the population. The modes of practising competitive status relations entail complex and often subtle tactical etiquettes rather than simple overt dominance through speaking the most forcefully in all settings.

A range of tactics and strategies were used in the process of politicking around the issue of country and associated matters. Commonly, an individual would feign indifference about getting the opportunity to speak authoritatively, or being acknowledged as expert on a matter; all the time knowing that no other person present had the requisite information, and that hence those present would have to wait for what he or she had to say. For example, at a meeting of men convened to form a regional 'Aboriginal law council' in response to an initiative from people at Mornington Island, one man was suggested (albeit circumspectly) as the person who should be the main Ganggalida 'representative'. While he knew that he was generally accepted as one of the most knowledgeable men about Ganggalida tradition, he stated: 'leave me out please'. After a period of about two minutes during which nobody made any further suggestions, a man began to introduce another subject but was immediately interrupted by the knowledgeable Ganggalida man, who maintained the focus on himself by asking: 'yes well, what we gonna . . . who we gonna get for that part now, Ganggalida?'. Again, people said that he should be on the proposed law council, but it was not until after considerable procrastination that he pronounced formally: 'put my name on there then, [be]cause not too many of these fellas here'll talk Ganggalida y'know — these younger people'.

In another instance of the use of subtle understatement of position, a man known to be a 'great singer' told me at the normal gathering place of the senior men that he would allow me to record on tape some of his songs. After I had recorded one verse (sung somewhat repetitively as usual) he gestured towards another man in the group, saying to me: 'I give it over langa [to your] *mimi* [fictive mother's father] here too, he wanna putim now'. This other man was known to be his main associate-cum-rival in the composition and performance of the major series of innovative song verses that he had started to sing, and the gesture indicated that I should also record some of this man's verses. The 'great singer' thus made it clear that his own status was sufficiently well established for him to not have to ignore his more junior rival; as an acknowledged expert he could afford to flaunt magnanimity. However, the rival was not to be drawn into the position of junior follower; he refused the opportunity: 'no, you're right, you can putim all yours — putim down all yours and I can putim mine some other day'. He thus implied that he was by no means dependent on the 'great singer' for the opportunity of an audience and a tape recorder. Yet the formality with which he made this statement contrasted with the relaxed and more secure attitude of the 'great singer'. Indeed, another man then somewhat trivialised the younger rival's statement with a jovial wordplay on its sexual innuendo: (to the 'great singer') 'you can putim yours tonight' (i.e. indulge in sexual intercourse tonight). Through skilful social manoeuvre, the 'great singer' immediately collaborated in the joke: 'mightn't be here tonight, might be la Burketown' (in this case a reference to sexual activity there). Soon after, he further assured the goodwill and responsiveness of his audience by jokingly downplaying his capacity as a singer. While himself beginning to clap his boomerangs in preparing to sing further verses he said 'killim finger [clap] please, makim good hey, I'm not very good singer y'know' (drawn from T83).

Such understatement is part of a tactical etiquette designed notionally to mask the quest for social honoúr in public settings, while making sure that one's indirect statements of personal prowess are recognised. Other politicking can be more direct, as in a case where two men deliberately played a tape recording of themselves singing a particular *gujiga* (song cycle celebrating the totemic features of a certain landscape). It was played very loudly, so that any conversation among the group of men sitting some 15 metres away was impossible. Despite their obvious purpose of flaunting their knowledge of the verses and their prowess in singing them, both men feigned indifference to the reactions of the group. After about ten minutes, one man turned the volume down and called to the group: 'you fellas right there, with your talk?'. Nobody responded that it was impossible to talk; everyone in the group remained silent and the singing was turned up loud again.

A further example of direct politicking for status occurred when a senior woman was giving me information about an area of country. When, during a break in the conversation another woman offered a short comment that added to those the older woman had just made, the former was forcefully rebuffed: '[X] you young generation — don't tell me: "[a]'long lagoon there", I been all over this country, I know every water!'. For the older woman, part of the integrity of her explication of the features of the country relied on that explication standing alone, certainly without qualification from a junior kinswoman. Similarly, when a senior man arrived at an estate with a middle-aged man who had never been to that part of his father's country before, the older man constantly made clear the younger's lack of knowledge. For example, within hearing distance of everybody as we disembarked from the motor vehicle, the expert patronisingly asked the younger man to indicate the totemic features and geographic dimensions of his father's country. The purpose was to joke about the latter's lack of knowledge and associated lack of status.

In unusual situations, protagonists argued vehemently. While the interchange of words nearly always finished when one party was no longer prepared to allow the disagreement to escalate, I observed one case where an old man flew into a rage, swore at his adversary, stood up abruptly and walked away. This man was regarded by most as always seeking to provoke an argument, and on this occasion he had interjected in a general discussion about an area of country, to ask aggressively and rhetorically of one of the other old men who had been speaking: 'now you tell me who [was] this boy's *mimi* [mother's father]?'. He was referring to a young man present whose country was being discussed. The argument occurred after the other old man replied to this question (correctly, according to most present). The younger man, whose country and relatives were being discussed, remained silent — behaviour commensurate with his status as a 'youngfella' whose knowledge of country was regarded as comparatively limited.

The overt seriousness of this particular argument was atypical, and after the aggressor's departure there was considerable comment that he was *murdu* ('mad'). There was also support expressed for the other man's explanation that under such provocation: 'a man got to say something back'. Indeed, the fact of quite divisive competitiveness among the senior Blackfella law experts was acknowledged reasonably openly as a routine aspect of social life. Details of various issues at stake were sometimes discussed in selected settings, away from people defined as rivals. For example, a senior man complained to me that one of his peers 'don't want to see me get ahead of him'. On other occasions, individuals asserted that their own knowledge was more expansive and accurate than that of their rivals, e.g. 'they tell you anything [not necessarily the truth] you know'. Experts at times expressed sympathy for my position, because of the way other senior individuals were (accurately) perceived as trying to have only their version of a contentious matter recorded. Some have even publicly chided others for giving me information in an allegedly biased manner: 'you wanna tell him straight way!' or 'right way', and so on.

These local-level political styles concerning country and Blackfella law illustrate a process whereby some senior people can achieve reputational social honour that stands out from that generally accorded to the senior age category. They achieve this status through the scope of their knowledge, their personality and their social skills. However, like all others, the extent to which particular senior people can win support throughout the village is influenced greatly by an aspect of their social identity yet to be discussed. This is the extent of an individual's network of close kin — a most critical aspect of village politics.

Kinship and social action

A pervasive principle structuring social relationships among village residents was kinship. Certain kin were distinguished in Aboriginal English as 'really', 'full' or 'blood' relatives; they were also referred to by the expression 'my *own* [X]' (where X is the kin category), emphasising the word 'own'. An actual genealogical link (either consanguineal or affinal) to such kin can usually be demonstrated, although the term 'blood' is not normally applied to affines. Kin were also referred to as 'close', and while these people were always among persons' 'really'/'full'/'blood' relatives, the range of people distinguished as 'close' varied according to a variety of social factors. Actual kin were thus ranged along a continuum of social closeness. Indeed, this was so for all Aboriginal people in the village, for those not designated as 'really' (nor 'close') relatives were referred to as 'long way' people. Ties to such 'long way' people were putative, and commonly based on the system of relationships implicit in the subsection system (cf. Maddock 1972: 86).

The complex traditional systems of kin terms and relationships have undergone considerable changes throughout the process of colonisation. It must suffice here to say that during my fieldwork most older residents knew (and variously used) the full sets of vernacular terms and the rules stipulating ideal relationships between different kin categories. Middle-aged and young people possessed this knowledge partially; some knew many more terms than they normally used. A small proportion of vernacular terms were used regularly across the entire village population (including children). Terms have been drawn from Garawa, Waanyi and Ganggalida languages in a mixed fashion and now constitute part of the contemporary Aboriginal English repertoire.

Older residents complained that young people no longer follow the traditional prescriptive marriage rules, and that they simply 'marry like dingo', that is, 'any way'. They pointed out that people who marry 'wrong' by contracting genealogically close marriages are breaking Blackfella law and are likely to suffer severe consequences. Nevertheless, my survey of marriages in 1980 shows that most individuals avoided marrying 'close' kin,[5] a fact that has led to a widening of kindred networks throughout the village population over the years.

Because of the extensiveness of broad cognatic groups throughout the population, residents' 'close' kin were typically spatially distributed quite widely among the ninety-six dwellings existing in 1980. In one of the largest cognatic networks, one old lady had consanguineal ties to one or more individuals in 47 per cent of households, and these households were not concentrated in any particular part of the village. The genealogies of other such groups indicate that most Aboriginal residents had similar networks of connection to a range of households, though some were less extensive than others. Even individuals who had come from outside the region were normally incorporated into such networks as 'really' relatives through their affinal tie to a member of the network. Without these links, individuals rarely stay at Doomadgee, for kinship is the primary basis for the distribution of social and material support.

Women appear to draw particularly on their siblings and husband's siblings for food (for example, when the family is short of cash or if something is needed for a child at night or on a weekend when the store is closed). Children were commonly sent to a close relative's residence to request basic items such as bread, tea, or sugar. Men without wives, in particular, as well as old people, would eat occasionally or regularly at the houses of certain close kin, but sleep elsewhere. Food was also sometimes sent to old people at their dwellings. Requests for food and other commodities would rarely be made to a person other than a close relative. Not only would such behaviour be considered a breach of etiquette, and the request usually refused, but also it is considered unsafe to take food from 'stranger people' (in this context genealogically distant people) because they may have a reason to perform sorcery against you and could do so through the medium of the food. For this reason, people are even more careful about who they allow to wash their clothes, for notorious forms of sorcery are known to be effected via the sweat lodged in a person's dirty clothes. While tobacco is requested and consumed with less concern about whose possession it has been in, it too is regarded as a prime vehicle for the performance of sorcery.

While economic support among close kin was a routine aspect of social life, the level of requests at times led to complaint and tension. People complained that their kin squandered their money or goods unwisely and then requested cash, food and other items. As one man put it when complaining to his mother's sister about her children requesting vehicle transport without contributing to the cost of fuel and other running costs: 'these people drive you *mad* you know'. However, this kind of tension did not typically develop into physical conflict as did other kinds of disputes. While serious conflict certainly occurred between close kin (e.g. between spouses or brothers, especially when one or both parties were drunk), a major role of kinship is to compell support for close relatives under attack from others, and this has been the more general aspect of village life.

Conflict was quite common within the village, and was carried on largely independent of the formal settlement administration. Consider the following comments by the chairman of the Aboriginal council, at a public meeting where he endeavoured (with a hint of futility) to convince people to involve the Aboriginal police (and hence the formal administration) rather than just fight it out among themselves. His references to 'domestic' disputes in fact refer to conflicts that commonly ramified throughout extensive kin networks, involved loud yelling of abuse and insult and often physical violence, and lasted for several hours:

> This has been a concern. I know, everybody has domestic problems — domestic trouble gets out on the street, gets out on the flat here sometime, and that's how domestic trouble can start [i.e. ramify], where it shouldn't come out . . . it should be kept at home. I know it's a little bit hard, but a lot of these problems that we have as domestic, as family affairs and so on, in relations [i.e. among relatives] — we have some trouble sometime and . . . it gets out of hand . . . Any problem come up, or you start a fight, or you hear something [i.e. rumours, gossip] that's not true . . . you take it straight to the police. (T71)

Conflict usually erupted over rumours and/or accusations about sexual activities of a pre-marital or extra-marital nature. People drew on what appears to be an established verbal and behavioural style used only in conflict settings. Such conflict is thus not regarded as aberrant, but as an inevitable part of social life. Even children can model their conflicts on this style. I have observed several young girls aged ten to thirteen years, while playing, emulate the adult style of conflict with great precision: i.e. with wild aggressive gesturing, waving sticks as fighting weapons and smashing them into the ground and against objects in a (mock) rage, and proclamations of personal prowess and fearlessness and of the strength of one's kin support, as well as invitations to each other to 'come out' and fight.

I have also watched some young children emulate adult behaviour to emphasise the haphazard, uncontrolled (and hence potentially very violent) nature of drunken conflict. In response to my query about their yelling and gesticulating on this occasion, they illustrated the emic conception of the drunken style as quite distinct from sober social action: 'we *gammon* [pretend to emulate] drunk talk'. Without addressing fully the subject of drunken comportment in village social life, I can say that fights involving drunk individuals typically developed haphazardly as compared to sober conflict. Most sober people tried to ignore drunks, or at least tried to feign indifference while observing them indirectly. While the antics of drunks were sometimes a source of entertainment for sober onlookers, it was said that one should not overtly 'take notice' of 'drunken fellas', close kin or otherwise, for this could attract their unwelcome attention.

If a drunk person did become embroiled in conflict with sober people who were not close kin (usually because his verbal and/or physical attacks had finally become intolerable), his own sober close kin would most likely intervene to support him. On one occasion, a sober man explained, while making ready to support his drunk wife's brother against sober people who had beaten him with sticks: 'you can't [i.e. shouldn't] hit a drunken fella!'. Indeed, his opinion was that in attacking a drunk person (though the behaviour may well have initially been a defence against the drunk's attack) those who had assaulted his brother-in-law had transgressed Australian law as well as Aboriginal etiquette.

Sober people occasionally become involved in conflict between two or more of their close kin where one who is drunk is regarded as the physically superior protagonist in a formally unequal match. For example, if a drunk man attacks a woman or an old male relative, other close sober relatives may intervene. This is much less likely to occur if the victim is also drunk. In any case, intervention by sober people against drunks (apart from in the case of the Aboriginal police) is usually circumspect, with the sober person(s) avoiding if possible direct involvement at the actual point of drunken physical conflict. One short incident illustrates such circumspect intervention.

A drunk (quite frail) man aged fifty to fifty-five years was punched and kicked to the ground by a young drunk close male kinsman. At the same point, this young man also kicked and punched a young drunk woman who was a close relative of both him and the older man. She had been trying to protect the older man with the aid of a fighting stick and by throwing stones, and the young aggressor forced her to retreat down the laneway in which the incident took place. He then moved off down the laneway in the opposite direction, loudly asserting his fighting prowess in typical drunken style. As he had advanced on the older man and made it clear that he was about to escalate from verbal abuse to physical conflict, the latter had called several times for his sober son-in-law, a big young man (and known as a strong fighter) to come and help him. While the violent encounter occurred, the son-in-law moved slowly from his house to a viewing position. He then moved to the end of the laneway to intersect with the aggressor's course and knock him unconscious with a single punch, and the Aboriginal police carried the young drunk man away to gaol.

The significant point here is simply that the son-in-law did not intervene with any speed to stop the (drunken) attack on the (drunk) older man and his female supporter. His initial avoidance of getting embroiled within a fight between drunks is quite typical of the sober behaviour of close kin in such circumstances. In knocking the young man unconscious, he behaved methodically and without saying anything. That is, he did not engage in the typical verbal-behavioural conflict style of sober people. He probably acted partly to stop the drunk doing any more damage, although revenge may have been an additional motive. The son-in-law's action was regarded as appropriate and necessary by all present, but he was not perceived as engaged in the social business of conflict with the young drunk man, simply because such 'full drunks' are not considered capable of rational social action. In such a state, people are regarded as not in normal control of themselves, and to this extent as unable to participate meaningfully in the social business of conflict (or for that matter in any other social action).[6]

In sober conflict, people routinely support their close kin with much greater urgency and emotional commitment. This is such a general aspect of village social life that it is rare for conflicts to involve solely two protagonists. People expect that their opponents will receive kin support. In the course of their verbal assault on others during conflict, people constantly refer to kin who will come to their assistance and to the fighting prowess of individuals among them. A wide range of relatives may come to an individual's aid, but most commonly groups of same sex siblings together with their parents and grandparents of the same gender, may be said to constitute fighting units, each of which is inevitably mobilised when one of its members becomes involved in a dispute. That is, a fight is commonly regarded as predominantly a 'woman fight' or 'man fight'; and in fact the former were more prevalent during fieldwork. Perhaps more accurately, the considerable number of sober conflicts I witnessed most commonly began with women as the main protagonists, and men then often became involved as the fight continued.

These conflicts can be very complex in terms of the kinship relationships between protagonists. The following partial account of a conflict shows how a dispute can ramify to involve a large number of kin on both sides. A young woman (*A*) had been living adulterously in a nearby town for some time with another woman's (*B*'s) husband. *B*'s mother (and other female kin of *B*'s) had therefore given *A* a 'hiding' in a public place in the town. Soon after all the protagonists returned to Doomadgee a long fight erupted in the early evening (the typical time of day chosen to express grudges against others).

I witnessed the early stages of the conflict from the perspective of certain people aligned with *A*. Several young children in the household I was in at the time were the first to hear sounds of a fight, and announced excitedly: 'they fightin, they fightin!'. As all household members moved quickly outside to observe, several asked:

'who fightin?'. People listened and watched keenly in the direction of the yelling, and quickly resolved the identities of the major protagonists by considering the general area of the village from which the yelling seemed to come; such assessments determine whether the location is 'top end', 'bottom end', or 'river side' of the village. By drawing on background knowledge of which families living in the area of disturbance had reason to fight, the 'mobs' involved were quickly determined. At that point, *A*'s father's sister came hurrying to the house to get the senior man of the household, the eldest son of another of *A*'s father's sisters, 'to try hold them back' (i.e. to try to restrain some of *A*'s kin who were incensed over the beating she had suffered). This man, together with his wife and children returned with *A*'s father's sister to the house of yet another of *A*'s father's sisters, where a group congregated that included at least four of *A*'s father's sisters plus the husbands of two of these women, *A*'s father's sister's son (plus his wife), and one of *A*'s father's mother's brother's sons. All these people were extremely upset. The group then moved to the house of one of *A*'s sisters (whose husband, also present, is *A*'s father's mother's brother's son). At this house a further large group of *A*'s relatives were gathered, including her mother and several of her siblings. *A*'s mother and sisters were trading insults loudly with the women of *B*'s grouping, located at a house several streets away.

Fighting eventually erupted in one of the streets and continued intermittently for several hours. I witnessed only part of it, and the following partial description of blows exchanged was given by one of *A*'s relatives. While it may thus be biased in terms of who were the victors, it demonstrates the range of close kin supporting the initial disputing individuals (*A* and *B*):

- *B*'s older sister was knocked down by *A*'s older sister.
- *B*'s father then aggressively restrained *A*'s older sister.
- *B*'s father was then cautioned by *A*'s father's sister's son, and simultaneously pushed back by *A*'s sister.
- *B*'s brother and older sister's husband were present but did not intervene.
- At one point just after *B*'s mother had been successful against a woman with her fighting stick, one of *A*'s father's mother's brother's sons warned her off with his own stick, but *B*'s mother then sent for *B*'s mother's mother's brother who came up quickly from his house several streets away, carrying boomerangs. However, he did not become involved in any actual physical clash. Men aligned with *A* later said that this man brought his boomerangs mainly as a bluff, for they claimed that he is not skilled in their use as fighting implements; however, his older brother is known to be an expert with these weapons and the implication

was that it would therefore have been dangerous to engage the younger man in physical conflict because his brother would most likely then have become involved.

- *A*'s own husband's brother apparently also threatened to attack *A* (for in forming the adulterous relationship with *B*'s husband in an open fashion she had also offended her own husband's family), but he was warned off by some of *A*'s male kin present.

Others who took sides in the dispute included *B*'s mother's sister's widower, who made comments in support of his deceased wife's kin during the next day. As well, the adulterous husband himself (who had remained in the nearby town throughout the conflict) was encountered several days later by his mother's mother's sister's son (structurally equivalent to his mother's brother, or 'uncle') while the latter was visiting the town. Both had consumed a small amount of alcohol, and the 'uncle' embraced the younger man, cried, and told him he would be safe if he came back to Doomadgee and stayed at his 'uncle's' house. After they arrived back at the settlement this was indeed the case, although the two young women protagonists and their relatives continued minor arguments over a longer period.

Apart from providing support in conflicts, individuals' social relationships with their close kin entail what is best thought of as an aspect of their status situation. That is, in village politics, the reputations of one's close kin are linked to and in part determine one's own status. To some extent, this is evident when people are very reticent to admit that a close relative has lost a fight or argument, unless the loss was absolutely clear (as in the person being knocked unconscious). Demonstrable physical injury to one's close kin is seemingly felt as an injury against one's self. Awareness of such injury to kin engenders the desire for retaliation, and I have observed those injured deliberately exhibit wounds to close kin in obtaining their support.

Pronouncements of loyalty when supporting close kin in such circumstances are made regularly during and following periods of conflict, e.g. 'I'll fight with my brother till I drop!', or 'fight one brother they fight them all!'. When people are quick to take the part of a close relative in the face of abusive or insulting comments from others, their actions are described by such statements as: 'she stood up for her aunty'. However in village politics this loyalty derives at least in part from concern about attacks on one's own public status because this status is tied firmly to that of one's close kin. The motives of those supporting their relatives in the encounter described above are best seen as oriented towards their own status situation as well as that of their relative under attack. To put the point succinctly, when individuals 'stand up for' their aunty, granny, brother-in-law and so on, there is an equally fundamental sense in which they are standing up for themselves.

The nature of Aboriginal politicking

There is a vibrant pattern of competitive status relations among Doomadgee's Aboriginal population, operating in terms of individuals' socially recognised affiliations to languages, areas of country and groups of close kin. These kinds of individual affiliations are inherited, although the point has been made that to some extent people are able to negotiate their public identity by managing their own genealogical and biographical details about their background.

An important generalisation is that I have not thereby described publicly accepted single-status hierarchies for languages, areas of country or networks of close kin. For it is basic to Aboriginal management of these aspects of identity and status that people do not agree on their ranking. The seeking and attributing of much status honour occurs in a fundamentally egocentric and chauvinistic manner. In this sense, there are as many emic status hierarchies of Aboriginal languages as there are languages to which people are affiliated, and the same point can be made for status hierarchies of areas of country and networks of close kin. The result is that these kinds of intensely competitive status relations entail cross-cutting assertions about the social honour of people, which are deniable or challengeable simply through the alternative chauvinistic proclamations of others. No individual or grouping of individuals can ever win widespread recognition for their assertions about the superiority of the aspects of their ascribed social identities discussed in this chapter.

A partial exception to this generalisation is that the senior age category is attributed high status across the village population, largely because older people are regarded as embodying 'law' knowledge. Nevertheless, only a relatively small number of senior individuals achieve substantial reputations as Blackfella law experts, through their success in the use of often complex and subtle tactical etiquettes. Those who lack sufficient social skills in asserting knowledgeability or prowess in the arena of Blackfella law are likely to be ridiculed just as are younger people who are regarded as illegitimately proclaiming their own esteem. In such circumstances people may be said to be 'skitin[g]', a term that does not so much express disapproval of an individual's actions as express an interpretation concerning his or her intentions. While it is accepted that many individuals will inevitably 'skite' in the course of relationships with other Aboriginal people, to so describe their behaviour embodies a culturally approved reciprocal competitive reaction to a person's statements and actions.

That is, the term indexes challenging sentiments about the person's competence and knowledgeability in taking a particular public stand.

The nature of village politics does not facilitate political unity among Aboriginal people in their relationship with the local White domain and the broader Australian society. The pattern of competitive status relations may in fact be regarded as reproducing a plurality of local level political interests that indirectly weakens tendencies for the formation of a unified political consciousness among Aboriginal people throughout the village. To an extent, the maintenance of this form of Aboriginal politics can be explained simply by reference to the imperative of tradition. By this view, village socialisation processes inculcate the legitimacy of the forms of politicking I have presented.

However, an important theoretical question to ask is why the traditional imperative has not been discarded so that Aboriginal people come to attribute status according to the kinds of (typically class) criteria institutionalised in the wider Australian society. Given their ultimate exclusion from all but the lowest levels of such class and status hierarchies, Aboriginal people at Doomadgee may well resist accepting the legitimacy of the criteria on which these hierarchies of the White domain are based. Whether or not this is a conscious resistance, maintenance of distinctively Aboriginal forms of politics can be regarded as further evidence of cultural resistance to the intrusive ethnocentrism of non-Aboriginal society.

While this chapter and the previous one have stressed the distinctiveness of Aboriginal social action and consciousness, and their partial independence from non-Aboriginal society, an ongoing set of social relations operates between the two domains of life at Doomadgee. From the White domain emanates the full force of the colonial administrative practices that mediate Aboriginal relations with the state. It will become clear that while the Blackfella domain, including its form of politics as described in this chapter, may be regarded as an arena of cultural resistance, we cannot disregard the ideological containment that has occurred as part of the wider colonial enterprise.

Notes

1 Among the early sources, see Palmer (1883: 277), Curr (1886: 314), Turnbull (1896: 13) and Old (25.5.1899); more recent consistent sources are Tindale (1974: 181) and Dymock (1977: 5).

2 It was quite likely in fact to have been within Nguburinji territory (see map 2), but (as with Min.ginda) there appear to be no people who now identify with this language.

[3] While I am not reviewing here the various relevant recent studies of traditional land tenure, Hiatt (1984: 20–1) makes an apposite comment about two tendencies that orthodox views on this subject have ignored:

> One concerns the incorporation of non-agnates; the other concerns competition *between* agnates. The former leads typically in the direction of land holding by cognatic formations . . . The latter tends towards fission or dispersal of agnatic cores, giving rise to the extreme case of individual ownership.

[4] The subsection system entails rules designating correct relationships of marriage and descent among the subsection categories; and it is in this way that four subsection-couples (or semimoieties) incorporate lines of patrilineal descent. These subsection-couples also divide the landscape into discrete parcels of country (or estates) and the totemic world into four categories (Sharp 1935, 1939; Reay 1962; Trigger 1982). While older Doomadgee residents suggest that before Whites came everybody had to 'follow the law' and marry 'straight', genealogies indicate that there has been a substantial proportion of 'wrong' marriages for as long as the old people can remember. Two surveys I conducted in 1978 and 1980, found rates of 56 per cent and 58 per cent wrong marriage (out of samples of eighty-eight and 139 marriages respectively). When the 1980 data were cross-tabulated with the age of the marriage partners, the result was that the rate of wrong marriage has been increasing over the past few decades. For the sample of 139 marriages, approximately 61 per cent of those aged over fifty-one years have married 'straight' to their current spouse, as compared with 39 per cent of those aged thirty-one to fifty-one years and 26 per cent of those aged under thirty-one years.

[5] Figures from my 1980 survey of marriages (see note 4 above) show that of the 162 people whose marriage was regarded as 'too close', thirty (19%) were wrong because they were 'too close' genealogically. Others who had 'wrong marriages' had married genealogically distant people who were not 'straight' for them according to the subsection system.

[6] Most drunks are recognised as 'full drunk' in this way. Only those whose drinking has been interrupted (e.g. if the 'grog' has prematurely run out) retain sufficient normal social composure to be referred to simply as: 'he been drinkin too', or as 'half-shot'. Drunk people can also be referred to as 'charged up' or 'sparked up' enough to be unpredictable and potentially dangerous, though not completely unable to control themselves in the way people are when they are 'full drunk'. It is not until 'full drunks' have gone through the process of becoming 'choked down' (they have collapsed into sleep for at least several hours) that they are regarded as once again largely in control of themselves (unless they begin drinking again).

CHAPTER SEVEN

Authority relations, the missionary staff and Aboriginal consciousness

Authority operated through settlement administrative processes and was apprehended differently by White staff and Aboriginal residents. Staff practices involved a substantial degree of factionalism and it is the diversity of views among the missionaries that I focus on first in this chapter. There were also several dimensions of the Aboriginal relationship to administrative authority. These included both support for, and opposition to, the historically familiar pattern of local paternalistic administration. After examining Aboriginal views on this matter, this chapter concludes with discussion about the extent to which Aboriginal people attribute legitimacy to the encapsulating political structures within which they are situated.

The nature of colonial authority: factionalism amidst collective staff commitment

Under the *Aborigines Act* of 1971 (hereafter referred to as the 1971 Act) and its amendments, the reserve manager was for many years the local administrative instrument by which the state authority of the Director of the Queensland Department of Aboriginal and Islanders Advancement (DAIA) operated. While that legal authority was much less extensive during the 1970s and 1980s than under previous Queensland law, some critics consider aspects of it to be in breach of various international human rights conventions (Nettheim 1981: 139–52). This criticism relates specifically to issues including access to reserves, the operation of local courts, the infringement of the privacy of persons' homes, the management of individuals' property, the manner of election of Aboriginal councils, and wage rates paid to Aboriginal workers on reserves. Furthermore, the apposite point has been made (Nettheim 1981: 32) that the more authoritarian official philosophies and policies of the past may have been continued in administrative practice after their repeal, particularly in such cases as Doomadgee where individual staff have remained in authoritative administrative office over long periods.

The number of White staff at Doomadgee remained quite small until 1975, having varied between five and eight during the late 1930s and the 1940s, increasing to between six and thirteen during the 1950s,[1] and while no data are available for the 1960s, by October 1975 the number had increased to eighteen staff (DAA n.d.*a*: 6). It is unclear whether there were also other spouses and children at that time. After 1975, the number of Whites increased rapidly due to the expansion of school and certain health facilities, so that in May 1979 there were thirty-four adults plus fourteen children (DAA n.d.*a*: 6). Staff have typically remained for substantial periods. Since the late 1970s the school teachers have generally been more mobile than other staff, but Murray's (1982: 3) data show that in 1982 the average length of stay among seventeen teachers was approximately 2.6 years (excluding the atypically long period of twenty-six years for the principal). Doomadgee staff have certainly differed from those in the contemporary Northern Territory communities described by Gerritsen (1982: 27); for he states of the 'service whites' that 'very few spend any [i.e. much] time in the community', and that these staff are seen as 'ephemeral'.

Accounts from senior missionaries indicate that only members of Brethren Assemblies were accepted as staff by the mission. Occasional exceptions to this rule appear to have included committed Christians of other fundamentalist faiths, mostly Baptists, and according to some accounts, one or two White Christians of other denominations underwent baptism by total immersion soon after joining the Doomadgee staff. Such baptism and being spiritually 'born again' were prerequisites for acceptance as a staff member. The first change in this situation was in 1982, when several teachers with non-fundamentalist backgrounds joined the school, and in 1983 the staffing of the school was completely taken over by the Queensland Department of Education. From 1983 the mission ceased to control all other staffing and the DAIA took over this role. However, a number of Brethren staff remained for varying periods of time.

Brethren Assemblies (i.e. church-focused congregations) are organisationally independent of one another.[2] There is no overarching administrative body. Thus, individuals have received 'commendation' from their Assembly to go as missionaries to Doomadgee. The Assembly has thereby given them religious authorisation and undertaken to support them financially when, and to the extent that, it is thought possible by the church elders. Such financial support may well be irregular. It has been suggested that the home Assembly would give according to a perception not so much of the missionaries' material needs but of what God wanted them to give. Apart from such direct receipt of money from the 'commending' Assembly, the missionaries have often received from the Doomadgee mission organisation rent-free furnished accommodation with electricity supplied, and in some cases, free food. At times, small extra amounts of money were apparently distributed by the Doomadgee church elders if, say, an amount had been sent to the church from an Assembly for all the 'voluntary workers'. The missionaries did not receive wages from the mission organisation.

All staff appear to have been unpaid in this way until 1975, when the teachers became paid employees of the Department of Education (Murray 1982: 11). By 1980, half of the fifty-two staff were 'voluntary workers', while during 1982, these workers numbered at least twenty-four out of a total non-Aboriginal population varying between sixty and seventy (although one source [Murray 1982: 1] has estimated it at approximately eighty).[3] Regardless of whether people had come to 'voluntary' or paid jobs, they believed they had come to do 'God's work' (however those not receiving regular wages could, from their viewpoint, certainly indicate a very tangible sense in which their wellbeing was in 'God's hands'). Several staff said that they expected to leave Doomadgee on the same basis as they came — when God told them it was his will for them to leave. People who grew up in certain Brethren Assemblies have usually heard about Doomadgee from a young age, through newsletters, personal letters from relatives and friends there, and other literature. A few Christian Aboriginal people have, over the years, also reinforced a widespread awareness of the mission through visiting some Assemblies and attending Brethren study courses at various 'Bible Colleges'. One young missionary related how she had always felt from a young age that she would go to work at Doomadgee. Thus, the missionary staff has consisted of people with very firm commitments to what they perceive as their evangelical task.

In Brethren Assemblies, no formal order of clergymen is established: 'There are no ordained clergy among the Open Brethren' (Van Sommers 1966: 30). Nevertheless: 'those who are gifted by God for the public ministry of the Word are gladly recognized' (Douglas 1974: 789). Thus, elders of the church generally hold considerable authority in relation to instruction and guidance on religious matters within the Assembly community. At Doomadgee, the manager was also a church elder. Indeed, according to the 1971 Act from which his secular authority derived, he was required to be 'the person in charge' of the religious organisation on the reserve. The manager was appointed in 1958 (DAA n.d.*a*: 2), having been at the mission since 1951. Not until 1975 did he formally relinquish control over any aspect of administration, when the affairs of the school were partially taken over by the Department of Education. In 1978, his personal authority over mission policy and financial matters, and over such issues as staff welfare, was (in formal terms at least) further reduced through the formation of a 'management committee' consisting of him, his wife and four other staff.

The school principal (also a church elder) occupied the only office of authority comparable to the manager in terms of influence over a large number of staff; he had also been at Doomadgee for many years, having first arrived in 1957 (Murray 1982: 10). These two men were the only Doomadgee residents who were members of a Brisbane-based 'Doomadgee Mission Committee', apparently formed in the early 1970s, and consisting of men from various Assemblies. This committee had little influence over the missionary administration until 1983, when it was apparently involved in a direction being given to the manager to resign. The latter and his wife then left the settlement, as did his son, accompanied by his own wife and children. No Aboriginal people were ever members of the 'management committee' or the 'Doomadgee Mission Committee'.

Two main administrative styles operated among the non-Aboriginal staff, which I characterise as the manager-centred and school-centred perspectives. The key administrative position was clearly that of the manager. Both he and his wife expressed clear commitment to the evangelical task: 'my commitment is to preach the word of God, so that they [Aborigines] can become Christians and know how to become Christians' (ABC *Nationwide* television program, 29.7.1982). From this perspective, the job is to lead people to develop personal faith in God and live what is regarded as the Christian life. Like many other staff, the manager and his wife regarded aspects of White Australian lifestyle as necessary for a Christian life. They could thus view with considerable satisfaction the material results of their labour over the years. Indeed, on at least one occasion during the study they were able to screen slides and movie film demonstrating to other (mostly younger) staff, the sequential establishment and improvement of material services (particularly, but not exclusively, in the White spatial domain) since their arrival many years ago.

These long-term missionaries have always been engaged in a tutelary relationship with Aboriginal people, encompassing both material and spiritual matters. They have indeed considered their relationship to Aboriginal people as akin to one of parents to children, although the manager's wife has argued publicly that they have not stifled Aborigines with paternalism:

> I feel exactly as I ever endeavoured to care for Aborigines as I've cared for my own sons, and my four sons had to be untied from mother's apron

> strings and the Aboriginal people just the same. (ABC *Nationwide* 20.7.1982)

As they put it they have received great affection in return: 'there's that bond of love that's grown over the years that nobody will break' (ABC *Nationwide* 20.7.1982). The following passage is from a statement made by the manager at a public meeting held in the village in 1980, just after a visit from the Commonwealth Minister for Aboriginal Affairs. While lengthy, it illustrates well the didactic paternalism that permeated his perspective as a missionary and an administrator:

> You know, I've said before: what sort of a place would Doomadgee be, if everybody in Doomadgee was just like me? Now you ask that question. If you're the type of person that throws a tin on the ground, and everybody was just like you we'd have lots of tins on the ground wouldn't we? If everybody did — and we could think of all the things that are wrong. But let's think the other way: what sort of a place would Doomadgee be if everybody in Doomadgee was just like me? If you had a desire to see Doomadgee as your home, [if] you desired to see it as we used to see it, with gardens around the home, ... with an interest in children. You know, there's nothing more rewarding and satisfying than to see the things which a child has been trained ..., as he gets older, to see him carrying on doing those things. You know [a certain Aboriginal woman] is not here tonight, but [she] was our house-girl back in the fifties, and I'm thankful for ... [three other women in their forties and one old lady] and others ... There was a time when Mrs ... [his wife] was sick and she had to go to Brisbane, and those girls looked after our boys [his own sons] as well as Mrs ... [his wife] did. They did it because they loved them. And we're thankful for that. But you know when ... [one of the women] had children of her own many years after there was an incident where ... [she] was doing something, and Mrs ... [his wife] commented on what she did. She said: 'Mrs ..., you used to do that'. So she [had] carried on. You know that gave us joy to think of that. You know if you train up a child in the way he should go, the word of God says when he is old he'll not depart from it. But that's your responsibility. Sometimes parents, they have heartaches, they have sorrows, because they've had no thought, they've had no care. You know Mr Read [when he was superintendent] used to say: 'Sometimes the people, they sits and thinks, but sometimes they just sit'. That means to say they sit and they don't think, and that's true isn't it? You know we can be like that. If everybody in Doomadgee was like the person who just sat, and he never thought, he didn't think, of his home, his family, his wife, didn't think of anything, what sort of a person would that person be? What sort of children would that person have? What sort of a family would that family be? ...
>
> He's [God] our leader, and as our lives are lived before him, you know we won't be worrying about cleaning up the house inside and outside, that just automatically follows. So we can be thankful tonight that we

> have, in spite of us, we have a God who cares, not only for our spiritual good but also for our welfare as far as our homes, . . . children, . . . the future is concerned. But the rest, as . . . [the chairman of the council, who was the previous speaker] said, is up to each one, individually, what they're going to do with it. So I'll just leave these words with you: what sort of a place is Doomadgee going to be, when every . . . person in the community is just like me? — speaking of oneself, not speaking of me, yet it includes me doesn't it? If I want to do things silly, if I want to act stupidly, and all those sort of things, . . . and everybody was just like that, what a terrible place it would be. If I want to be more kind, more loving . . . So let's see that with the good news that we have [following assurances of substantial funding from the Commonwealth Minister for Aboriginal Affairs], with the hopes for the future, with plenty fishing down at Old Doomadgee, and all that sort of thing, let's see [if] we can't revive some of the old interest that we had in the past. (T64)

From this perspective, there has been little question of learning anything worthwhile from Aboriginal people. Indeed, some other staff suggested that in the manager's view, the role of 'White people' as morally senior to (and thus as the teachers of) 'Black people', had 'scriptural authority'. For such is apparently an interpretation of Genesis 9:21–29 and 10, by which the descendants of one among Noah's three sons were cursed to be the servants of others, and it is interpreted by various means that the cursed son was the ancestor of the dark-skinned people of the earth (see Buckland 1929:189 and Pettingill 1971: 338–9). I am unable to confirm or deny whether any staff held to this interpretation during my fieldwork or whether those working there in earlier times did; the majority of staff appeared to reject it. However, it must be noted that the Aboriginal church elder quoted below appears to have held this view, and it is most unlikely that he would have developed it without White tutelage.

The manager claimed that he would like to be able to have administrative positions taken over by Aboriginal people:

> As far as the administration is concerned, well with administration goes accountability, and if there are those who rise to that situation, who can take over the administration, well it would give me a greater opportunity to do the main [spiritual] work which I came for, and that's to be able to move and sit with the people, to be able to talk to them. (ABC *Nationwide* 20.7.1982)

However, he further pointed out that Aboriginal people did not usually complete the training needed for administrative jobs:

> and if we were only looking at the results [of our attempts at training people] that we get from what we put into it, well then one would give up — but there's no thought of giving up, we're out here to help the people. (ABC *Nationwide* 20.7.1982)

The following passage, extracted from the 1980 public meeting cited earlier, illustrates his constant concern that Aboriginal people develop 'responsibility' in order to work in administrative positions:

> The matter did come up [with the Minister] as far as responsibility is concerned, taking positions. It's not Mr . . . [the Minister's] idea nor the Commonwealth Government's idea, that one day we're just going to change things just like that. He realises that it requires those, as . . . [the council chairman] has said, who are prepared to put themselves out and have an aim to achieve something. And when that person has achieved something, it won't be very long before he'll be given a responsible position. (T64)

According to this view, the earlier (dormitory) generation was more responsible and better suited to jobs in the White domain than contemporary young adults. The methods of the past were favoured, and such new approaches as the teaching of 'culture' in the school and the development of 'indigenous' (or 'distinctively Aboriginal') Christianity were firmly rejected. As mentioned in chapter 1, there was seen to be no scriptural authority for such notions; to again quote the manager's wife: 'We'll all be together in heaven so why separate now?'.

It is important to understand the manager's view that the 'hand of the Lord' was evident in *all* things, including whatever administrative processes may have been occurring at various times. Thus, also at the 1980 public meeting, he explained for the edification of Aboriginal listeners how a number of then current events reflected God's work: during the Minister's visit a request had been put to him about funding for construction of a direct road to Old Doomadgee; then some White men arrived to say they were establishing a new cattle enterprise on the property between the 'old' and 'new' reserves, and if they could hire the mission grader and operator to make the road the Doomadgee people could use it to get through to the coastal country. Some of the manager's comments were:

> You know, the Bible says: 'Before they call I will answer', and we've had so many instances here in the past of God answering prayer . . . but there's so many circumstances in connection with these things, they all dovetail in together. These [station] men came back Sunday morning, and they saw me and one man he said: 'Well I know some of your friends, I know some of the Brethren down there in Dalby, and . . . in Toowoomba'. So he mentioned a name, and I said: 'Well, you might know some of the Brethren, do you know the Lord?'. And he said: 'Praise the Lord I do, I'm born again'. He said: 'We were coming back this morning to come to church but we couldn't make it'. Then one of the other fellows that was with them — I don't think he was a Christian — he said: 'You know, things have happened on this trip . . . everything has just gone well'. And

> you know what the Bible says about the person who's blessed? He that God blesses is blessed indeed. He can't be unblessed. God is in control. And so we give Him the thanks tonight, for the Federal Minister. We're told in the word of God, to pray for those who are in authority. We're to pray for men in authority that they might be given wisdom, so that we might live a quiet and peaceful life in all Godliness and honesty. (T64)

In fact, at least some of the station men turned out to be charlatans engaged in various criminal activities such as the growing of marijuana, and departed owing the mission a large amount of money for stores, equipment hire and wages. Yet from the manager's perspective, all things must continue to be viewed as part of God's plan.

The school-centred perspective diverged from the practices and ideology of the manager-centred perspective. Many school staff during the late 1970s and early 1980s developed quite different views from those of the manager and his family (and various others). Some teachers sought administrative changes in an attempt to improve the school's relationship with Aboriginal residents and the general educational servicing of the community. Most significantly, some teachers tried to monitor the degree of success of the school, and were prepared to acknowledge certain problematic issues. For example, a survey attempting to establish community awareness of aspects of education was carried out, and came to conclusions including:

> Aboriginal parents seemed to be uneasy about approaching the school personnel or environs because of lack of information about procedures and layout. (in Murray 1982: 26)

While it is not clear that the various steps taken by the teachers completely achieved their aims (nor even as much as some teachers argued had been achieved), the increasing awareness of problems on the part of a majority of teachers distinguishes them from many (though not all) other White staff. From the teachers' perspective, the formation of various Aboriginal advisory groups presented consecutive attempts to facilitate information flow between the school and Aboriginal residents. In analytical terms, they may be viewed (at least partly) as attempts to legitimate the school's role in the broader administrative servicing of the Aboriginal population.

The school innovation known as the 'culture program' may be regarded in just this way. As mentioned earlier, the initiative taken by the few Aboriginal people who had applied for government funds to form what was locally termed the 'Ngurduri culture company' (Ngurduri being the Aboriginal place name for the settlement site) was eventually coopted by the teachers. They organised the formation of a 'culture committee', which advised the school on how 'culture' could best be taught during school hours. The 'culture committee' was formed as a sub-committee of the Parents and Citizens Association, which began in 1975 after the first involvement of the Department of Education (Murray 1982: 11). The 'culture syllabus' consisted of a list of topics thought to be important (e.g. food collection, bush medicine, history of the arrival of the missionaries). A teacher's written review of the culture program (Murray 1982: 34–8) outlines varying degrees of success over the years, and such developments as the appointment of a full-time Aboriginal culture teacher in 1980, then his replacement in 1982 with a younger Aboriginal teacher-aide to assist older 'culture teachers' maintain pupil interest.[4]

From the early stages of the 'culture program', the school principal (and other teachers) were concerned not to foster anything 'sinister' (i.e. the parts of local Aboriginal culture perceived as unacceptable from a Christian Brethren viewpoint). Examples of such unacceptable cultural forms are initiation rituals where, it was believed, unwilling young men were in the past forced to participate, and beliefs in such malevolent bush-dwelling 'spirits' as the 'short people' (about which the principal had heard snippets of information over the years). The principal's aim was to 'foster a sense of pride' in the pupils about the fact that they were Aborigines, by having them taught the 'acceptable aspects of their culture' (from his viewpoint) that their people 'once had'. However, it appears that as the program progressed he and some other teachers learned more about various Aboriginal beliefs and about their contemporary currency, and adopted a less uncompromising attitude about precisely what was 'unacceptable'.

If most teachers' support for the 'culture program' is to be viewed analytically as partly an attempt to legitimate the authority of their occupational role, the manager-centred faction was certainly not concerned with such legitimation. Regardless of undertakings from the teachers that they would control its content, there was considerable opposition to the culture program from the manager and some other staff. As mentioned in chapter 1, the reasons for this opposition included the viewpoint that it is not possible to separate the acceptable aspects of Aboriginal 'culture' from those that are unacceptable; that to teach pupils that they are different (or at least distinctively Aboriginal) would lead to racism (though it remains unclear whether this was envisaged as racism on the part of Aborigines or Whites); and that there is no 'scriptural authority' for the fostering of separate 'cultures'.[5]

In the context of this disagreement, as with others, the school principal was the only staff member with influence among a number of staff (and probably among Aborigines as well) comparable to that of the manager. The principal appeared to be very popular among his subordinate staff. A survey of teacher attitudes (Murray 1982: 17–9, 45–50) found that he was believed to be 'sensitive', 'interested', 'warm and supportive', and 'dynamic, energetic, innovative, hard working, caring'. The survey also found that all teachers (numbering eighteen) agreed that there was 'a high level of positive staff morale' in the school. The principal's capacity for change contrasted with that of the manager. For example, he stated his belief that children should not have been separated from their parents in the dormitories and coerced (through physical punishment at times) to live a highly restricted and routinised lifestyle, and wished that he and others had simply come in as missionaries preaching the Gospel, allowing people to make their own decisions about 'their culture'. He also offered the view that one consequence for those in the dormitories for so many years was that as adults they had no adequate parenting model in the care of their own children. He was certainly aware of (and somewhat uncomfortable with) the way he was still perceived as an authority figure by those (now adults) whom he and others supervised in the dormitory for so long. Murray's report on the school comments (1982: 12):

> The Principal who is the 'authority figure' of their youth is still in charge of the school today. For some this may inhibit their full participation as adults in the life of the school.
>
> Most parents of school age children have not lived in a normal nuclear or extended family during their youth. Consequently they have not had models in decision making for the day to day business of life. The missionaries provided everything and directed their lives. As a result, we now have a generation of parents who are used to 'white' people making decisions for them.

Unlike the manager, the principal took an interest in some historical research on early race relations in northern Australia and in some of the broad dimensions of Aboriginal affairs (e.g. the issues surrounding a treaty between Aboriginal and non-Aboriginal peoples, and Aboriginal land rights). A DAA report on Doomadgee (DAA n.d.*b*), compiled during May 1982, reports the author's unconfirmed understanding that the principal 'has found an increasing idealogical [*sic*] rift with . . . [the manager]'.

The rift was substantial, but set within a strong commonality of commitment shared by these two influential men together with all other staff. The readiness to admit past mistakes and present problems on the part of the principal and other teachers by no means displaced their continued commitment to evangelism. The coordinated Christian message from teachers to pupils was transmitted informally as much as formally. In response to some media criticism that the school was 'Christianising' the children at 'the taxpayer's expense' (ABC *Nationwide* 20.7.1982) the teachers issued a statement arguing that the time allocated to religious education was no different from that in other state schools and that 'our religious program is essentially educational rather than evangelical'.[6] Nevertheless, the first two of six general aims of the school, presented in a booklet apparently prepared as a teacher's guide, were: (1) to present Christ and encourage personal faith in him; and (2) to teach the scriptures in relation to practical Christian living. The principal appears to have varied in his opinion on whether the teaching staff should have remained exclusively Christian. Certainly, from his perspective, the Doomadgee school operated much more successfully (e.g. had a higher pupil attendance rate) than the school on Mornington Island, where teachers did not have to be Christian. And while the pupils' record of academic achievements was by no means outstanding,[7] all teachers would most likely have argued (together with other staff) that Christian teachers would have more commitment to their work and produce better results than would non-Christian teachers.

Nevertheless, the factionalism among staff was at times quite divisive. One staff member mentioned during 1982 that the extent of disagreement meant that any possibility of a meeting of all Doomadgee staff to discuss the issues was precluded by the fact that it would be too volatile. The two major factions derived their bureaucratic role (and authority) from two state government departments (DAIA and Education), and the two senior people in these factions (the manager and school principal) were both long-term missionary residents with personal followings among the White staff (as well as among some Aboriginal residents). There was strong antipathy on the part of certain non-teachers towards what were thought of as the teachers' unrealistic ideas and opinions, arising out of their more extensive education (any social science or non-technical expertise was particularly resented as impractical and based on 'highfalutin' ideas). The latter feeling was described by one staff member as 'reverse snobbery'. A small number of staff had little formal education, and very few seem to have had much education about Aboriginal society. When I explained that radio-carbon dating had established that there had been occupation of the Lawn Hill Gorge area (to the south of Doomadgee) for up to 30 000 years, one non-teacher seriously asked me if I meant occupation by Aborigines or Whites, and another (non-teacher) couple rejected this information because it was inconsistent with the biblical account, which indicates that the entire universe is no more than approximately 6000 years old.

However, disagreements among White staff were by no means confined to the teachers versus the rest. Several nurses were, like the teachers, paid workers, and some 'voluntary workers' felt that it was inappropriate to receive wages for what was supposed to be 'God's work' because the work thus did not involve sufficient personal sacrifice. Furthermore, during the late 1970s and early 1980s an increasing number of non-teachers aligned themselves with widespread staff opposition to the manager, his wife, and his son and his wife. Thus, the manager-centred faction lost members and support throughout this period. In some cases, people resented the manager's and his wife's assumed role as senior staff who should oversee all matters regardless of their competence in the different occupational areas. The clearest example of this problem was their perceived interference in the affairs of the medical clinic.[8] As noted in the DAA report compiled during 1982 (n.d.*b*), the manager did not always order drugs and other goods requested by the clinic staff, and he had the 'final say' on whether or not the Flying Doctor was called (p. 12). The report also refers to complaint from certain medical staff that, despite continual requests for 'the management' to rectify what the nurses considered unhealthy and potentially dangerous problems with equipment and the material environment of the clinic, their requests had been to 'no avail' and 'fallen on deaf ears' (p. 13). The author of the DAA report points out that one nurse was 'grateful for the opportunity to speak to me out of earshot of the Mission Management' (p. 16), that the manager attempted to stop him getting access to various data concerning health matters, and that the feeling among two nurses (who apologised for not being able to be frank in the manager's presence) was that the manager and his supporters did not want to lose control of the clinic as they had in the case of the school some years earlier (pp. 17–8).

Further hostility towards the manager focused on his perceived autocratic role in appointing some office staff to various jobs, and on his alleged desire for his son to occupy certain positions (and apparently eventually succeed him as manager). Furthermore, as self-appointed guardians of morally appropriate behaviour, the manager and his wife were accused of interfering in the personal lives of staff (e.g. attempting to control both public and private courting behaviour among several young White couples).

Many staff were also critical of various aspects of the manager's administrative practices as these pertained to the Aboriginal residents. Criticisms from individuals included concerns over his total loyalty to the senior DAIA administration in Brisbane, and alignment with its policies, instead of pursuing a more open-minded approach to other policies and initiatives being developed by various state and commonwealth government departments. Some were worried about the possibility of the manager using funds for purposes other than those for which they were intended. Many staff disliked what was perceived as the patronising attitude often taken by him and his wife in interaction with Aboriginal residents. Reported examples include a case where he apparently embarrassed a person seeking readmittance to church fellowship by asking her to state in a public setting the reason for her previous expulsion. In another case his wife is said to have told an Aboriginal person to 'put her false teeth in'.

A few staff criticised the manager's failure to separate administrative and evangelical tasks. At times this criticism centred on somewhat minor issues, such as his preaching on biblical themes at a public meeting in the village called to discuss a politician's visit. At least one person espoused the position, however, that it was just not possible to administer secular affairs and carry out effective evangelical work at the same time. To quote (personal communication from a Doomadgee staff member), 'The whole institutional concept is wrong' and:

> When does an administrative body recognize the fact that the institutional work has outgrown the spiritual work to an extent that the original aims and objectives are hampered or in fact no longer achieved.

This person's position was that the church should withdraw completely from its administrative role.

The majority of staff would have vehemently opposed that position, another indication that amidst factionalism and disunity there was a collective commitment. A broad common commitment to a shared interpretation of biblical precepts united them all; for example, there was simply no questioning of the firm mission opposition to any use of alcohol and tobacco (such use being regarded as a 'vice').[9] Disagreements over the interpretation of scripture certainly occurred: several school teachers objected to (and refused to attend) open air evangelical meetings held regularly in the village; several female staff (also mostly teachers) expressed frustration with and opposition to the subordinate position to which women were relegated in public life;[10] and in 1980 there were apparently at least four people who (albeit in idiosyncratic fashion) regularly and conscientiously objected to voting in any elections, because of their view that God rightly controls the world and it is not for people to interfere in such 'worldly' matters. These kinds of disagreement did not, however, overshadow a firm degree of collective commitment to the broad evangelical task.

An important aspect of the unified commitment among the missionaries may be viewed in terms of their collective sectarian relationship to the broader Australian society, many aspects of which they disapproved of with deep conviction because of the 'vices' common there. Tonkinson's (1974: 120) comment concerning apostolic missionaries at another Aboriginal settlement in the 1960s makes the same point:

> By coming to Jigalong these people are escaping from a society in which a majority of people are steeped in many 'vices' that the Apostolics cannot tolerate or bear to witness: drinking, smoking, swearing, blaspheming, gambling, dancing, fornicating, wearing 'indecent' clothing, breaking the sabbath, and failing to attend church.

That a number of Doomadgee staff found it psychologically difficult to live in the wider Australian society was suggested to me by one staff member, although another strongly denied my suggestion that in going to live at Doomadgee the missionaries were concerned as much with a need in themselves as with the needs of Aboriginal people. No doubt this man's denial would have met with agreement among the majority of staff. For despite the divergent practices and factionalism I have reported, the staff shared a fundamental belief that both the evangelistic and administrative aspects of their tutelary role served the interests of Aboriginal people.

Aboriginal consciousness and the state

Various government departments had increasing administrative influence over the settlement from the mid–1970s onwards. Direct grants from the Commonwealth Department of Aboriginal Affairs began in 1974 (DAA n.d.*a*: 11) and in 1975 the Queensland Department of Education began taking over the administration of the school from the mission (Murray 1982: 11). In January 1978 a Queensland Department of Health mobile community health team was stationed permanently at Doomadgee (personal communication, Sr M. Sault Queensland Department of Health).

The strongest external government influence has clearly been the Queensland DAIA, largely via the agency of the local White staff, most particularly the office of the manager. Under section 15 (3) of the 1971 Act, the manager was formally 'subject in the administration of this Act to the Minister and the Director [of the DAIA]'. The historical continuity of strong influence from Queensland government law specifically concerning Aborigines has meant that 'the Act' has been known by the majority of Aboriginal people as the most critical external government influence. Indeed, being 'under the Act' was perceived as having always been coterminous with being resident on the reserve.[11] Consider the following quotation from the Aboriginal council chairman, made during a public meeting in the village, where he reported on how he had responded to delegates at a regional DAA meeting who were bidding for government funds in competition with the Doomadgee community.

> I told 'em [delegates from the Gulf region]: 'Any you fellas been under the Act?'. None of them fellas could give an answer for that because

> they been live in a place, live free, they been brought up free . . . I said: 'The Act was the Act and we were well under it!'. We're gradually getting away now — we don't want to say the Act gonna abolish or something like that [when] it's helping us a little bit; it helping us to get up, look, and stand up strong on our feet a little bit more, give us more understanding, more knowledge you young people gotta take this stand for it. (T55)

Implicit here is the chairman's view that most other delegates who had lived in the larger towns of the region had been able to avoid the kind of institutionalised state surveillance to which reserve residents had historically been subject. However, he also suggests that the legislation enables necessary tutelary and educative support for Doomadgee residents, and his sentiment reflects a view that I will argue is an important aspect of Aboriginal political consciousness.

Aboriginal consciousness in relation to 'the Act' is not easily represented because of the multiple views expressed from time to time throughout the village population. One informative source on this subject is a recording (T62) of what eight Aboriginal speakers said at a public meeting held just before my first fieldwork, early in 1978. The meeting was called specifically to discuss residents' feelings on whether 'the Act' should be abolished or continued in some form, as the state government was considering that issue at the time. The statements made at such public meetings do not necessarily represent a valid cross-section of village opinion. The manager was present (DAA n.d.*a*: 8), and this may have dissuaded some people from making statements known to be contrary to his views. Nevertheless, much of what was said indicates entrenched Aboriginal support (at least among a vocal minority) for the state sponsored paternalistic tutelage that had been provided by the familiar missionary staff over a long period.

Only the first speaker said that 'the Act' should be abolished, although he was sceptical that this would lead to substantial benefit for village residents:

> We're no better out of the Act than what we are under the Act. I been a long time under the Act . . . I got nothing when I started, today I still got nothing, so what can I do? Try another way, get out of the Act . . . I came here in 1946, I had nothing from that time, right till today.

This man's sentiments were not echoed by the seven speakers who followed him. The first was the council chairman, who stressed that the Act did not curtail Aboriginal residents' freedom to 'handle' their personal money (and property) if they so chose, unlike the situation in earlier times, when legal provisions had authorised the manager to control this aspect of residents' lives.[13] Similarly, the chairman commented that people are now free to move off the reserve if they so wish:[14]

> You're free as the breeze today, if you want to handle your own [bank] account, you can do so . . . go anywhere you want to go, you can do so, transfer to another settlement, you can do so; you got all that, but the thing [issue] is if you abolish it and to be equal with the White . . . Yes or No?

Later in the meeting, the chairman restated his support for the existing legislative and administrative arrangements, when commenting favourably on similar sentiments expressed by other speakers:

> Yes, it's quite true you got everything, . . . award wages,[15] . . . education, slowly getting your homes, and what more? . . . you can amend the Act, take away some, . . . and you've got your UB [Unemployment Benefit] on top of it, hundred dollar, you're given it, while you're waiting. There's no complaint. I'm glad that few here got brains and can explain these things. Now we don't want radicals, . . . heard lot about 'em, and I don't want 'em, . . .

The chairman's wariness of 'radicals' refers to those (mostly outside of Doomadgee), calling for the abolition of state legislation concerning Aborigines, and generally expressing anti-White sentiments. However, the basis of his support for 'the Act' was put more clearly by the speaker who followed the chairman early in the meeting. This speaker was also a member of the Aboriginal council. In his view, Doomadgee people were not ready to manage their own affairs; they needed more education and required continued 'protection' before they could handle the 'responsibility' of self-management. His comments particularly stressed current Aboriginal ways of handling money as incommensurate with what is necessary in the broader White society:

> [if the Act is abolished] the bigger responsibility come back to the council, . . . all the authority the whole lot of it, the heap of it. It's gonna push on us [the councillors who have got] no education, no spelling right sometimes comes with me, no adding up . . . yet you want to heap it all up now to abolish the Act so that we can have the power, more power, that's the idea of it — not on your life! My boy might . . . if he climb the ladder; every other children might if they climb the ladder; only few here that did climb the ladder — I don't have to tell you the names of the few. You see education got to come first . . . The responsibility, that's what I'm scared of . . .
>
> But I was told, and asked the question that I can't even work out yet: 'What the Act? How we gotta abolish the Act? What are we abolishing? What are we, doing away with everything and live like a White man?' . . . We say like this, abolishing the Act, we gonna hold our own affairs . . . we gotta think first, get ourselves up first on higher ground . . . I tell you what we're gonna let go a real big protection, and a protection that

> I agree to stay under ... I don't think I can handle my affairs good enough yet, I think I'll get robbed for writing a cheque out and make a mistake about that, and I think I might make too much money and end up wouldn't keep up the account of it, and lose half of it, and couldn't care less about what I lost, and give ten dollar to anybody who come along and ask for a loan. You see? I'm not ready for it; all these things what we not ready for ... I'll let my children agree with that [become more independent].

This speaker also commented on the difficulties for Doomadgee people of living in predominantly White towns or cities, without the 'protection' available within the home community on the Doomadgee reserve. He associated 'the Act' with the continuity of such protective environments for Aboriginal people in the face of the essentially hostile White world.

The next speaker was the sergeant of Aboriginal police (although he finished his comments by saying that he was speaking 'on behalf of the police force and the council'). He opposed views that had apparently been expressed by a visiting Aboriginal researcher who had surveyed opinion about 'the Act' at Doomadgee (and in other Aboriginal communities). She was conducting the research on behalf of the Brisbane-based Foundation for Aboriginal and Islander Research Action (FAIRA) and the Aboriginal and Islander Legal Service, both organisations opposed to Queensland government policy and law concerning Aboriginal people. This researcher's visit may have been what prompted the chairman's earlier comment about not wanting 'radicals' at Doomadgee. As the sergeant put it:

> [the FAIRA researcher] said to me: 'The council here and the chairman has not got the power to remove anybody off the community'. Then I said to her: 'Where did you get this idea from?'. She said: 'Oh it's laid out in the law book'. And I said: 'Show me'. So she refused to show me the book and I told her: 'Here, amongst my own people I can say for myself they have a real fair go'. She say: 'In what way?'. I said: 'Well, many many times here, I [as sergeant of Aboriginal police] bring people before the [Aboriginal] court here, lay a charge against them, and the chairman of the council lays a penalty on them, give 'em a light penalty here, like fine ten or thirty dollars, without getting sending away [to a state gaol]'. I said to her: 'They have the power to remove you off the community for twelve months or more, if they want to be nasty'. So I told her that the council do have the power to put anyone off the communities, doesn't matter who it is, even if it's a White bloke, we not all by ourself, we got somebody else behind us [referring to the authority of the state police].

Thus, in the sergeant's view, the Aboriginal council and police were empowered under 'the Act' with sufficient authority, which was appropriately supported by the authority of the state police.

Three further speakers expressed their support for the state law partly in terms of their loyalty to the administrative role of the missionary staff; the following woman also spoke of the long-term benefits of colonisation:

> to abolish the Act, it means that Aboriginals take over into the mission, and the councillors supervise in the office, and White men come under them and whoever supervises . . . he gives the White man the job to work in the mission. But, take it from long way back, from years back before we ever was born; you know, if it wasn't for the White people that discover Australia, us Blackfellas wouldn't be as we are today — educated. And you know, there are some Aboriginals that got too educated that they want to be on top of the Whites, well that's not right you know we want to be all the same. And now they want to be the big boss, and you know what — they are making trouble for us Blacks. Soon there'll be White and Black fighting against each other if you don't wake up . . . I've only come back from Mt Isa last week and I've heard few stories in Mt Isa where the Whites are beginning to complain about Blacks throwing all the blames and troubles on to them for everything that they do and what's wrong. Now we don't want that, we don't want trouble in the mission, we don't want to have any troubles with our missionaries here; they come from a far away, just to teach us education, and I'm very thankful for what I've learnt . . . and I want my children to grow up not to think himself better than the other. We all want to be on that same level.

Another woman, who was then working outside Doomadgee but returned to live at the settlement soon after, spoke of the great value of having a Christian Aboriginal community to return to:

> just like to let you know I appreciate coming home here [for a visit] and it's been a home to me, and [the FAIRA researcher] said: 'Well, forget about the missionaries'. And I pointed [out] to her that it took the early missionaries, White people that were interested in Aborigines to come out here and raise us. And I'd like to tell you some of the experiences I've had, away from here. On the money line it's very hard, . . . you've got to save up, and . . . it took me three months before I could get a job . . . I do know there is discrimination [against Aborigines seeking employment], but . . . Black people discriminate against White too. When she [the FAIRA researcher] said to get rid of the European people here, and to have Doomadgee just run by all Blacks, I said: 'Don't you think that's discrimination?'. She didn't have a right answer; but people like that who come in here and try and influence us and talk you into things . . . you gotta be very careful . . . You must remember that Satan is very active in the world today and that he's using people like that to come in and break down the Gospel from going through to us . . . It's not a woman's privilege to preach in public but this is some experience that I've had away from home . . . I just like to tell you young people that when you go out to the world to be very very careful and to put things

> right with God if you going to get away from here and try and look after yourself and also, that with your money the White man will cheat you if they're not Christian people.

An Aboriginal elder of the church began by referring approvingly to the biblical basis for White tutelage and administrative authority over Aboriginal people. His reference to 'White man' breaking the word of God was probably in relation to those Whites outside of Doomadgee who supported the notion of Aboriginal self-determination and abolishing 'the Act':

> And . . . about the White man coming under the Black, y'know what White man is doing today they going against the word of God really. You know when Noah had three sons, he had Shem, Ham and Japheth . . . one of them was a Black man, one . . . was a White man and one . . . was a Yellow man. And you know, because the Black man saw the shame of his father, God gave this command, he said: 'From this time on . . .', because the White man corrected this young dark man, God said: 'From this time on, . . . for all throughout life on earth, the dark man [will] come under the White man'. And . . . men are trying to change this today, they're trying to break the word of God . . .

This speaker also supported the current administrative and legislative arrangements because, since his youth, more government-funded welfare monies flowed to Aboriginal people:

> But, about changing the Act you know, . . . what I heard the other day, you'll get no money. But . . . way back . . . over twenty-one years ago when I last stick a brand in a calf . . . [and worked at other stockman's tasks] we were getting something like fifteen bob [shillings] a week. And if it to be on the complaint of that time to abolish the Act I would've said yes. I won't say it now. You know why? . . . today you get a big cheque [referring to social security benefits], bigger than you can handle — what are you talking about abolishing the Act, what do you want to get out for? . . . and the cheque that you get today from just sitting down here, and the man sit in the office down in Brisbane, he writes out a cheque for about one thousand, fifteen hundred or something like that and you just go up and spend it just as you like. What more do we want? You're getting enough aren't ya? And if you're talking about getting equal with White man, . . . you know some of the poor White men today they would like to have your profit. We need to climb up, . . . before we can handle anything — we won't know where to start, won't have the faintest idea where to start about caring for ourself.

These passages have been presented at some length because they illustrate very well the nature of Aboriginal support for the system of White administration. Apart from the first speaker quoted, the views expressed argue (albeit indirectly) for no change in 'the Act'. I will shortly address the nature of opposing views held strongly among other village residents.

Plate 1: Aboriginal workers obtaining salt from saltpans in coastal country northwest of Burketown circa 1914 (courtesy Mrs M Walden)

Plate 2: King Jimmy Dawudawu wearing his king plate, and standing in front of a large ant-hill located adjacent to the old road from Burketown to the 'Old Doomadgee' Mission site; a second man stands on top of the ant-hill, posing for the photograph (circa 1933, courtesy Mrs D Akehurst)

Plate 3: Mrs D Read, one of the early missionaries, bathing a child at 'Old Doomadgee', among a group of other Aboriginal children and adults. Two of the missionaries' small children are standing among the group, under the supervision of two Aboriginal teenage girls (circa 1933, courtesy Mrs D Akehurst)

Plate 4: Boys' house at Old Doomadgee, early 1930s (courtesy M and D Read)

Plate 5: Doomadgee, May 1982, looking westwards, with the 'Village' in the foreground and the 'Mission' in the background (courtesy Connah/Jones Aerial Archaeology, University of New England)

Plate 6: Looking from the White domain across the median strip towards the Village, May 1978 (photograph D Trigger)

Plate 7: Returning to a typical old style home in the Village with goods purchased at the store in the White domain, June 1978 (photograph D Trigger)

Plate 8: Returning to the vehicle after shooting two wallabies on a road near Doomadgee, June 1978 (photograph D Trigger)

Plate 9: New style (high set) Aboriginal home in the Village, September 1983; note author's caravan in yard (photograph D Trigger)

Plate 10: A large crowd including performers and spectators disperses after a long bout of traditional (secular) dancing at the back of the Village in the afternoon, November 1978; this was a time of 'revival' of such dancing (photograph D Trigger)

However, several issues emerge from the statements made at the 1978 public meeting. Some indicate considerable confusion about the nature of the law, its current administration and the consequences of changing it (e.g. the notion that if 'the Act' were repealed, and possibly if it were changed, people would no longer be able to maintain sufficient social and physical distance from the broad White society — they would then have to 'live like a Whitefella'). There were several confounding issues not relevant to the question of whether the Act should have been changed. These included: the fact that material conditions (particularly wage rates and social security benefits) and personal liberties were believed to have improved greatly since earlier times; local Aboriginal opposition to perceived anti-White beliefs and actions on the part of certain Aboriginal groups and individuals outside Doomadgee (and indeed some local Aboriginal expressions of approval of the long-term consequences of colonisation); and certain beliefs stemming from the Christian commitments of some speakers. Local White administrative assistance without the operation of 'the Act' also seems to have been wrongly thought to be impossible. Indeed, the relationship between the existing external law and its administration and settlement life, as well as the question of possible alternative options, were not understood clearly by those who spoke at this meeting.[16]

This was generally true for all administrative processes stemming from the laws of the state. While commonwealth and state government funded services, benefits and projects engendered continuing, though mostly irregular, visits to Doomadgee by various officials (and occasional politicians), these rarely involved many Aboriginal residents. The visitors simply carried out their business within the relevant section of the White domain. To the extent that the visitors were noticed by Aboriginal residents, they were mostly lumped together as 'government people'. Visits from the state police (usually from Burketown, although also from Mt Isa in the case of more serious criminal investigations) were different in that they would typically involve Aboriginal people and hence were the focus of great interest and comment. Royal Flying Doctor (a non-government enterprise) visits were also important to Aboriginal residents.

Because people in the village rarely sought meetings with visiting officials and politicians it cannot be assumed that they remained uninterested in putting a case to such people. The following complaint was made after one visit by the Commonwealth Minister for Aboriginal Affairs in 1980. The speaker was blind, but his lack of awareness of, and involvement in, the visit is by no means atypical:

> [official visitors] see nobody, talk to nobody, ask nobody question, everybody down here [in the village] waiting with their question . . . They

> come out here [and we] never get one single information, [about] what we want, what we would like to do for our self, we never get anything like that from government man what comes out here. Then . . . [chairman of the Aboriginal council] and . . . [manager], and they broadcast it over the loudspeaker [at a public meeting in the village]: 'Oh we're sorry, we wanted so-and-so to remain for a little while . . ., we're sorry we didn't bring him here, we had too much to talk about [in the White spatial domain]', and all the rest of it. No, I reckon that's a big excuse. We hardly ever see anyone. Sometimes they [official visitors] come and go here and I hear after they've gone, and I hear the plane going away [and I ask]: 'Who's them group?', [and the reply is]: 'Oh they government — Aboriginal fellas [i.e. people working on government matters concerning Aboriginal affairs]'; think they'd make a speech or something but they never make a speech. (T75)

While the world of White officials beyond the settlement thus remained completely remote from most Aboriginal residents, 'government' personnel were conceived (sometimes wrongly) as having an important status and considerable power in White society.

However, there was an ambivalence in this Aboriginal view of officials. Most Whites known as 'government man' were conceived as 'flash', a reference that typically connotes a derisive attitude towards what is perceived as individuals' ideas of their own self-importance. One good example of this perception are some unelicited joking comments made during part of an initiation ritual (held away from the settlement in 1982). Several elaborately decorated men, performing important tasks in the course of the ritual, were jokingly referred to by others present as 'government man'; and, for example, when light-heartedly giving such a man the cue to carry out part of his task in the ritual: 'Where that man from Canberra?'. Greeted with much hilarity, this reference to those who come from the seat of national government embodies good-natured sarcasm about any equivalent sense of self-importance the Aboriginal men may feel, or feign to feel as part of the joke.

Aboriginal consciousness and the missionary staff

Sentiments of both support for and opposition to the local missionary staff were evident in village social life. The nature of supportive views, of both 'the Act' and the tutelary missionary presence, is illustrated in several of the quotations from the 1978 meeting. However, it must be said at the outset that some individuals expressed verbal support for certain administrative practices on some occasions and then opposition to the same and/or other practices on others. Consider the blind church elder quoted earlier, and below, who on the one hand lauded the paternalistic care provided by the mission administration and on the other hand voiced his resentment about not being given the opportunity to meet and talk to visiting White officials.

An important factor to be aware of is what the manager's wife called a 'bond of love'. It is probably better termed a 'bond of familiarity', although some Aboriginal people undoubtedly have had great affection for particular missionaries who lived at the settlement for a long time (including a number who had left Doomadgee before I began my study). The record of the 1978 public meeting to discuss 'the Act' provides further information on this issue:

> really we should be thankful here . . . I've had the wonderful Christian upbringing and I'm not ashamed to tell people . . . and that's one thing that Doomadgee has offered to us . . . in the early years when I was brought up here, . . . when I go away from here . . . the thing I miss very much is the Christian fellowship, and the love that was shown here over the years. (T62)

And again (from a person who was then a councillor):

> And another thing, . . . she [the FAIRA researcher] said openly — me and her had a tongue-bang [argument] . . . — wipe away with the missionary, wipe away with the White people. Look I reckon I'll see [be happy for] somebody *coming in* with a White somebody, hey? And I said: 'You go back now to where the missionary first got who to build the place, who to form a mission, what tribe of people . . . where all the heart came from to form a mission?'. You see, it was all God's plan . . . that's where it all comes from. (T62) [speaker's emphasis]

These quotations are typical of statements expressing affection and support for the missionaries, in that the speakers were at the time committed to a Christian outlook. The second speaker went on say how important it was that the missionaries continue to provide religious and associated administrative services:

> and I thought of something really solemn then straight away, and I think you'll help me to think about this very hard. I'll try say it, from the bottom of my heart on this. We think of the death at times, we think of the Service at times we have, we think of important time of our life when we can come to a position concerned about a loved one been put to the grave. Who takes all the funeral service and all that sort of thing? You see, we got no actions yet of nothing, we not putting nothing into practice of what we know. We're gonna go bury our people like dogs and cats [if the missionaries leave], like they're doing outside now, even putting 'em to ashes [a reference to cremation]! We want a decent funeral here. We want a decent mob of people here on this place! (T62)

Not all support for the missionaries stressed the importance of a specifically Christian staff presence. Some older residents expressed support for them simply because they were seen to 'look after' people: 'he helps me when I need him' (said in relation to the manager). This sentiment is similar to that reportedly felt in the past for certain 'bosses'. The manager was apparently referred to over the years as 'father boss' (or the equivalent terms in the local Aboriginal languages). One person remarked how the manager and his wife were: 'the biggest part of the grandfather for these people' (i.e. virtually like grandparents). Some older people exhibited an openness towards several staff by attributing subsection affiliation to them, and hence including them indirectly within the fictive kinship system. This occurred despite the fact that no White staff at Doomadgee ever understood the subsection or kinship systems. Similarly, one of the manager's sons was apparently given an Aboriginal language name when a baby, which was the name of an old Aboriginal man, and the manager himself was known familiarly by a nickname derived from an animal he was said to look like (one of the normal ways that nicknames are apportioned to Aboriginal people). Indeed, even some of those Aboriginal people (of all ages) who were consistently opposed to the manager (at times quite bitterly), appear to have felt sorry for him in the circumstances of his departure in 1983. Comments included the observations that the church had unfairly insisted that he resign, and that he had 'kept the place together' for a long time and it would 'bust apart' without his paternal controlling administrative presence.

Nevertheless, prior to his departure, there was certainly widespread general feeling that the power of the manager was too great. A comment that was made quite routinely was that 'he been here too long', and that he ultimately controlled the administration of settlement life despite the token role of a small number of Aboriginal people, particularly the councillors and police:

> if we want anything we go up and ask somebody up there [in the White domain] who is responsible [White staff or Aboriginal councillors] — they [are] all put on responsible places . . . some jobs or something up there — and we go and see them and they say: 'Oh you go and see [the manager]'. [He] seems to have the last say in everything — [Aboriginal] police, you can't say anything to the police. He always make [directs] the police, and the police are doing wrong, [of] course they're doing wrong, they're not doing things right. But then he argue he says: 'You can't put [say] the police [are] in the wrong . . .'. He make the wrong look right . . . I tell you another thing, I don't like [the manager] in that [Aboriginal] court, I don't like him coming down here . . . I can't understand why [the manager] got to come in. (T72)[17]

Though to a much lesser extent, the school principal was also occasionally similarly accused (e.g. in relation to school Parents' and

Citizens' Association meetings: 'he doesn't get the mind of the people — he's got everything in his mind what he wants to talk about'). While all missionaries were known to have very firm ideas on what should happen at Doomadgee, the manager and school principal were recognised as having authority to put those ideas into practice. The capacity of other staff to implement their personal views was perceived accurately by Aboriginal people as more ambiguously held.

Aboriginal statements of opposition to staff were mostly associated with personal issues relevant to the speaker's circumstances at the time. Such statements were often made when people were dissatisfied with the way office personnel seemed to them to be handling such financial affairs as wages or social welfare benefits. Some people would regularly complain that 'the mission' was stealing 'half the wages' (and had been doing this for years), or that office staff were stopping their welfare payments because they were either deliberately vindictive or just insufficiently motivated to properly present the Aboriginal person's case to the relevant government officers. There was widespread resentment among Aboriginal workers concerning their receiving wage rates well below award levels. People also mistrusted what they saw as the manager's handling of rent monies paid by all families in the village.[18] The rate of material improvement in the village was compared unfavourably with that in the White domain, and the manager was said to be mainly responsible for this inappropriate allocation of materials and labour. Office staff generally, and the manager in particular, were also accused of withholding information from people. The most common example concerned incoming telegrams, which were simply kept at the office (or, according to several people, deliberately misplaced); Aboriginal residents felt that such messages should have been immediately taken (either verbally or on paper) down to the village and delivered to the relevant person. These telegrams were considered particularly important if they concerned residents' relatives in other settlements or towns and on several occasions the manager and office staff were said to have given wrong or incomplete messages, either deliberately or through incompetence.

It was again the manager (together with his wife, and to a lesser extent, his son) who was most commonly accused of 'stickybeaking' into the private affairs of Aboriginal residents. This was often said with reference to the habit of these staff of driving slowly through the village looking at people's houses and yards, and indeed occasionally taking visiting Whites (some of whom took photographs from within the moving minibus) for a drive up and down the village streets. One woman also complained that the office staff would never help her with the paperwork for certain training courses she was enrolling in, unless her dealings with the outside organisations were completely known of and controlled by the mission. In her view, counter staff at the office would intrusively ask her in relation to the relevant forms: 'Where did you get this?'[19]

Aspects of the evangelical process were also regarded as uninvited interference in Aboriginal lives. Personal interactions with some missionaries were said to be fraught with the possibility of a sermon on the need to live a Christian life, and this was felt by various Aboriginal people to impose an uninvited pressure on them. One man requested me to deal with the manager on his behalf concerning a personal administrative matter, because if he had to hold a discussion with the manager the latter would most likely 'bore it up him on religious matters' because he no longer lived a Christian life. A further example concerns an Aboriginal widower's account of how the missionaries interfered after they learned he had 'run away *gunjiwa*' (i.e. in this case spent a couple of days in the bush engaging in sexual relations with) another man's wife. When the adulterous couple returned, there was little, if any, negative response among the relevant Aboriginal families.[20] However, according to the man's account, at least two missionary men (including the manager) heard of the incident and came after 'morning prayers'[21] to the man's front yard to ask him: 'why did you take another man's wife?'. He answered: 'wouldn't you if a woman took off her clothes and tempted you?'. By the man's account the missionaries then apparently turned away with shame, and knelt and prayed in his yard. He regarded the adulterous incident as none of the missionaries' business, and took great offence at their visiting his house in this way.

Apart from such specific events the more general imposition of the evangelical enterprise was felt by some to be the weekly open air religious meeting held at rotating positions under street-lights in the village. A loudspeaker would be set up at the meeting and those preaching would 'blast the Gospel'[22] into the night atmosphere. Most speakers were usually White. While some Aborigines attended these meetings, most ignored them and those in houses near the meeting site either extinguished lights, kept their fire low and watched while seated in their yards, or totally withdrew into their dwellings. The open air preaching had been carried on at Doomadgee for a very long time, and Aboriginal people mostly appeared to treat it as a normal fact of life. However, negative comments were occasionally made, such as the following complaints after the White manager had, in the course of preaching at one such meeting, loudly and repetitively used much reference to biblical passages to stress the constant theme that if you die before being spiritually 'born again' you are in for a terrible time from Satan and his realm. One woman among those watching from some distance complained at this point: 'make me wild, these missionary people, they're so worried about Blackfellas, why they go on and on about it?'. Another person added: 'they just come down [to the Blackfella domain] for what they want, they don't even spend five minutes for a yarn or anything'. The latter speaker went on in a sarcastic parody to predict (accurately) what some of the final stages of these meetings would involve:

> [the manager] will start soon, he'll cover [generalise from] everything others've said [and say]: 'What Mr . . . [an earlier preacher] has said reminds me of when I was in the army . . . [etc.]'.

An important implication of these complaints for any discussion on Aboriginal Christianity (chapter 9) is that opposition to the manager's administrative style (and that of other staff) had consequences for Aboriginal people's Christian commitment. It was sometimes said of people who were once, but no longer, 'in fellowship' that certain missionaries turned them away from Christian beliefs by not showing them 'brotherly love' or by making people grovel socially when seeking readmittance to the church after a 'downfall'. Several people who appeared to have maintained a Christian commitment had been discouraged from church participation during periods of hostile feelings towards the manager (and at times other staff) (e.g. 'I felt like to go to church today but I didn't go'; or 'a lot of Christian people here, some lonely Christian people too, but they don't go to [church] meeting'; or 'they [missionaries] haven't even got the guts to ask me why I don't go to meeting'). Village residents also expressed the view that the missionaries did not themselves live up to the Christian standards they set. For example, in reference to their alleged tendency of not stopping on the roads away from the settlement to assist Aboriginal people with broken down cars: 'they Christian people, they shouldn't do that hey?'.

The final aspect of hostility towards the evangelical process concerns its attempted elimination of many aspects of Aboriginal belief and behaviour. The following statements (Aboriginal Land Commissioner 1982: 61–3) are from a man giving evidence at Najabarra, an outstation on the Nicholson River just inside the Northern Territory (see map 1). The setting was the Waanyi/Garawa land claim hearing, which involved many Doomadgee residents claiming traditional lands under the *Aboriginal Land Rights (N.T.) Act*. This claimant's statements illustrate a perspective towards the administration at Doomadgee which was held by a substantial number of people (particularly older ones, although the speaker was only in his mid-forties) who had, over the years, felt unable to pursue openly aspects of their traditions. The questioner was the Northern Land Council lawyer acting for the claimants.

(Q) Do you sometimes talk with the people about this land?

(A) We talk a lot because today is one of the happiest moments in our life, today we can talk freely, and I hope that it remains that way, the days that lie ahead. There have been talks, but we haven't talked this way before as a group of people as a big number of people. Our talk had been secretly, only in family groups. We have lived in the State of Queensland where there was fear that rides us. We couldn't talk freely. Today and the days that lie ahead [i.e. following the land claim, with the prospect of moving permanently away from Doomadgee into the Northern Territory] we feel free to speak how we like, and we speak things that are very important to us on the Aboriginal culture side of things.

Q What sort of things do you feel free to talk about . . .?

A We are free to talk about our dreamings, secrets of men, of women, these secrets that are very close to our people as Aboriginal people, our way of life — that we can['t] speak freely,[23] say, in the State of Queensland.

Q Why do you say that . . .?

A Because I believe that there is a difference. There is ill-feeling [towards such things on the part of the administration at Doomadgee]. It may not be law, but there is ill-feeling, and we don't want to cause ill-feeling in a State where it is hard for us to believe that we have a right to speak about our way of life.

Q The people in Doomadgee, when you are in Doomadgee — can they talk freely about dreamings and that sort of thing?

A There is to a certain point . . . I believe that if it got out of a group of people [i.e. received overt expression] it may cause an inquiry [by the administration] into something, you know? Along these lines, we have to think that way.

Q You might want to have some sort of ceremonies and *yarambaja* [ceremony] at Doomadgee. Do you think you could do that?

A I don't think so, . . . I believe that there would be a very, very ill feeling in the place. I mean, it is in us as Aboriginal people. We feel that we carry on; we must pass this on to our children, but we are in a place that we are not free, in a State that we are not free to be able to practise and go on with that.

Thus, for this speaker, living away from the Doomadgee administration (and outside the jurisdiction of the Queensland 'Act') was a means of ending the stifling of parts of Aboriginal tradition. Furthermore, he and others knew of the manager's opposition to the land claim, and (although certain staff were thought not to oppose it) some claimants were worried about repercussions for them and their families resident at Doomadgee after the hearing. One worry was whether the large number of children absent from school (because their parents took them to the hearing) would cause some administrative 'inquiry' or lead to the children being excluded from the Doomadgee school altogether. However, these feared consequences did not eventuate.

Aboriginal people recognised that the desire to evangelise was entwined throughout most staff action. This sometimes emerged as a subtle form of constraint entailed within aspects of the 'help' offered by certain missionary staff. One man expressed his suspicion about an offer of assistance in establishing an outstation: 'I know that trick. They cunning bastards — [they say]: "Can I help you? I'll pray for you" '; that is, the assistance was invariably cloaked with the expectation that the recipient would embrace Christian practices and beliefs. Offers of material assistance were genuinely appreciated by some, but at times there was also cynicism in the Aboriginal response. This was again demonstrated when a group of men were generally discussing the prospects of leaving Doomadgee for outstations in their country on the land claim area. Much to the amusement of the group, a young man in his late teens parodied the predicted bewilderment of the school principal when he heard of the departure of two individuals present. One (X) was a talented painter the principal had tried to assist some years before by arranging a display of his art in White society, and the other (Y) was a man who had been teaching 'culture' in the school. While parodying the principal's bewildered reaction the young man said, 'and . . . [X] was my painter-boy, and . . . [Y] was my culture-boy!'. The cynicism on which this joke rests seems to derive from Aboriginal recognition of the power relation implicit within the occasions of familiarity and support between the principal and the two Aboriginal men.

The old entrenched pattern of missionary control through 'advice' and 'assistance' was foremost in the minds of these men. Again, despite the good intentions of the manager's son when he was appointed (on DAA funds) to be an 'advisor' to the council, there was considerable suspicion and resentment about his appointment:

> you know . . . [the manager's son] went with . . . [two community representatives] for that meeting last time [in Mt Isa] . . . [one of the representatives, also a councillor] said: 'I'm a bit disappointed to see . . . [the manager's son] there'. [The council chairman made the decision to appoint him] I said to . . . [the chairman]: 'I don't think I'll agree with you . . . In time to come government gonna say: "What he doing there? All this . . . new law, and the rights for Aboriginal is given to the

> Aboriginal . . . we want your voice not the White man voice" '. He [the manager's son] could be say anything what he think up in his mind. It might please you, it mightn't please you, it mightn't please the rest of the Aboriginal. It'll only please him. I don't agree with that and I reckon it should be the Black man. (T75)

On one occasion a councillor who got drunk in Mt Isa rather than attend the meeting he had gone there for said he had done this because he had not been happy having the White adviser with him in the meeting.[24]

Finally, many diverse complaints about the staff surfaced routinely in village discourse. One man told a school teacher about a relative of his having been shot by a White man during Wild Time, but concluded from the teacher's reaction that 'they don't want to hear'. Another complained that some years earlier the manager had taken with him to Brisbane a small bag containing secret sorcery and healing implements and later (very inappropriately) referred to it publicly when preaching at Doomadgee. Allegations were made public on an ABC radio program (A.M. 29.8.1978) when one man claimed that the manager gave jobs to Whites instead of Aborigines, that council elections usually resulted in councillors who were loyal to the manager being elected, and that the banning of alcohol from the settlement led to drinking sessions totally away from medical facilities, thus risking dangers associated with drunken fights and the episodically acute illnesses suffered by some drinkers. Another man alleged that 'those White people cause disturbance between families' at a time when his wife had made a prior commitment to assist some female teachers with a 'girls' camp' and he wanted her to accompany him elsewhere. The last two complaints were made by two of the small number of Aboriginal people who were known by the reputation: 'he's not frightened of *Mandagi* [Whitefellas]'. That is, unlike the majority, they were known to be prepared to speak their mind to White staff when sufficiently roused, while others would wait until the Whites had gone, or until they themselves were 'charged up' with alcohol, to engage in routine conversation which gave voice to their disapproval.

Opposition and consent within Aboriginal consciousness

Staff factionalism was a significant aspect of social life among Whites, and thus had implications (albeit indirectly) for the nature of services provided to Aboriginal people. Aboriginal consciousness exhibited both support for and opposition to the system of administration. Sentiments of opposition and resentment were articulated strongly, though at times expressed very subtly. An important summary point is that this opposition and resentment operated in a context where Aboriginal people had to continue to deal with the structures of White authority. This authority was underpinned by both the law of the state and the senior missionaries' control over the settlement's essential services. To quote consecutive DAA officers' reports: in 1979 (DAA n.d.*a*: 23), 'the mission is more firmly in the hands of the Christian Brethren than it has ever been'; and in 1982 (DAA 1982) the manager and his wife were still 'almost indispensable because only they know the exact details of Mission funding'.[25]

Chapters 5 and 6 presented evidence of an Aboriginal capacity to retain a degree of autonomy in the face of this authoritarian control, through maintenance of a Blackfella domain of social life in the village. The existence of deeply felt (albeit diffuse and disorganised) resentment towards the White system on the part of Aboriginal people strengthens this argument for an oppositional Aboriginal culture. However, it is clear that the missionary administration intrudes into the Aboriginal domain in terms of both practices and ideology. Thus, if we are to stress Aboriginal resistance, what of the support offered the missionaries as part of relations of familiarity stemming from the didactic paternalism of the long-serving staff? To what extent can Aboriginal consciousness be said to attribute legitimacy to the system of White authority?

The economic dependence of Aboriginal residents on the provision of commodities and services has led to most perceiving no realistic alternatives to the continuance of the administrative processes by which these commodities and services have historically been provided. However, when people make use of the services controlled by the White staff they do not necessarily thereby regard the structures of authority underpinning the services as legitimate. Again, in the context of their historical institutionalisation, Aboriginal people have typically considered bureaucratic dealings with government departments to be inevitably part of the White domain. Many have therefore felt it necessary that there be a benevolent White staff presence to deal with this bureaucratic discourse. In the words of one councillor quoted in this chapter, the alternative would be to 'let go a real big protection . . . and a protection that I agree to stay under'. This is not to suggest that all, or even most, residents have found the associated White administrative authoritarianism desirable.

People may well attempt to make use of the extant authority structures in the course of everyday social life (e.g. individuals might actively align themselves with White authority in disputes with other Aboriginal people). The threat to report an opponent to the 'White police' was commonly made during arguments and fights, and people did sometimes attempt this course of action. Indeed, there were a number of occasions when Aboriginal residents proclaimed openly that they had vigorously abused the White manager because he had failed to support them in a dispute with other Aborigines (i.e. he had failed to heed their requests to get their opponent(s) charged by the White police). Similarly, there were occasions when Aboriginal women were reported to have 'run up la house' (i.e. retreated into the White domain), knowing that the manager's authority and ultimately his access to the White police would preclude their being attacked in that domain by their Aboriginal opponents. In one case a woman was fleeing from a furious attack by the wife of a man with whom she had allegedly had a recent sexual encounter, and in another case a woman (and her young children) were fleeing from the threatened attack of her drunken husband.

While such active Aboriginal attempts to use the administration again indicate the lack of unity across the village population in its relationship with the system of White authority, they do not necessarily represent a widespread intellectual embracing of the appropriateness of that system. The same point can be made in relation to Aboriginal statements that point out the practical necessity of continued missionary tutelage without necessarily endorsing all aspects of the system of White authority. Nevertheless, the next chapter examines further the extent to which Aboriginal thinking has been constrained by White administrative practices and ideology.

Notes

1 See *Australian Missionary Tidings* magazine for the months during 1939, and Annual Reports of Queensland Government Department of Native Affairs for the years 1940–1960.

2 All unreferenced data below concerning the missionaries have been drawn from field notes based on informal discussions with them. However, on this particular point, note also Van Sommers (1966: 29-30):

> Each of their assemblies or local congregations is entirely self-governing. There is no central governing body and consequently no centrally laid down policy. Each congregation bases its activities on its own interpretation of the Scriptures . . .

3 An official account given for 1980 (*Australian Missionary Tidings*, September 1980, Daily Prayer List insert) lists seven married couples with nine dependent children among them, plus three single people, as 'voluntary workers'. Three of the couples and the three single people received money for food from the mission organisation, as well as the free accommodation given to all 'voluntary workers'. Fourteen school teachers (three with non-working wives and two couples with five children between them) and four health personnel were employed on normal award wages by government departments. During 1982, there were eighteen teachers employed in this

way (Murray 1982: 3), plus at least four nurses, and twenty-four 'voluntary workers' (DAIA 1982: 32).

4 A DAA community study of Doomadgee (n.d.*a*: 8–9) points out that the initial letter sent to the Arts Board from Aboriginal residents was signed by eighteen people including three councillors, one of whom was the chairman. It is broadly correct in describing the company as an ill-fated formal attempt at self-management, though incorrect in describing it as the only one apart from the council (the 'Ganggalida Society' was another). Further comments in this report are also instructive:

> The Company was suppressed by the mission on the grounds that it received outside advice (from Mornington Island) and was not a mission initiative. It nevertheless aroused enough community support to convince the school principal to take the cultural program on under the administration of the school rather than the Company.

5 The DAA community study (n.d.*a*: 17) notes that: 'In 1975 strong opposition to teaching of Aboriginal languages was expressed to a DAA visitor by the Superintendent [i.e. manager]'.

6 *North West Star* newspaper July 1982 p. 16; also see *Queensland Teachers' Journal* July 1982. The difference between 'educational' and 'evangelical' religious education remains unclear from the teachers' defence, as does the extent of such possibly *ad hoc* routine Christian practices as hymn singing at morning assemblies.

7 The first pupils to attend high school (away from the community) went out in 1967; in 1968 and 1970 two men received one year's assistant-teacher training; in 1969 the mission opened Woongoora Student Hostel in Malanda on the Atherton Tableland in northeast Queensland, and all students deemed to have academic potential were sent there and attended Malanda High School; in 1979 the first Doomadgee student completed grade 12 at Malanda High School; in 1981, 16 Junior (Grade 10) Certificates were presented (Murray 1982: 11).

8 This facility was known by both Aboriginal and White residents as the 'hospital' but despite its fully qualified nursing staff, it was formally administered by the mission, which meant the manager in real terms, and he was medically unqualified.

9 The relevant biblical passage is 1 Corinthians 6:19–20, which directs that 'your body is the temple of the Holy Ghost'. These substances are believed to defile the body.

10 Note the comment in Van Sommers (1966: 30):

> Women take no part in Church government, doctrinal or administrative, but act as teachers and workers in Church welfare undertakings . . . They are not permitted to speak at meetings for worship.

11 The 1971 Act and its amendments largely focused on reserve residents although the legislation could be used to manage the property of Aboriginal people not living on a reserve, subject to their consent. Consent

had to be obtained in such cases because of overriding commonwealth law (see Nettheim 1981: 73–98, 117). The 1965 *Aborigines . . . Act* (Part III) concerned non-reserve residents who were declared 'assisted Aborigine(s)', however I am not aware of any data on the number of such persons in the study region. Prior to 1965 the relevant state law automatically applied to all Aboriginal people, although there was a provision for the exemption of individuals from 1939 to 1965 (*The Aboriginals Preservation . . . Acts* 1939 to 1946, section 5 [3]), and of 'half-castes' only, from 1897 to 1939 (*The Aboriginals Protection . . . Acts* 1897 to 1934, section 33).

12 Prior to this comment, the chairman also made the point that most of the delegates were of mixed racial descent. I will deal below with the complex issue of the significance of skin colour and ancestry in Aboriginal social life (see also Trigger 1989).

13 Nettheim (1981: 78–84) discusses gradual improvements in freedom of choice in this regard, from the situation according to the 1965 Act, through the 1971 Act, to the 1974 *Aborigines . . . Amendment Act* and also certain commonwealth legislation during the 1970s. While the office at Doomadgee still handled a substantial number of DAIA 'trust accounts' for Aboriginal residents during 1978, only a few (mostly of old people) appear to have been maintained after an agency of the Commonwealth Bank was opened there in 1979.

14 See Nettheim (1981: 42–52).

15 In fact, Aboriginal workers on reserves were not paid award wages at the time of this meeting (early 1978). The payment of under award wages was permitted by Regulation 68 of the *Aborigines Act* of 1972. After considerable industrial disputation between the DAIA and the Australian Workers' Union (acting on behalf of workers on reserves), the wages of reserve workers were increased to the level of the Queensland state minimum wage (still normally below award levels) following a decision in the Industrial Court of Queensland in May 1979 (Queensland Government Industrial Gazette, June 1979: 133). However, this raise was not actually received by workers on reserves until May 1980 (Nettheim 1981: 73–78).

16 The DAA community study (n.d.*a*: 8) makes a similar point. However, it also inaccurately suggests that the opinions on the tape can be summed up by the first speaker's declaration that he had received no benefit from 'the Act'. In fact, all other speakers expressed either directly or indirectly their belief that they had benefited from the Act over the years. In presenting the results of the FAIRA/Legal Service survey, Pryor (n.d.: 147–8) gives a more balanced account; after describing 'considerable discontent toward management and administration' on the basis of sixty-two completed questionnaires, she deals with the opposing view:

> I feel that those who spoke in favour of Church Mission Control were so used to this life and did not want to see the Missionaries leave in fear there would be no place for them to go. These were staunch believers in the church who had a christian outlook. I respect their opinions as individual people. One

thing I did notice though, was most of these people with this outlook were housed in the new homes, whether by coincidence or otherwise can be only left to one's discretion to judge. I found the ones in the old shacks and tents with more of a militant attitude.

The question of whether distribution of new houses has favoured particular groups is dealt with later.

17 As at other Queensland Aboriginal settlements at the time, the Aboriginal Court was presided over by the chairman of the Aboriginal council (together with other councillors). These courts typically dealt mostly with offences under reserve by-laws (e.g. being under the influence of alcohol; behaving in a disorderly manner; assault; and gambling). A report compiled in May 1982 (DAA n.d.*b*: 1) states that the most common offences were 'disturbing the peace and resisting arrest'. No. 45 of the *Aborigines Act* Regulations (1972) stipulates that Aboriginal Courts be constituted by two or more Aborigines who are Justices of the Peace or, where such people are not available, at least three members of the Aboriginal council. However, this speaker is complaining that the White manager had undue influence over the proceedings. The 1982 DAA report (DAA n.d.*b*: 1–2), based primarily on consultations with mission staff and members of the council, indicates that 'the Mission Management only occasionally sit in on court', but, it is likely that during previous years the manager had considerable influence over the court's operation. Cf. discussion of these general issues in The Australian Law Reform Commission (1979: 18–25 plus Appendices 6 & 7; and 1986: 66–8).

18 In 1979, the weekly rent on the twenty government funded European-style houses was approximately $10 to $12, and on sixty-seven older (dilapidated) mission-owned huts was $3 (DAA n.d.*a*: 10). From the Aboriginal perspective this money went into the White domain and was controlled by the manager.

19 The DAA Community Study (n.d.*a*: 18) also reported that after she completed a course as an alcohol counsellor at a Brisbane institution this woman's qualification was not accepted by the medical staff in the clinic at Doomadgee. However, it is unclear what approaches she made to the White medical staff.

20 This should not be taken as a necessarily typical consequence of such a situation.

21 Indeed, the adulterous relationship may have been announced at this prayer meeting as a 'downfall' (see chapter 9) for one or both of the people involved.

22 This phrase was first suggested to me by a Brethren man who had visited Doomadgee for a short period and disapproved of the way the open air meetings were held in the village.

23 There is almost certainly a mistake in the transcription here, which renders this word as 'can'.

[24] This should not be taken to indicate that any White person would have been unacceptable as an adviser to this councillor.

[25] The popular press has given varied accounts. For example, *The North-West Star* newspaper's (25.3.1980: 1) story describes Doomadgee as 'another world' where Aborigines 'have to do very much as they're told by their administrators', although the Aboriginal council was 'slowly changing' that situation. However, the *Sunday Sun* newspaper (22.5.1983: 19) portrayed a place where Aborigines 'dream of a place for all, white and black' and where people 'had hoped [the manager's] son . . . would perhaps take over' when his father had to leave.

CHAPTER EIGHT

Councillors, 'Yellafellas' and the influence of colonial ideology

Two aspects of settlement life particularly exhibited the influence of White practices and ideology on Aboriginal thinking. The first concerns the incorporation of a small number of village residents as councillors into the apparatus of White administrative authority, and their associated role in settlement power relations. The second is the extent to which White notions about distinctions between people of solely Aboriginal descent and those of mixed Aboriginal/non-Aboriginal ancestry have been embraced intellectually among the village population. Both these matters raise the question of whether Aboriginal thinking has been constrained hegemonically, that is, in a way contrary to Aboriginal interests.

The incorporation of Aboriginal councillors

Membership of the Aboriginal council was the major means by which a small number of Aboriginal residents were incorporated into the apparatus of settlement administration. Other means included becoming a church elder, working as an Aboriginal policeman (particularly the sergeant), or serving on one of the advisory committees associated with the school: the Parents' and Citizens' Association, the 'culture committee', or the School Advisory Committee (formed in 1982). However, unlike the council, these advisory committees did not have a broad impact throughout settlement life.

Queensland law appears to have first allowed for the office of Aboriginal councillor on reserves under the 1945 Regulations (Nos 45- 50).[1] Through a number of stipulations in these Regulations, the council remained firmly under the control of the local protector or superintendent. Regulation No. 50 (5) precluded the council from having any jurisdiction over:

> the aboriginal police, aboriginal workers while so employed, or any person, matter, or thing, unless such jurisdiction has been allocated to it in writing by the Director through the protector or superintendent. (QGG 1945: 1067)

Whereas the 1945 Regulations (No. 45) ruled that three to seven members (all male) were to be elected by majority vote,[2] the 1966 Regulations (No. 19) provided for four-member councils, with two members elected and two appointed by the Director. Regulation 19 also simply stated that the Director could remove any members of an Aboriginal council. According to the 1972 Regulations, (No. 18 [1]), three councillors were to be elected and two appointed by the Director, however this was amended in 1974 to stipulate that all five councillors were to be elected. The 1972 Regulations (as amended), and also a set of standard by-laws, applied during the research period and I will refer to them selectively below. However, I first note Nettheim's (1981: 60) summary opinion of the legal situation:

> a perusal of the [1972] regulations establishes that the councils are completely subordinate to the management, just as managers, district officers and councils are all responsible to the Director [of the DAIA].

What follows in this section is partly concerned with examining the nature of this alleged subordination.

According to comments from the Doomadgee manager in 1982, certain Aboriginal men were used as 'welfare liaison' personnel during M. Read's period as superintendent (from 1936 to 1951). It appears that the first formally constituted Aboriginal council began in 1966 or soon after. By the late 1970s, the council was an established institution with widespread interest being shown by both Aboriginal and White residents in its role and affairs. In the 1978 election there were eight candidates[3] who received a total of 1198 votes. Although the 1972 Regulations (No. 35) stipulate that each elector shall have one vote, the manager told me that Doomadgee electors were given five votes each (and that the five candidates with the five largest numbers of votes were then considered elected to the five available positions in a first-past-the-post fashion). As the total number of votes cast in 1978 is not divisible by five, I can only assume that some electors did not cast all their five votes, yet the votes they did cast were not regarded as informal. Assuming that only a few people did not cast all their five votes, the number of voters would be approximately 235, or 55 per cent of the 429 people shown in mission records to be aged over eighteen years in 1978 (stated in *Annual Report Statistics* prepared 31.3.1978). Two hundred and thirty-five voters may represent a somewhat bigger percentage of eligible voters than it first appears, because official population numbers for Doomadgee typically included a substantial number of people who were away from the reserve at the time of the count.[4]

Both councillors and other Aboriginal residents regarded the official role of the council as substantially derived from, and appropriate to, the White domain. Indeed, on the occasion I attended a council meeting (for part of its business), the procedure was very much organised according to formal White Australian bureaucratic procedure. One report (DAA n.d.*a*: 8) commented for 1979 that:

> The Council's room [within the general office building in the White domain] is used mainly for storage. Council meetings are held in the office of the Superintendent in his presence, and the Superintendent's wife takes shorthand minutes.

While this arrangement did not always operate, it was the common one throughout the research period. Chapter two of the settlement by-laws (Commissioner for Community Relations, 1977: 102–3) stipulates that various aspects of bureaucratic meeting procedure must be followed: ordinary meetings are to be held regularly at set dates and times; the chairman or deputy chairman is to preside; no business is to be transacted without a quorum; resolutions or motions are to be carried formally by a majority; and written minutes of all proceedings are to be kept and subsequently confirmed. Indeed, it appears that the minutes of all council meetings were sent to the Director of the DAIA for his routine perusal. The meeting I attended was opened with brief prayers, and according to several councillors this has been standard practice over the years (as has been closing the meetings with prayers). While the practice has no doubt been considered appropriate by many councillors (though not all), my point is that the prayers would impress on meeting participants the formal authoritative nature of the proceedings.

Aboriginal conceptions of the formal written procedures necessary in official dealings with state bureaucracies are evident from the following statements, made at a public meeting in 1980 by the then council chairman. In assuring listeners that the formation of the mooted 'Ganggalida Society' would not be advantageous solely for Ganggalida people, the speaker referred to the '*Mandagi* [Whitefella] way' of written discourse:

> But if this Society ever comes up we must remember, there's constitution sort of thing, laws, rules and all that — you get a big length of paper. You gotta read what that say, and you gotta do what that paper say on it. That's *Mandagi* way about it. (T55)

Later in the same meeting, the chairman mentioned that:

> to do this [form the Society] I think it have to go through channels properly. You know, we've got to bring it to the note of our Director, and finalise the thing properly there. (T56)

Such public meetings, though usually held in the village, were themselves associated by most residents with council business pertaining to the Whitefella domain. A microphone and loudspeaker were usually set up near the village centre (at a road intersection, and mostly at night), so what was said could be heard by a substantial number of residents, whether or not they actually moved over to the meeting site. However, many people typically did not take much notice of what was said and most were disinclined to speak themselves. To take only the most obvious point, women rarely spoke at such public meetings. The small number of people who did speak were usually councillors, police, church elders, or people who had once occupied one of these offices .

The council chairman and manager in particular spoke for long periods at the meetings I attended, and indeed they appear to have been responsible for organising most public meetings. As other White staff were not routinely informed of these meetings, the manager, his wife (and at times his son) were often the only staff present. While these persons' presence may well have deterred larger numbers of Aboriginal people from speaking, their reticence was also due to the prevailing general Aboriginal conception of the meetings' business as derived from the Whitefella domain and hence as appropriately expounded by councillors (particularly the chairman). There was a general antipathy towards asserting oneself publicly on matters that remained hypothetical, or at least peripheral to individuals' immediate life-concerns. Speaking at the meetings was one among a number of aspects of exhibiting public behaviour about which people used the concept of 'shame'. In this context they would imply by use of the concept that they did not wish to be the focus of public attention in such settings. The more confident speakers would allude to this fact by commonly exhorting other people not to be 'frightened' to speak at the meeting, or if they were too 'frightened', to speak to councillors during the next few days.[5]

Other factors supporting the notion that councillors were the appropriate people to deal with administrative matters included the fact that in 1979 a number of councillors' houses were linked to a new internal settlement telephone network, which included most dwellings in the White domain. Though this enabled them to communicate with many of the White staff, it was the fact of communication between the council chairman and the manager that Aboriginal residents appeared most aware of. The only other homes in the village to have telephones installed were those of the police sergeant, the senior Aboriginal church elder and a man then working in the administration office (although telephones were installed in the homes of some other residents several years later).

Furthermore, as noted in chapter 7, the councillors formally administered the proceedings of the Aboriginal court, which had the power to impose fines (or imprisonment in the local gaol though it appears that the punishments were usually fines).[6] Under Regulation 54 (1), these fines were to be paid into a local community fund managed and administered by the council in the exercise of its local government functions (The Australian Law Reform Commission 1979: 22). At Doomadgee, this was termed the 'Council Welfare Fund', and (according to Regulation No. 4) the council could use these monies to provide minimal welfare assistance to residents judged to be in dire need. In May 1982 (DAA n.d.*b*: 2) assistance seems to have been given in such circumstances as residents having to obtain sufficient money to attend relatives' funerals at places throughout the region. The council's power to sit as a court and carry out these functions was known throughout the village population to be underpinned by the authority of Whitefella law.

To a significant degree, councillors embraced what they perceived as the status accorded to their office by the law of the state, particularly as this status was expressed by senior people among the missionary staff. Key concepts in councillors' discourse were thus the 'authority' and 'responsibility' of their office, although those occupying the office of chairman were most forceful in expressing this sentiment. When he exhorted people at a public meeting to speak their mind, the council chairman said: 'I might be in authority but I'm not speaking strictly or anything like that' (T62). At a public meeting in 1980, another council chairman voiced his concerns about people 'living together' without being married:

> you know, it's my responsibility here because I'm in authority, and I feel it's wrong to continue like that . . . [living together when not married]. (T71)

And again:

> I only say this here tonight because it's [being married] an honouring thing, and I feel responsible and I'm guilty before God, upholding somebody else responsibility about living [in a sexual relationship] and not getting married . . . because there is a by-law here in this community saying it can't continue to happen. I might do something about it. (T71)[7]

The White manager's commitment to an administrative perspective entailing hierarchically organised legal authority is clear from a number of passages quoted in chapter 7, and his influence over council chairmen in this regard appears to have been considerable.

However, at public meetings on a number of occasions, the two men who alternated as council chairman between early 1978 and 1983 also indicated their dislike of having to enforce local rules. One chairman made his point while also speaking of the difficulty he experienced in having always to be the one who bore the brunt of dealing with matters involving White bureaucratic discourse:

> I feel sometimes I'm alone in my position as a chairman, as a representative for you people. I feel it. I had this complaints [discussed and complained about this] first thing this morning with Mr . . . [manager]. I feel myself alone, and I feel sometime, I shouldn't be talking . . . but I have a job and I have a responsibility, and that is all of your concern.
>
> I don't want to get any praise or backing up and saying: 'Look you're a good chairman', or something like that; but sometime I do feel I'm alone. You've got to have backstoppers, you got to have people to encourage you, . . . to give you strength and you're the people, think what you want, and think for yourself for the future. Just imagine, we're gonna take the control of [administrative] things and all that — how it's [going to] come about I don't know. But one thing — and I don't like to say it here tonight before youse all. You don't want to be a depending type of people, and depending upon the few. We want to come to the point where we want to be independent. Not saying [i.e. people like councillors having to say]: 'You clean up, keep your rubbish clean, keep your children together and so on'. [The speaker then refers to how people should seek training and employment at the settlement.]
>
> It might take us a long time before we can be a self-management and so on, but it's got to come . . . I know I can never be it [part of a council which takes control of the 'whole of Doomadgee'], 'cause I wish sometime I don't like to be a chairman, but I'm here for you people, you put me here. (T64)

As the next speaker, the manager spoke of the 'loneliness of leadership' with reference to the chairman's situation, and strongly requested the Aboriginal public not to worry the chairman with their personal requests, especially at inconvenient times:

> The person doesn't [i.e. shouldn't] go along to the chairman with all sorts of problems that are only his and he's only using the chairman for what he can get from him . . . And the chairman doesn't do something just for his own aim, as we know he doesn't. There's a time and a place for everything. (T64)

Pressure on councillors (particularly the chairman) derived partly from requests for the use of several vehicles controlled by the council. Such requests from close kin were especially difficult for one of the chairmen to handle. Several people stated that on one occasion the pressure of many people constantly taking their problems to the chairman had led him to lose his temper and use a tyre lever to kill one of three of his dogs that had been fighting each other. On another occasion, this chairman apparently refused to 'judge' his brother in the Aboriginal court when the latter had broken a local by-law. He also supported his close kin, with great anguish, when his wife's sister was allegedly beaten up when drunk by certain of the Aboriginal police. For their part, the police denied this allegation. The sergeant of Aboriginal police explained to me on one occasion that he tried to get the manager to appoint policemen from a number of families, because if they were 'close relation' of only one or a small number of families the 'public' accused the police of 'favouritism' (i.e. nepotism).

Despite the theory of representative government, according to which the authority of the council was supposed to work, confounding influences flowed from individuals' strong alignments to close kin. In chapter 6 I quoted the chairman's appeal to the public to work their conflicts out through the settlement's administrative authority structure, particularly the Aboriginal police. On the same occasion, he also mentioned the difficulties the council had in operating authoritatively in relation to such matters:

> I was only talking to . . . the [White] constable from Burketown the other day, and we don't want to let Doomadgee get it over us y'know [i.e. allow a bad situation to develop at Doomadgee], we want to be the right sort of people . . . live by the Regulations, the rules and the law and so on, we uphold it, it's good because it's you people who have respect for it. There are certain things, domestic trouble, we [the council] can not enter unless the [Aboriginal] police [have] been called upon, and we leave domestic trouble to Mr . . . [manager] and . . . we usually talk to husbands and wife when they having domestic trouble, but we only talk as a help-out, and some other people say we should look into it and muck into it and get stuck into it and so on [take a more active role in solving disputes]. (T71)

Councillors found enforcing by-laws concerning the control of conflict among Aboriginal residents a most difficult task. They did indeed leave most such attempts to the manager, who (under the Regulations) directed the operations of the Aboriginal police.[8] However, the police also of course operated in the strongly kin-aligned Aboriginal domain. A final indication of the importance of kin ties for the operation of the council is that there were references to people voting for councillors according to kin-aligned interests. As one person put it: 'People vote for [their] countryman'.

Aboriginal consciousness and the council

Throughout my fieldwork there was widespread and sustained dissatisfaction with the council on the part of other Aboriginal residents. The dissatisfaction was evident from continual complaint focused around two issues: that councillors pursued their own interests; and that the council was merely a means by which the manager achieved his will. In relation to the former criticism, councillors did receive regular economic benefit from their office, apparently in the form of a small nominal fee.[9] An irregular benefit was the possibility of travel to Brisbane, Mt Isa and occasionally other places for official meetings, however some councillors in fact disliked such travel and tried to avoid it. Councillors did not appear to have regular access to council vehicles for their personal use, although some benefits accrued to the chairman in this regard, particularly concerning his mundane weekday transport needs within the settlement.

There was criticism from some residents that councillors (particularly the chairman) would at times ensure that they and/or their own close kin received employment. Most (under-award) employment involved working in service jobs within the settlement. In May 1979 there were sixty-four men and twenty-six women so employed. Eight of these were teacher aides and two were health workers, whose appointment would have been supervised by the school principal and senior Aboriginal health program personnel respectively. The remaining eighty people were employed by the council — in the store (as cashiers and storemen, and in the butcher shop where mission cattle were killed and sold as meat), the administration office (as clerical workers), the mechanical workshop (assisting in the maintenance of various vehicles and machinery), at the stock camp (as stockmen maintaining the mission cattle herd), as Aboriginal police, at the bakery (which produced the settlement's bread), and on sanitary, cleaning and general services (DAA n.d.*a*: 14).[10] Together with the manager, the chairman of the council most likely influenced the filling of these jobs.

A small number of people worked off the reserve, on cattle stations or for the local Burke Shire Council (mostly on roadworks), thereby receiving award wages (but usually for relatively short periods). During previous decades, employment of Doomadgee people on cattle stations was very high,[11] but by May 1979 only twenty-one men and one woman were employed off the settlement (DAA n.d.*a*: 13). The manager and council chairman would most likely have less influence on the choice of people for outside employment than would be the case for jobs within the settlement.

The council also had considerable influence over who was to occupy the new housing that became available. There was some feeling in 1983 that the then chairman's 'own people' (i.e. close kin) had been favoured in the apportioning of recently completed houses. The alleged evidence for this was that six out of the available twenty-one new houses were occupied by the chairman's 'own people'. In fact, two houses went to two of the chairman's married daughters, three went to married siblings of one daughter's spouse, and one to the married sibling of the other daughter's spouse. The chairman was thus said by one person to have favoured his daughters and his 'in-laws'. A spouse of one of these in-laws was in fact the deputy chairman of the council (who thus got a house himself).

Furthermore, prior to 1983, most councillors themselves occupied the newer European-style three-bedroom housing in the 'top end' of the village. These houses had been built and occupied between 1972 and 1976 (DAA n.d.*a*. 9), and from most accounts the manager had considerable influence on deciding who would occupy them. Yet, apart from their awareness of this fact, Aboriginal residents also acknowledged the truth of what councillors, White staff and others implied directly and indirectly a number of times, namely that the criteria for getting a new house included the demonstrated capacity to maintain rent payments and 'look after' the house.[12] Thus, any simple analysis of housing allocation that looks only at favouritism by the manager towards councillors, or at nepotism by councillors themselves, is confounded by these other factors. Most of those who occupied the new houses in 1983 were regularly employed and thus most likely to be able to meet rent payments. This was the case for the chairman's 'own people', although these persons may have been favoured over some others with regular incomes (and records of maintaining the material condition of their dwellings). However, my general point here is that some qualification is necessary when acknowledging the possibility of councillors having obtained material benefits for themselves and their close kin by virtue of their office. Being a councillor or the close kin of a councillor was one of the variables associated with obtaining better housing and regular employment, but not the only one; being of mixed racial descent, for example, was another, and I will discuss the political significance of this aspect of identity shortly.

The second criticism of the council among Aboriginal residents was that it was merely a means by which the manager achieved his will. The general criticism was that councillors 'took orders' from the manager, that they were 'too frightened' to speak their mind on issues and were generally unable to assert any administrative independence. Specific criticisms varied from solely local government issues (such as the council allegedly not organising a truck to provide people with firewood or transport from the store to the village with their purchases on shopping days), to issues with wider political implications, such as the council allegedly not providing backup logistic support for those attempting to establish outstations away from the settlement, and also not actively pursuing broader land rights issues on behalf of residents.

Though it is not easy to determine the indirect influence of the manager on the council, the following cases are relevant. In 1979 a DAA official visited Doomadgee for a short period and compiled a report (DAA n.d.*a*) that was in part critical of the administration. After examining the report together, the manager and the council apparently sent letters to the DAA rejecting it *in toto*. While the report certainly contained some inaccuracies which were no doubt rejected by the councillors, the rejection of all of it appears to have reflected substantially only the manager's opinion. When, at a later date, I discussed with some of the councillors the criticisms of administrative practices contained in the report, I found them in agreement with those criticisms (as was a staff member who perused the report and concluded that 'much of it' was accurate). An important point here is that the manager was able to influence the councillors by extracting from them agreement with his own views. He achieved this in the context of being the mediator between the councillors and the large amount of written bureaucratic discourse (such as reports by public servants) with which they had to deal.

The manager's influence also derived from his being able to predict authoritatively the official governmental reaction to courses of action being considered by the council. For example, a school teacher put to the council that adult education funds were available to employ one or two young people with high school qualifications to conduct a short voter education course shortly before the federal election in 1980. The teacher reported that the councillors were initially very enthusiastic about the idea as it would increase local Aboriginal understanding of the voting process; however, they were ultimately persuaded by the manager that this would be inappropriate in terms of official procedures.[13] Thus, when the manager stated something to be appropriate or required at law, councillors would often accept his pronouncements as legal fact. At times the manager was proved to be broadly correct (e.g. when he persuaded councillors that increased DAA funding would not be obtained by forming an incorporated organisation separate from the council — the mooted 'Ganggalida Society'). On other occasions he was not correct (e.g. in his reputed claim that I could not be allowed to reside in the village because it was against local by-laws). However, the fact of his influence in both cases lies in the councillors' having to accept the manager's interpretation of the official requirements without the means of confirming it independently of the bureaucratic process under his control.

This aspect of the manager's power derived from his position within the prevailing political structure, but a clearer example of his hegemonic influence was evident when certain councillors embraced his personal authoritarian style when operating in a setting that focused on their office. One chairman's style of discourse (see the quote earlier in this chapter, where he stresses the sinfulness of *de facto* sexual relationships), is very similar to the manager's style, which I have labelled didactic paternalism. The following statement (made at a public meeting in 1980) illustrates the chairman's inclination to take on aspects of the manager's role — in this case checking on how people were maintaining the material standard of their houses:

> I think we're a really needy mob of people. I walk from time to time, I drive all of this street, every day, trying to take up notes on who looking after home — the older home better, who's keeping it up, who's [has] interest in keeping their old home up. They might be the one that might enter into some of them [new] houses over there, into a new home, because that person's showing the interest. That's the way it just have to go about it. Other people just want to get out from where they're at and go into a new home. Others want to go into a home and not finishing [paying] off their bills, y'see because of all money, because of lack of it. These things will be going up . . . money on the rents of the house, it goes back on the repair, for breakdown of that house, that's the maintenance. Y'see all this has to come about. (T56)

The chairman thus embraced intellectually the rhetoric of what was ostensibly a very practical administrative perspective. His style entailed presenting his own position as one part (albeit a pivotal one for the village residents) in the broader administrative process that engulfed the settlement. Both chairmen and a number of councillors during the research period adopted such a position in relation to the wider Aboriginal public, and in doing this they emulated important aspects of the manager's style of legitimating the authority of the administrative process.

This incorporation of councillors' thinking by the ideology of the colonial administration is discernable clearly, despite occasional assertions by some of the individuals occupying these offices that they were gradually seeking independence from the manager's control. A few councillors mentioned their having complained directly to the manager. For example, the chairman related how he had complained bitterly about tradesmen on the staff putting most of their efforts into construction projects in the Whitefella spatial domain, while important maintenance (and construction) work was required in the village. The chairman suggested with some pride that these complaints had resulted in the building workers being instructed by the manager to leave their jobs in the White domain and begin work in the village. On another occasion, the chairman said that he controlled the Aboriginal Court, whereas in the recent past the manager had done so.

This latter conviction may have led the council, together with the Aboriginal police, to express the view to a DAA official in 1982 that the court was fair and just (DAA n.d.*b*: 1). But the point is that the council was bound by both the political structures of the administrative hierarchy and its ideology. While the chairman's complaints led the tradesmen towards work more directly beneficial to Aboriginal residents, the administrative hierarchy was such that it was still the manager who had to give the workers new directions. And if we accept that the councillors (together with the Aboriginal police) genuinely controlled the Aboriginal Court, they did so in terms of an ideology of 'responsibility' and 'authority' that underpinned the paternalistic tutelary relationship between White staff and Aboriginal people.

Councillors (along with many other Aboriginal residents) were aware of the widespread debate on the media and in government and bureaucratic circles about Aboriginal self-management. On one occasion, two councillors (one of whom was also a church elder), together with several other people from Doomadgee and Mornington Island, were able through a DAA-funded project to visit two Aboriginal settlements in the Northern Territory in order to observe 'leadership' there. As stated in the report prepared after their return,[14] one of their most significant impressions was of the increasing extent of Aboriginal control over a variety of administrative matters. There is no doubt that the manager's influence over the council decreased throughout the late 1970s and early 1980s, due in part to the council's increasing access to the policies of government departments other than the Queensland DAIA (with which the manager had always been closely aligned). Nevertheless, the councillors' increasing independence did not mitigate their attribution of greater legitimacy to the prevailing administrative system than was forthcoming from those not holding such office. This was particularly so for chairmen, who worked closely with the White manager on administrative matters. But the partial cooption of councillors did not serve to engender legitimacy for the White administrative system throughout the Aboriginal population. On the contrary, Aboriginal consciousness in general remained quite unwilling to regard the councillors' role as anything more than self-interested behaviour on their part.

To the extent that the thinking of councillors was derived from their experience of incorporation into White political structures, the colonial ideology concerning the appropriateness of authoritative

White tutelage penetrated the consciousness of a small number of Aboriginal residents. Furthermore, an instrument for indirect White domination thereby operated through these individuals. Yet the influence of other aspects of White ideology and practices operated more widely across the Aboriginal population. The complex nature of Aboriginal thinking concerning the distinctiveness of people of mixed racial descent is a striking case of such influence.

Racial ideology among Aboriginal people

As discussed in earlier chapters, the attitude of White officialdom (in both Queensland and the Northern Territory) towards mixed-race children on cattle stations and in fringe camps was that they should be separated from 'native camps' and that they were more assimilable into White society than were those termed 'full-bloods'. At Doomadgee, similar convictions seem to have been historically extant among White staff. During my fieldwork, some staff suggested that mixed-descent people were generally more 'trainable' for work roles entailing responsibility, and others mentioned their belief that the 'mixing' of 'the two races' (i.e. Whites and people solely of Aboriginal descent) would naturally produce the 'best workers'.

Thus, the thinking of the Whites has been part of a racial ideology, in that the socio-psychological characteristics of mixed-race people (and others) have been seen as inherited biologically. The idiom used to express this notion is that such characteristics and capacities are inherited through 'the blood' or 'the genes'. Non-Aboriginal ancestry (or 'blood') has been regarded as partially 'breeding out' or displacing what have been viewed as Aboriginal socio-psychological characteristics, leaving mixed-descent people 'racially' distinct from both Whites and full-descent Aborigines. In the rest of this chapter I will examine the extent to which Aboriginal thinking has been influenced by this European ideology (and associated body of historical practices).

In their attribution of meaning to phenotypic distinctiveness, Aboriginal residents regarded those of mixed descent as a socially separable category within the village population. The significance of skin colour in Aboriginal social life is a complex issue. When a speaker focused on mixed descent as a feature of an individual's identity, he or she might refer to the person being 'half-caste', 'quarter-caste', or more usually a 'Yellafella'. In more general designations, mixed-descent people were included within the wider category of (predominantly full-descent) Aboriginal people, and hence could be referred to as 'Blackfellas' (or by various other terms used routinely for Aboriginal people). While skin colour was the main criterion for emic recognition of a person as a Yellafella, the process was subject to other considerations, in particular, knowledge of persons' parents and grandparents.

A continuum of skin colouration was recognised within the village population, and generally understood as derived from parentage and grandparentage. For example, a woman distinguished her full-descent brother's children as looking 'fair', 'because they mother colour', i.e. they inherited a 'fairer' colour from their mother, whose own father was the child of a European man and a full-descent woman. The children's mother's mother was of full Aboriginal descent, and their own skin colour is quite dark; their fairness is regarded as simply reflecting the 'fairer' or 'lighter' colour of their mother (and the greater 'fairness' of their mother's father). It is unlikely that the children would be referred to as 'Yellafellas', though their mother could be (and, typically, her own father would be). She and her siblings have been referred to as 'that real dark [kind of] Yellafella'. Similarly, a person can be said to be 'Yellafella, but little bit dark', or 'Yellafella, but real light'. These kinds of qualificatory comments simply locate people along a colour continuum including all Aboriginal people. The further physical feature which can be discussed as indicative of a person's parentage or grandparentage is eye shape, as a degree of epicanthic fold is taken as evidence of some Asian ancestry, typically Chinese.

Persons' actual ancestry, particularly the identity of their father (or grandfathers) may not be known widely, yet their 'light' (or 'bright') skin colour will be simply taken as evidence of a non-Aboriginal or mixed-descent person in their genealogy. For example, several people were simply said in general conversation to be 'too light' to be descended from their socially acknowledged full-descent Aboriginal fathers. Nevertheless, in the case of people regarded as only 'little bit light', such views are normally offered tentatively, for a degree of individual variation in skin colour is accepted as normal within the recognised full-descent population. In one case, a full-descent man (deceased for a long time) was simply said to have been 'copper coloured' (and hence known as 'Yellow Jack'); while another full-descent man was said to have been of 'light' skin colour because his conception totem was 'rock possum', which apparently has light-coloured fur.

A further important criterion relevant to people of mixed descent being constituted in public discourse as members of a socially separable category was aspects of their behaviour. The issue is whether or not persons' behaviour leads others to conclude that they regard themselves as 'classed' with people who are routinely designated publicly as 'Yellafellas'. For example, a person descended from a full-descent Aboriginal mother and a father apparently of Aboriginal/Chinese descent may only very rarely be tagged in discourse as a Yellafella, or have his personal identity constructed situationally by reference to his skin colour or physiognomy, because: 'he don't class himself as a Yellafella', or 'he got no time for them Yellafellas'. The fact that the skin colour of such a person is likely to be quite dark plausibly influences his or her lack of social distance from the full-descent Aboriginal majority. However, the public identity of a person with quite 'light' skin colour, can also be constructed without much reference to his or her status as a Yellafella, if he or she is regarded by those of full Aboriginal descent as somebody who 'class himself with us all the time'. Alternately, somebody such as a young man who was regarded as 'that quarter-caste fella [who] don't class himself with us, won't talk to us', will have a public persona constructed around his skin colour and status as a Yellafella.

The core of people conceptually constituted as the Yellafella minority thus varied somewhat in terms of skin colour. While this minority was made up of those of 'mixed descent', we must note that some people of mixed Aboriginal/non-Aboriginal ancestry were only occasionally placed in the Yellafella category, subject to flexible assessments about aspects of their behaviour. Recognition of persons' part non-Aboriginal ancestry and consequent physical distinctiveness was not routinely pejorative (cf. Shaw's [1983: 238] similar comments for the East Kimberley region)[15] and people of mixed descent themselves at times referred in public settings to the non-Aboriginal components of their ancestry. Where the identity and/or reputation of their non-Aboriginal ancestor (typically their father, or less commonly, grandfather) was widely known in the region, individuals might well acknowledge their consanguineal link to him with considerable pride. Nevertheless, social relations between those of full- and part-Aboriginal descent exhibited substantial tensions.

A survey in 1980 showed 15 per cent (fifty out of a sample of 324) of adults to be unambiguously regarded as 'Yellafellas' in the opinion of those consulted. The proportion of mixed-descent children (while not surveyed) appeared similar to that of adults. In many cases, these adults and children were residentially distributed throughout otherwise full-descent families, and in one sense, virtually all mixed-descent people routinely engaged in social relations with full-descent people. However, the conceptual separation of the two categories was evident from such discourse as the following where an Aboriginal man explained why some Aboriginal residents feared the consequences of White men coming to live in the 'Blackfella domain':

> Some people are saying . . . 'Oh if we let one White man come into the village, they'll all be wanting to come . . . and live, . . . and marry our Aboriginal race, dark race, and . . . biggest advantage of children be here

> then be all half-caste. What going to happen to the black ones? They all gonna die away. The black one will be destroyed in fifty years time, won't be a black race in the village . . .'. Old Blackfella, he's waking up to himself now [laughing]. (T75)

Mixed-descent people were said (by full-descent people) to prefer marrying each other; one man stated that this was particularly so for mixed-descent women who would not want to marry full-descent men. The 1980 survey found that of a sample of thirty-eight mixed-descent married residents, only thirteen (34%) were married to full-descent residents and, given the much larger full-descent population, this represents a substantial degree of endogamy among people of mixed racial descent.

Moreover, there was clearly considerable tension in status and class relations between people of full- and part-Aboriginal descent. With some exceptions, those designated as Yellafellas were commonly said to 'reckon they're next to Whitefella' (i.e. to indicate that their status was higher than that of other Aboriginal people — somehow in between Blackfellas and Whitefellas). Evidence of this assumed higher status was identified by non-Yellafellas with reference to the fact that Yellafellas commonly adopt a 'flash' style, predominantly in their domestic life, and that they have been able to attain a comparatively higher socio-economic status (and associated class position) than others, mainly because of more favourable treatment from White officials and employers over the years.

It has been suggested that predominantly mixed-descent families (though not normally individuals of mixed descent within otherwise full-descent families) have desired, and been able to achieve, material aspects of a domestic lifestyle that are closer to the White Australian ideal than those of other Aboriginal families. The houses, yards, cars and general physical appearance of these mixed-descent families have thus been known as 'flash'. An unelicited statement on one occasion provided an informative indication of the emic association of mixed-descent status with spruced-up cleanliness and the outward signs of good health as they are known to be defined within White ideals. In a comment about an old full-descent man who in 1982 was frail, crippled and decrepit, a woman of full descent contrasted his appearance with how he once looked very healthy, and thus described him as having looked 'real half-caste', 'like properly clean and Yellafella'. The implication that Yellafella attributes are comparatively closer to Whitefella status than are Blackfella attributes, was again indicated when women of mixed descent were occasionally referred to as 'mijiji' ('missus', a word for White woman), although this most commonly occurred in reference to mixed-descent women who had left the settlement to live permanently or semipermanently in predominantly White towns.

The conception of Yellafellas (held by other Aborigines) as noticeably 'flash' is tied closely to their perceived greater ownership and use of commodities obtained from the Australian market. It was alleged that Yellafellas were disproportionately favoured in the allocation of jobs and housing at Doomadgee. For example, it was said that 'If half-caste fella miss a day he still keep job; if Blackfella miss it, he get sacked'; and a full-descent member of the Aboriginal council reportedly said in 1983 (quoted in Brisbane's *Sunday Sun* newspaper 27/11/1983: 10–11):

> The full bloods respect me but the half-castes say 'He's only a black fellow'. The half-castes get all the best jobs and the responsibility. They also get the best houses while we are in the humpies by the dump.

Indeed, in October 1983 (not long after the departure of the missionary administration) there were apparently seven Aboriginal full-time staff employed by the DAIA and hence on award wages (personal communication from the new DAIA White manager), and all were publicly regarded as Yellafellas.

The fact that a substantial number of jobs and advisory roles in the DAA bureaucracy (centred in a town adjacent to the immediate study region) have increasingly come to be occupied by people of mixed descent, has also not gone unremarked among the majority full-descent Aboriginal population at Doomadgee. Furthermore, there has at times been resentment that certain mixed-descent people resident in nearby towns have allegedly emphasised their Aboriginality only during the last decade or so, when government funding for Aboriginal organisations has increased. Consider the following complaint made by the council chairman at the public meeting following his attendance at a regional DAA meeting (he was referring to certain people of mixed descent, representing various organisations, who were bidding competitively for government funds in competition with the Doomadgee community):

> I went as a council[lor] [to a DAA area conference]. When I went in there I saw hardly any fella look bit like me colour. They were Yellafellas, half Whitefellas . . . and here with their top education lot of fellas never got, and they been fighting for Aboriginal money! When there been no grants given out to Aboriginal [after that] they been come back and put themselves as Aboriginal, that's how I criticise them. (T55)

This is another part of the passage quoted in chapter 7, where the chairman pointed out that Aboriginal people who had lived off the reserve had not been 'under the Act' and therefore not subject to the type of state surveillance reserve living had entailed. Implicit here also is the chairman's view that mixed-descent people living off the reserve were able (if they wished) to downplay their Aboriginality in a way not possible for those on the reserve. In the view he put, these people therefore had less right to government funding than did the residents of reserve settlements such as Doomadgee and Mornington Island. In other conversations, he also suggested that mixed-descent people on the reserve had historically enjoyed greater freedom than those of full descent to leave and obtain a better material standard of living within the wider non-Aboriginal society. While he simultaneously referred approvingly to those mixed-descent people who chose to continue living at Doomadgee among the full-descent Aboriginal majority, what is relevant here is the fact that the chairman uses the idiom of skin colour to frame his criticisms of a particular category of persons within the Aboriginal population.

Quantitative data from my 1980 survey of the Doomadgee population indicate an association between publicly attributed Yellafella status and proportionately higher employment rates (both full-time and part-time), greater access to operational motor vehicles, and occupation of newer European-style housing. In the case of employment, Table 1 indicates a best estimate of mixed-descent adults being just over twice as likely as full-descent adults to be in employment. Cross tabulation between racial descent and access to operational motor vehicles (Table 2) shows that mixed-descent people were more than six times as likely to be living in a household where there were one or more working motor vehicles. On housing, while the dwellings constructed between 1972 and 1976 do not appear to have been distributed to favour mixed-descent people, of the further twenty-two new houses occupied around mid–1983, nine went to mixed-descent couples and a further two went to families where one of the spouses was of mixed-descent, indicating disproportionate occupancy by mixed-descent people in a population where they constituted only 15 per cent of residents.

Table 1

Racial descent by employment situation (Doomadgee 1980)*
(Column percentages, chi square = 17.96, $p < .001$)

	Racial descent	
Employment situation	Full descent (N = 245)	Mixed descent (N = 46)
Employed	66 (27%)	27 (59%)
Unemployed	179 (73%)	19 (41%)

* No distinction is made in the Table between part-time and full-time workers. Informants included a small number of people as workers who had ceased working just prior to the survey period.

Table 2
Racial descent by residence in a household with one or more working motor vehicles (Doomadgee 1980)
(Column percentages, chi square 37.15, p < .001)

	Racial descent	
Access to vehicles	Full descent (N = 273)	Mixed descent (N 48)
Vehicle(s) at house	13 (5%)	16 (33%)
Vehicle(s) not at house	260 (95%)	32 (67%)

To obtain regular employment (and therefore the ability to pay rent regularly, and to purchase and maintain vehicles) may, in some types of jobs (such as office work, and jobs as teacher aides and health assistants), require a high school education. And some data indicate that, compared with the general population of Doomadgee, mixed-descent people achieved disproportionately high education levels. The first two Doomadgee students to attend high school (in 1967) and the first to complete high school (in 1977) were of mixed descent (Murray 1982:11). In 1983, all fifteen Aboriginal pupils in the special program grade (along with all the eight non-Aboriginal pupils in the school) were of mixed descent. According to the relevant teachers, the criteria used for selection of children into the special program grade were: parents' high aspirations for their children's education; standard English competence; previous academic achievement; and the ability to work for periods independently of teachers in the classroom.

Associated with the assertion that Yellafellas enjoyed higher socioeconomic status were complaints that they were sometimes able to thwart the authority of the Aboriginal council and even of the Aboriginal police. For example, it did not go unnoticed that the council chairman was quick to aggressively warn and threaten the full-descent protagonists of a fight one night that they would be arrested, whereas several nights later he did nothing when drunken and disruptive conflict broke out among a group of mixed-descent young men (at times termed the 'top end boys'). Given the chairman's sentiments (as documented above) we might assume that his inaction was not necessarily due to a desire to favour the 'top end boys', but perhaps to a lack of confidence in confronting them directly.

These 'top end boys' were a small group of mixed-descent young men who lived (until 1983) predominantly with their mixed-descent parents and affines in the northwest corner of the village, and formed a particularly separate grouping. On an occasion when one such young man accompanied his wife on foot to my camp in the eastern area of the village so she could deliver a message to me, he made it clear that he did not usually travel very far from the 'top end'. In response to my comment that I had never seen him walking there before, he replied that I would never see him doing it again for he would always drive a car or ride a horse, and in any case he would: 'stay up in the corner [of the village], where I belong'. The fact that this group of mixed-descent young men collectively maintained a degree of social discreteness was known routinely throughout settlement social life, e.g. they were said to drink alcohol among themselves rather than with others: 'Those top-end boys don't drink down there [at a nearby site where most drinking of alcohol was done], they go bush in their cars when they got grog'.

A further issue in status relations between Aboriginal people of full and mixed descent was the expectation among those people committed to 'Blackfella law' that Yellafellas were typically uninterested in it. Thus, discourse would at times link the lack of 'law' knowledge of several mixed-race men with their perceived preference for pursuing a lifestyle derived from European traditions: 'He don't know law — he *Mandagi* [Whitefella] too much'. One full-descent councillor pointed out that: 'The half-castes have taken the place of the missionaries [who had ceased to formally administer the settlement that year] . . . But they don't seem to respect the black man's culture which is being wiped out' (*Sunday Sun* newspaper 27/11/1983: 11).

However, it is clear that mixed-descent status does not necessarily entail a lack of interest in Blackfella law. A small number of older men of mixed ancestry were acknowledged as 'law men'. Others were recognised as appropriately interested in and respectful of certain aspects of the knowledge associated with ceremonial life. Nevertheless the attitude of such people was regarded as distinctive among the broader Yellafella group: 'No matter he Yellafella, he can sabby [understand and embrace] law!'. When three young men of mixed descent were among eight Doomadgee young men initiated in 1982 at an outstation to the west, one 'law man' of full descent marvelled: 'That three Yellafella got me beat [have me very surprised] — that's big thing that' (i.e. the initiation is highly important in terms of Blackfella law). Similarly, some Yellafellas warranted specific comment when consulting 'Blackfella doctors' whose practices demonstrably draw on 'Blackfella law'. As one man put it:

> Even this Yellafella here, [he] believes on the Christian *Mandagi* [Whitefella] way, but when White doctor couldn't fix his wife he came to . . . [a prominent Blackfella doctor, and said] — 'I'll give you $50 if you can fix her'.

Accounts from mixed-descent people themselves focused typically on how the system of White administration has sought to separate them from other Aborigines. People of mixed ancestry speak much less than do those of full descent about comparative material benefits which they may have derived from White practices, but other aspects of their special treatment are spoken of quite openly. For example, one mixed-descent woman described how, during the 1950s, the missionary staff at Doomadgee arranged for her to marry a man from a station across the border, despite her only occasional previous contact with him and her mother's opposition to the marriage. While this man 'had Aboriginal in him', he was 'raised as a European' and looked more 'White' than Aboriginal. The staff view was that they were looking after the girl's interests by organising for her to 'leave [the] reserve and go and live as a white person'. After thirty-one years away, this woman returned to assist her invalid full-descent mother, and in 1988 she forcefully proclaimed her Aboriginality: 'it doesn't matter how light the skin goes, you stem from the Aboriginal race and you'll always remain an Aboriginal'.[16] However, other mixed-descent people who had similar experiences did not return to live among their full-descent relatives, and some have established lifestyles that are much closer to those of local working class Whites (in terms of material style of living) than to those of their full-descent relatives who stayed in the region of their birth.[17] From the perspective of those resident at Doomadgee, such people demonstrate the way mixed-descent individuals have historically been presented with the kinds of opportunities for socioeconomic advancement that have not been available to the majority of Aboriginal people in the southern Gulf region.

The influence of colonial ideology

The incorporation into the administrative apparatus of a relatively small number of Aboriginal councillors and Aboriginal police (both offices with changing memberships over the years) suggests hegemonic aspects of the colonial social relationship. Given the material presented in both this chapter and chapter 7, it is clear that councillors (and the police sergeant at least) typically accorded greater legitimacy to the administrative authority of which they were structurally a part, than did the general population of Aboriginal residents. Some councillors embraced significant elements of staff ideology, particularly the notions of 'responsibility' and 'authority' as attaching to their office. To the extent that this ideology can be regarded as not congruent with their own interests as members of the broader Aboriginal public, its effects can be considered to entail a form of hegemonic domination. The material advantage able to be derived (for oneself and/or one's close kin) from the position of councillor might be viewed as serving the short-term interests of people occupying these offices; and the individuals themselves might feel that some status attaches to the position as it is valued within White society, and also by virtue of the power to enforce the regulations and by-laws of Whitefella law. However, the ideology that entails compliant councillors who are reliant on continued White paternalistic tutelage does not serve broader (or longer-term) Aboriginal interests, and to the extent that this ideology has been embraced we see the hegemonic aspects of colonial domination.

Councillors have been typically perceived by other Aborigines as seeking material advantage and status from within the Whitefella domain, partly by emulating the administrative style of the key senior staff. Despite the view among many White staff that the council legitimated the wider administrative system through representing the desires and sentiments of those administered, it is clear that the concept of representativeness was simply not given much credence within the Blackfella domain. Hence, the operation of the council did not engender throughout the wider Aboriginal consciousness, an experience of incorporation into the White administrative system; nor did it facilitate the major degree of attribution of legitimacy to that system which could have been expected to follow from such an experience of political incorporation.

However, I have also discussed the influence of other aspects of colonial ideology and practices throughout the wider village population, through an examination of the socially distinctive identity attributed to people of mixed racial descent. From the perspective of those in the village regarded as non-Yellafellas (i.e. essentially the majority who are solely of Aboriginal descent), characteristics of Yellafellas have included their comparatively 'flash' lifestyle, material advantage, and lack of interest in Blackfella law. This view has been part of a degree of tension in social relations between Aboriginal people of full and mixed descent.

I have made it clear that diversity among those referred to situationally as 'Yellafellas' was recognised among village residents. Specifically, some were distinguished as having 'never been flash', particularly those who were not removed from the influence of their mothers by White officialdom (either police protectors or missionaries). In the words of one old lady, a group of younger mixed-descent people quite closely related to her have: 'never been flash, because . . . [their] mother was still alive . . . because they been told'. Thus, many Yellafellas were known not to warrant the negative evaluations described in this chapter. Furthermore, those who were conceived as behaving 'flash' and enjoying economic advantages were still regarded as part of the broad Aboriginal domain. But the conceptual category 'Yellafella' is tinged with an entrenched historical association of distinctive negative characteristics. As a principle of classification among Aboriginal people the idiom of skin colour is not neutral in evaluative status terms; and this remains so, despite the not uncommon occurrence of relationships among Aboriginal people of full and mixed descent where colour appears to be ignored.

Aboriginal thinking on this issue has been influenced by colonial administrative and general social practices, or, more specifically, by the material consequences of these practices for social relations between Aboriginal people of full and mixed descent. But the further question is whether specific European ideas about 'racial' inheritance of characteristics have been embraced among village residents. There is some indication that similar 'racial ideology' constrains Aboriginal thinking, in the form of elicited comments about *why* certain Yellafellas have in the past or do now pursue a 'flash' lifestyle, and hence do not generally 'class' themselves with Blackfellas. Reasons given will include references to their non-Aboriginal ancestry (e.g. the reason why a mixed-descent man was 'terrible flash when he young fella, fightin against Blackfella', was described as due to his 'Chinese start I think'). Moreover, Aboriginal people (like Whites) not uncommonly discussed the behavioural characteristics of domesticated animals (cattle, horses, and especially dogs) in terms of their breeding and 'blood'. The prospective or current behaviour of one's own dogs can be regarded with apprehension or disapproval, and the reason for this bad behaviour described in terms of them having 'bad blood'.

Yet my conclusion is that, in general, Aboriginal thought does not attach inherited behavioural concomitants directly to skin colour or ancestry in the way this view pervades White ideology. In the most general terms, like Whitefellas and Blackfellas, Yellafellas are said to have their 'own way'. But, unlike White ideology, the Aboriginal perspective on the origins of this 'way' is circumspect. Also, in contrast to what has been reported for the northeast Queensland settlement of Hope Vale in the early 1970s (Terwiel-Powell 1975), Aboriginal people at Doomadgee (and more generally in the southern Gulf region) have not associated innate intellectual and cultural superiority with fairer skin colour. Moreover, Aboriginal speculation about reasons for the fact that 'Yellafella got his own way' differed markedly from the White perspective by emphasising the importance of mixed-descent people having been provided with different opportunities by the world of White officialdom and employers. Thus, while White racial ideology has derived directly from an imported intellectual tradition (cf. Banton 1987), Aboriginal consciousness concerning this subject has been greatly influenced by the material experience of White colonial practices derived from White ideology.

Finally, while this chapter has discussed two important ways in which Aboriginal consciousness and social action have been enmeshed within the influences of White ideology and administrative practices, consideration of power relations at Doomadgee is incomplete without treatment of Christianity as a key legitimating ideology for colonial authority. This is the subject of the next chapter.

Notes

1 In the Torres Strait a system of elected Islander councils was instituted in 1899 (Beckett 1987: 45).

2 If an insufficient number of councillors were elected or if no candidates offered for election, the required number could be appointed by the Director (No. 48 [1]). As the nomination of every candidate had to be supported by no fewer than ten electors, in writing (No. 4 [27]), it is quite likely that insufficient numbers of councillors would have been elected on many occasions. Councils appear not to have operated consistently on many reserves until after the 1966 Regulations were established.

3 One further person attempted to stand for election, but was disallowed by the manager because he had broken a local by-law. Under the 1972 Regulations (No. 31), a person convicted of an offence in an Aboriginal Court in the two years immediately preceding the election was disqualified as a candidate.

4 On the basis of access to mission records, a DAA report (n.d.*a*: 5) gives the example of March 1979, when 22.5% of the 903 Aboriginal people officially recorded as associated with Doomadgee were in fact 'away at the time on a long-term basis'.

5 Cf. Myers' (1979: 361–5) comments on 'shame' among Pintupi Aborigines:

> The concept of 'shame' is usually associated with the discomfort of being observed by others in the public domain, especially at being seen to do something that is poor etiquette, ill-mannered or wrong.

He notes (p. 362) that considerations of 'shame' make individuals 'reluctant to overtly impose themselves or their wishes on others', and refers specifically to 'embarrassment' often accompanying public speaking occasions.

6 Pursuant to Regulation 79 (2), the fine could be up to $50, or according to by-law Chapter 24 (4), up to $40 or fourteen days imprisonment (The Australian Law Reform Commission 1979: 22). At Doomadgee, the gaol was used mostly (if not exclusively) for drunk people who had become disruptive; they were locked up there overnight (or occasionally over a weekend). A report compiled in 1982 (DAA n.d.*b*: 2) states that the usual fine imposed by the Aboriginal court at Doomadgee was $10 to $20.

7 The standard council by-laws applying in all Queensland Aboriginal Reserves (and originally formulated by the DAIA) do not contain any specific reference to living in a *de facto* marriage relationship. However, it is quite likely that a by-law making this illegal was passed by the Doomadgee Council under the supervision of the manager. A government bureaucrat suggested to me that this occurred during 1980.

[8] Under the 1972 Regulations (No.'s 64–6), the manager appointed, promoted, suspended or dismissed Aboriginal police, and made rules for them. Although these Regulations include references to the manager carrying out certain of these tasks in consultation with the council, in practice at Doomadgee the police sought direction from the manager.

[9] Section 56 (20) of the 1971 Act enables Regulations to stipulate fees to be paid for the purposes of the Act; however I am unable to say how much councillors were paid. The chairman apparently received a marginally higher fee than other councillors.

[10] Wages for council employees came out of the community fund, which was in turn mainly derived from the profits of the retail store, although the DAIA also subsidised these wages to an unrevealed degree (DAA n.d.*a*: 14). In 1982, the DAIA staff quota for Doomadgee was sixty-eight full-time salaries, however, as the manager's wife reportedly pointed out, through use of part-time salaries, the money was extended to employ around ninety people (DAA n.d.b: 8).

Estimates of the unemployment rate are 60%, on the basis of 1976 DAA data (Altman and Nieuwenhuysen 1979: 39), and 57% (using Australian Bureau of Statistics 1981 Census data. A substantial proportion of residents aged fifteen years and over received social security pensions or benefits, 35% according to 1976 national Census data, 36% according to (unpublished) Department of Social Security data for May 1978 or approximately 40% according to (unpublished) DAA Community Profile data for 1981.

[11] For example, Long (1970: 153) reported that between January and December 1965 (when the official settlement population was 528), 274 employment agreements were signed for jobs at seventy-four cattle stations (for 188 men and fifty-five women) as well as for jobs with ten contract drovers and musterers (for twenty-six men), and for jobs with two other employers (for five men).

[12] Aboriginal residents say that the manager and his wife used to inspect persons' houses, although they had apparently ceased doing this by early 1978. Indeed, their legal authority to carry out such inspections was confined under the 1971 Act 'to situations where the occupier consents or where a justice issues a warrant' (Nettheim 1981: 33). Even prior to 1971 state law appears to have enabled only visiting justices to make inspections without consent or warrant (section 15 of the 1965 Act, and section 10 of the 1939 Act), but a by-law in force right up to and throughout the period from 1978 to 1983 states that a householder shall allow 'an authorised person' to enter his house for the purpose of inspection (Commissioner for Community Relations 1977: 106). In practice, the manager would certainly have had few problems in asserting a right to carry out such inspections up to the early 1970s.

[13] Instead of the house-to-house educative visits envisaged by the adult education teacher, there was a public meeting in the village not long before the election. The manager explained the voting procedure without favouring any particular candidate, while the council chairman briefly

expressed his personal preference for the National Party candidate, with whom he was acquainted personally.

[14] *Aboriginal Leadership: Sharing Impressions on Aboriginal Community Leadership*, by Aboriginal Leaders from Doomadgee and Mornington Island, June 1982, published by Aboriginal Training and Cultural Institute, Sydney.

[15] The term 'Yellafella' is not necessarily regarded as pejorative, despite its clear association with a social position intermediate between Blackfellas and Whitefellas (cf. Meggitt 1962: 34). However, while it is used as a term of reference, the label is not normally used in addressing a person. Furthermore, it is not used routinely throughout those areas of Australia where the Aboriginal population is predominantly of mixed ancestry and, like the term 'half-caste', it can be regarded as very offensive. Consider, for example, the bitter comment of a mixed-descent man from southeast Queensland, made with general reference to Aboriginal people in the Northern Territory: 'They call us Yellafellas . . . [and] they'd rather trust a White man than a Yellafella'.

[16] Transcripts of evidence given to the Royal Commission into Aboriginal Deaths in Custody, during hearings at Doomadgee, 21 October 1988 (pp. 382–3, 396).

[17] One woman who spent her youth in the dormitory at Doomadgee and now lives with her White husband in a small, predominantly European town, was presented with a 'Citizen of the Year' Award by the local shire council (see *Kimberley Echo* newspaper, 7/11/1988, p. 14).

CHAPTER NINE

Christianity, domination and resistance

The question of the significance of Christian ideology in the consciousness and social action of residents at Doomadgee is complex. My discussion centres on whether Christianity operated historically to legitimate the domination of Aboriginal society, or provided a basis for forms of Aboriginal resistance. Considered thus, Christianity's primary sociological significance is located within the operation of settlement power relations.

Becoming a Christian

Avowedly Christian Aborigines described the process by which people become Christians as involving three stages. The first is that the person is 'saved', which involves approaching a church elder and making 'a profession of faith'. (During most of the research period there were five church elders: two Aborigines and three Whites. A third Aboriginal church elder was appointed in 1983). The second stage of becoming a Christian is when, largely it seems at the discretion of the church elders, the person is baptised by means of total immersion. The third stage involves the person continuing to live an authentic Christian life. If they fail to do so and commit sins of various kinds they are said to have had a 'downfall'. They are then publicly named at a Christian meeting and must wait some time until the church eldership readmits them to 'fellowship' and allows them to 'take bread and wine at the Lord's table' (i.e. participate in what is referred to within mainstream Christian denominations as the rite of Communion).

The following passage presents the senior Aboriginal church elder's account of this process:

> What the Gospel says: you get saved — you don't have to get baptised

> to be saved. Two things — being saved and being baptised are two different things. You're saved, what I mean being saved, the Gospel here preaches that Christ . . . was crucified, and it preaches his death, burial and resurrection, and if a man believes that he died and that he was buried and rose again, and in his faith if he see that he's a sinner . . . we believe that, we're saved. Then we follow up that salvation with baptism . . . person who is saved, the next step is baptism. We show in our openness, righteousness, publicly that we have died with Christ, and buried with him and raised in new life — so he [the person to be baptised] walks in the water and he is put under the water, that's what you do when you bury people, you put them right under, you don't put 'em half-way down and hold his head up, you don't put'em in the grave and leave his head out, but you put him right down underneath the water . . . He died and buried and then you lift him up from under the water and [he] walk out — he's raised with Christ, he's shown now that he believes inwardly, this is the work that has been done inwardly, he believes that he has died with Christ, was buried with him and raised again. (T57)

The same speaker went on to point out that the trouble with many people was that they had only 'a bit of religion, just to last you about a month':

> I know one fella come up here one night and he said: 'Oh I'm going to change my life'. You know when Ben Mason was here?[1] He walked out there [to the public speaking position at the evangelical meeting] and he said: 'I'm finished . . . with the old ways, giving up drinking . . . everything. I'm not having anything more to do with it'. All right, in three days time [laughing], we heard he was in . . . [a known grog-runner's] car blind drunk . . . See they fell on that stony ground,[2] he only had religion for about three or four days. (T57)

The process of having a 'downfall' and then being 're-dedicated' after some time appeared to be quite common, although many people would not 'return to the Lord's table' until such a life-crisis as the death (or perhaps near-death) of a close relative. The most common form of sin constituting a downfall was drunkenness and associated violence and sexual promiscuity. Indeed, drunkenness was posed by Christians (both Aboriginal and White) as the inevitable converse of embracing Christianity.

By the Christian perspective, those who were not 'saved' from a life of sin were inevitably destructive of themselves and others, and this was quite apparent in the widespread drunkenness among Aboriginal people not 'in fellowship'. As Tonkinson (1982a: 126; 1988: 68–71) has suggested with reference to Christian Aborigines' fundamentalist objections to alcohol use, their interest in Christianity 'may prove to be less focused on its theological content than on its coercive potential'. Thus, alcohol use was perceived as a 'vice', involving a substance representing the 'work of the Devil' and therefore as something which typically led to sinfulness and the life-crises associated with sin. The senior Aboriginal church elder told me (T75) that 'the first flagon' was made at the time of Noah's drunkenness as described in the Bible. One of the consequences of this drunkenness was believed by some to be that the descendants of one of Noah's sons were cursed forever. The sinfulness and destructiveness of gambling were also perceived by Christians to be evident from the fact that many Aboriginal people lost money that was needed to support their other family members. While large numbers of once baptised people certainly remained out of fellowship for long periods after a 'downfall', others were keen to return to active fellowship as soon as possible. One man told me that he had complained to a (White) church elder about how he was being made to wait too long (several months according to his account) before re-acceptance.

This distinction between the large number of people who had made a 'profession of faith' and been baptised over the years on the one hand, and the small number who at any one time were 'in fellowship', is an important one. I noted in chapter 4 the manager's statement in 1970 that approximately 150 people (then living) had been baptised over the years, that few had 'maintained a consistent testimony', and that an average of thirty to forty then attended meetings regularly. Twelve years later (in 1982), the overall number of people (then living) who had been baptised had increased to approximately 260, however the number 'in fellowship' remained at thirty to forty.[3] These numbers refer mostly to people aged over eighteen years, apart from a small number of younger teenagers who had been accepted as having sufficient 'understanding' and faith. Children are not baptised according to Brethren doctrine.

A similar distinction between kinds of pentecostal Christian Aboriginal converts has been made by Calley (1958), in his study of a community in northeast New South Wales during the late 1950s. He distinguishes (pp. 300–310) 'crisis' or 'contingent' converts from 'permanent' converts: the former most commonly experienced 'salvation' and began to participate in the pentecostal cult when they were ill, and 'hard core' cult members would attempt to cure them through prayer. In contrast, illness at Doomadgee was most commonly understood in terms of Blackfella law, and to the extent that non-medical cures were drawn upon, these were deliberately obtained in consultations with 'Blackfella doctors' rather than Christians. Nevertheless, illness or injury had marked the time of 'salvation' among several of those saved 'permanently' at Doomadgee (to borrow Calley's term). The senior long-term Aboriginal church elder explained, for example, that he had been 'saved' soon after an accident that resulted in his becoming blind. Calley points out that 'very few hard core members had been converted during illness' (p. 307), but also that some crisis converts continued to participate in the Christian cult long after their illness had passed (p. 306). His point that '[t]here is no definite dividing line between contingent and permanent converts' (p. 306) is relevant to Doomadgee in that many of those who have been actively 'in fellowship' for lengthy periods have eventually had a 'downfall'. Only a small number of Aboriginal residents at Doomadgee have thus been really 'permanent' in their active participation in the Christian Assembly.

Revivals such as that in 1953 (chapter 4) have occurred on a few occasions over the years, and they have involved much larger numbers of people being 'saved', baptised and then attending church meetings for a period. The most recent of these events was during late 1980. The following letter was published in the *Australian Missionary Tidings* newsletter (January 1981); it was written on 16th December 1980, at the height of the revival and published under the names of the manager and his wife. I quote a large section of the letter because of both its factual content and its representation of an important staff perspective at the time.

> There certainly has appeared to be barrenness, particularly among the teenagers, which has caused us concern. Only three weeks ago hardly a soul sat to hear the gospel message as it was told out on the basket-ball court in the village on a Sunday night.
>
> Our concern has been heard before the Lord, and we are full of joy as God's Holy Spirit has worked in the hearts of many, some making a profession of faith for the first time, some having made a profession in their childhood days and never gone on, and others wanting to be restored from lives of sin.
>
> It began through last week when . . . [two missionary staff] distributed Don Stanton's booklet *The Great World Holocaust*. Thursday, Friday and Saturday nights saw European and Aboriginal Christians counselling many — till about 1 a.m. Saturday. On Sunday night after the open-air meeting there were many more, and we are hearing of others who want to talk with someone but said they could not get near. It makes one think of those who wanted to see the Lord Jesus when He was on earth, and of those who let down their companion through the roof of the house.[4]
>
> Never before can we remember using every available seat for the Sunday morning meeting, but the people just flocked to the hall. Friday morning saw the village hall full for morning devotions, and so it was decided to hold this meeting in the larger main hall this week. Every morning the hall has been so nearly full that it has been decided to use the P.A. system so that the speaker can be heard above crying babies. On Sunday night at the open-air meeting, crowds sat round and listened.
>
> Our house-help, . . . who had never previously made a profession of faith and for whom we often had prayed, accepted the Lord on Saturday

> night, and her twin sisters and her brother, on Sunday night. So, with others of the family wanting to put things right, they are a united happy family. . . . our other house-help, and her husband, . . . were among the multitude who came on Sunday morning, and each morning since.
>
> Twenty-seven were baptized last Sunday, and yet more are requesting baptism — the most ever in one day since we have been here. Our hearts were full of praise to God, yet prayerful knowing that there will be many attacks of the evil one when the strength of the Lord will be needed to be drawn upon. Be with us in constant prayer that those who have turned to God, and those who have returned, will be steadfast in their Christain faith, growth and walk.

Another missionary suggested to me that 'about 200' people were attending Christian meetings regularly around this time. According to another, the large number of people came to a dozen or so meetings over the Christmas holiday period, but by March 1981 the 'revival' was finished (i.e. numbers had returned to normal). This person also stated that what had started the 'chain reaction' remained unexplained.

The booklet referred to in the letter above,[5] warns in graphic fashion of the 'great tribulation' (referred to in the Bible [Mathew 24:3]) about to descend on people everywhere. The 'Coming Holocaust' would be directed by a satanic figure known as the 'Antichrist', and would involve horrific suffering and death for those who had not been 'born again'. At one point, the author suggests that the great tribulation may well begin in 1982. Thus, no doubt fear of such a holocaust played a considerable part in so many people seeking salvation for a short time, through baptism and attendance at Christian meetings.

From my discussions with the senior Aboriginal church elder about those who were baptised and attending Christian meetings (see note 3 above), the following facts emerge. Firstly, of the 164 baptised people among those discussed, ninety-six (59%) were female; more significantly, of the sixty-seven people he said were attending Christian meetings regularly or irregularly, forty-five (67%) were female. Apparently no people under thirty-one years of age attended church meetings regularly, though some were said by the senior Aboriginal church elder to attend irregularly.

The Christian routine

A pervasive routine of Christian meetings operated. Note the 'events of the week' as listed in a typical Assembly newsletter (21 September, 1980):

Sunday: 8.30 a.m. Sunday School in the Village Hall

10.00 a.m.	Morning Worship Meeting, followed by Bible Study Time for men.
7.30 p.m.	Prayer Meeting in Village Hall and then Open Air Meeting.
Monday: 7.45 a.m.	Women's Meeting Youth Centre — boys.
Tuesday: 2.30 p.m.	Mini Rally, in the Meeting Hall . . . [for children].
7.45 p.m.	Prayer Meeting and Bible Study, Speaker: Mr. . . . [the manager, though speakers rotated week to week].
Wednesday: 7.30 p.m.	Boys' Rallies [involving different school grades having games, outdoor skills and Bible talk, under the supervision of members of the male missionary staff].
Thursday: Youth Centre -– girls.	
3.30 p.m.	Good News Club . . . in the Village Hall — for interested young Christians and their friends.

Morning Prayers — every day 7.35 a.m., leader: . . . [this job also rotated week to week among the male missionary staff].

While Christian Aborigines and missionary staff formed the majority of adults attending these meetings, many unbaptised children and teenagers would go to the 'rallies'.

The newsletter also lists 'prayer points', thoughts centred on scripture passages for 'quiet times' during the week, and provides general news of the Assembly's affairs (e.g. the distribution of Assembly money to some missionaries in other places is noted). Much additional Christian literature from the White domain circulated among Aboriginal residents: 'Do-it-yourself Bible Study' lesson booklets prepared by the United Aborigines Mission and other similar organisations; 'Home Bible Study' leaflets prepared by local missionary staff, which typically pose questions that the reader answers by referring to biblical passages; and various fundamentalist Christian magazines.[6]

The two largest gatherings of people occurred on Sundays, at the morning worship meeting and the open air meeting in the evening. The morning meeting was held in the church hall (the old girls' dormitory) in the White domain (until the construction of the new church in 1983). Between twenty to forty Aborigines and a minimum of thirty Whites usually attended. The meeting would proceed by interspersing hymn singing with individual men standing and praying out loud while others listened silently. Only White men stood and prayed in this way at the meetings I attended.[7] The manager would typically preach for some time, before those present (except for the few like myself who were not baptised 'believers') would partake of 'bread' (considered to be Christ's body) and 'wine' (which was in fact cordial, considered to be Christ's blood). Before the meeting's conclusion, the manager would make any necessary announcements, including the naming of any individuals who had recently been sinful (e.g. had been 'overcome by drink'), and who were thus being prayed for and 'grieved for'. Any persons being re-admitted to 'fellowship' would also be named.

The open air evening meetings were held in the village, usually under a streetlight, at different locations each week. A mission truck would bring seats to the site; but most Aborigines preferred to sit on the ground. Although the use of a microphone and loudspeaker, as well as a piano accordion and guitar, meant that quite a large number could overhear the proceedings, fewer people actually attended the open air meeting than the Sunday morning meetings. Approximately ten to fifteen Aboriginal people were usually present at these meetings, although the number has varied from five up to twenty-five. The number of Whites was usually fifteen to twenty. The procedure again was hymn singing interspersed with individual men standing at the microphone to preach. It was more common for individual Aboriginal Christians to preach (and occasionally sing) at the open air meetings than at the morning meetings in the White domain. Many residents ignored the open air meetings despite their intrusive style.

The content of the open air meetings was similar to that of other such gatherings, though speakers were more aggressive in 'blasting' their message at the Aboriginal public. The following is taken from an open air meeting in 1978; the speaker was a White Brethren man from a southern state who was visiting Doomadgee at the time:

> You know this evening . . . there is a need to take refuge from the coming storm of judgement that God is going to bring upon the world of the ungodly, who know not God and who obey not the Gospel of our Lord Jesus Christ . . . [etc.]. (T11)

Although the local missionary staff usually preached in language more readily comprehensible for most Aboriginal residents, their message was similar to this passage in being always aggressively didactic and paternalistic in its warnings about the consequences of not embracing a commitment to Christian Brethren belief.

Funerals were an integral part of Christian procedure at the settlement, and a setting in which the inevitability of death and the clear choice of heaven as against horrific hell after death were put forcefully to mourners by those preaching. No alternative to a Christian funeral has ever existed at Doomadgee, although certain other traditional practices have also been carried on within the Blackfella domain. While many people not 'in fellowship' at the time of a funeral simply attended the church meeting as 'unbelievers' before proceeding to the cemetery for the burial, others committed to Blackfella law waited outside the church and then participated more actively in the mourning process at the cemetery. Some who faced the crisis of a close relative's death subsequently re-entered the Assembly and attended Christian meetings for a period, and this was seen by others as perfectly understandable (e.g. 'he got to go to meeting, he lost his wife'). However, more often than not, such a person would not continue to 'live a Christian life' after the crisis of the relative's death subsided.

Tension between Christians and others

The view among many village residents 'in fellowship' has been that becoming a Christian necessitates rejecting Blackfella law. This view was put to me quite consistently by the most senior of the Aboriginal church elders. Consider, for example, his rejection of male initiation: after agreeing with me that Jesus was himself circumcised, he went on to talk of the unacceptable way that circumcision had developed in Blackfella law:

> But since our people took it over, Aborigines, they've added things to it that wasn't suitable and it wasn't . . . right in God's law, . . . made it very hard even death come into it. This squaring up too . . . they have to give . . . whatever young fella was circumcised his family have to give over to the man who done it [i.e. to the 'doctor' who performed the operation], to their family . . . Otherwise [if] they didn't do squaring up, there would have been death . . . It sort of got out of hand, . . . that put fear into the circumcision, . . . fear of death. (T57)

As mentioned briefly in chapter 1, in 1978 a group of Christian Aboriginal councillors (who formed the majority of the council at that time) directed the organisers of an initiation ceremony not to conduct the ceremony anywhere on the Doomadgee reserve. Two of these councillors[8] went so far as to assert to me that Ganggalida people (their own 'tribe', as they put it at the time) had never had male circumcision as part of their 'law', though it is doubtful whether they put this assertion directly to the old Blackfella law experts. They pointed out that their own fathers, like themselves, had not been initiated in this way (nor in any other way). Three of these Christian councillors argued that I was encouraging people to perform the ceremony, and that most of the Aboriginal residents 'don't want it'.

They said the ceremony was based on fear, and that people were coerced into participating, and also that if the ceremony were to be held at a good waterhole, people would subsequently be precluded from fishing and hunting there because it would have achieved ritual importance. This latter concern indicated that they did not regard the ceremony as unimportant or to be scoffed at in any way; if anything, they regarded it as dangerous in some spiritual sense. One of these men was particularly upset because, the night before, he had driven down to the back of the village where *bandari* (rehearsal of the dancing and singing to be performed at the initiation) was being held. He had come without realising the nature of the proceedings, thinking they simply involved secular matters. What made the situation very bad from his viewpoint was that he had his wife (and daughters) with him in the car. After the car stopped, he and his wife sat there watching for several minutes before one of the junior 'law' men told him that women should not be there. He immediately left with his wife, and both of them were very upset about the unintentional transgression. The very next morning this man met with the other councillors and the manager, before the three councillors came to my camp to tell me that they had made it known that the ceremony (or even such rehearsal as had occurred the previous night) could not go ahead on the Doomadgee reserve.

The Christian Aborigines opposing the initiation ceremony also claimed that it would not be carried out properly, because the novices would not adhere to the relevant restrictions on their behaviour for the required period after the ceremony. Some referred to several initiation ceremonies that had been held in recent years on Mornington Island, and pointed out how the novices there 'were breaking the law' by engaging in unrestricted social interaction (and even getting drunk) too soon after the ritual had finished. Indeed, certain Christian Aborigines opposed what they glossed as 'Blackfella law' *in toto*, on the grounds that this law was 'too strict' in requiring immediate death as punishment for transgressions. This kind of punishment was held to be totally impracticable in contemporary times:

> Some of them saying: 'Let the old Aboriginal law come back again. Let them have their own law', . . . and if they going to have their law they going to be pretty sick. You can't hang'em in Australia now but that means that if they break Aboriginal law, they'll be speared to death. (T57)

Their stated view was thus that Blackfella law was 'too heavy' — 'it can't be made any lighter' (T57) — a view that certainly takes Blackfella law seriously, while yet rejecting it.[9] The Aboriginal Christians appear to have intellectually embraced the missionary characterisation of the 'old beliefs' in their emphasis on the uncompromising physical punishment of transgressions. Aboriginal Christians' knowledge of actual practices within Blackfella law during earlier times was by no means always accurate, as the denial of male circumcision indicates.[10]

From the viewpoint of the 'law' experts, the younger councillors simply did not 'know law'. Some resistance against the ban on the initiation ceremony was mooted. For example, the assertion was made that if the ceremony were banned the old experts would be more strict about stopping people from visiting a certain good fishing place, potentially dangerous because of the dreamings there. However, everyone knew that the only thing that had temporarily stopped people visiting this site over the years (at least since the early 1970s when residents began obtaining motor vehicles and could thus get there quickly) was the fact that some people had become sick after a visit there. The old people also knew that the councillors had the manager's authority behind them, indeed some said that the councillors were just enforcing the manager's opposition to the ceremony. The result was that the ceremony was not held, and many people continued to complain that the council and the manager (along with other missionaries) should not be able to stop Blackfella law.

It was not until some residents came to realise that they were going to be able to claim their own 'country' under the *Aboriginal Land Rights (N.T.) Act* that they held an initiation ceremony in 1982 at the site of the main outstation (Najabarra), on the Nicholson River land claim area. The ceremony was held immediately following the land claim hearing, and was regarded as part of the demonstration of 'law' knowledge to a White judge. This was the first initiation ceremony to be held predominantly by Doomadgee people (though with substantial assistance from Borroloola ritual experts) since the early 1950s. In successfully applying to a commonwealth government body for some financial assistance for provisions and travel of people from Borroloola and Doomadgee to the site, a senior organiser referred to the opposition to such ceremonies at Doomadgee over the years:

> Well we been havim plenty young boy there la Doomadgee, we wanna put'em longa smoke y'know,[11] la Doomadgee, and people there wouldn't [al]'low — Councillor wouldn't [al]'low run that place there. Turn Off Lagoon before, we been havim [initiation ceremony] place, they [Doomadgee administration] wouldn't [al]'low that place [in recent times], and while we here la Najabarra I want to putim all the boy la this place la Najabarra. Too much this'un our country now.[12]

On many other occasions a section of the older people similarly vigorously discussed how Blackfella law (sometimes termed 'culture') had to be maintained:

> See this culture now we want to talk up see, White man can't stop the Blackfella culture; see White man got his way, never mind about this missionary, God made everything, create everything for the Aboriginal too see, that been start early days. We gotta keep on our great-grandfather culture see. (T8)

A further example of such discourse is the following conversation, between myself and several men, on initiation ceremonies:

> Speaker 1 They don't [al]'low it here . . .
>
> Speaker 2 Yeh missionary don't [al]'low . . .
>
> Speaker 1 Missionary don't [al]'low. They [some male novices] go away to Borroloola and Mornington Island, you know, get fixed up [initiated] but not in this mission. They [the missionaries] don't [al]'low.
>
> Speaker 3 Can do it here if Aboriginal fight strong for their culture.
>
> Speaker 1 They never ever, they very weak . . .
>
> DT This missionary here, what happen if this mob [referring to Aboriginal residents] got together [and] they said: 'Oh well, we're gonna do it our way'?
>
> Speaker 2 Oh they can, but council gotta say [agree], big mob [of those desirous of holding ceremonies] here, and I don't know, they won't try it you know.
>
> DT Council won't try it?
>
> Speaker 2 Won't try it, even the [Aboriginal] police, won't try it, all this native police . . . they can talk up you know . . .
>
> Speaker 3 Even the . . . see they're [police and councillors] trying to stop the culture too, you know.
>
> DT Why they trying to stop it?
>
> Speaker 3 Well I just don't know . . .
>
> Speaker 2 I can't go over there to Brisbane or to Cloncurry and stop White man not to dance. I can't do that, that's his dance, I can't . . .
>
> Speaker 3 Like we still said, that's our culture, that's our great-grandfather culture, we can't go without it.

Speaker 2 Long way back that's the way it's been. You can't stop White man dance, that's his, he gotta dance everywhere [wherever he likes]. (T7)

The implication of the last statement is that Whites should therefore not be able to stop Aboriginal dancing and associated ceremonial activities. A similar complaint referred specifically to missionary opposition to initiation ceremonies:

> But now I gotta ask you [D. Trigger] another question: Why the government b'long to Queensland they don't [al]'low people to make a young man longa Queensland — like a [in the] Territory? This law b'long to Aborigine he b'long to our father after this place land been drainin[g] away see,[13] and alright this law he b'long to here, because they only White man they come from Egypt, England, somewhere. (T16)

These old people would on occasions state that most young people were 'lost' (i.e. no longer interested in, nor properly controlled by, Blackfella law). Some appeared resigned to this fact, although they would complain vociferously about it at times, particularly when young men or boys committed crimes. The following comment was made after an alleged attack by a young Aboriginal man on a White nurse:

> This country got no [Blackfella] law. Young boy cross-breed, marry wrong, that's why they get loose, they lost — still *juga* [uninitiated] this country [as compared with across the border in the Northern Territory where ceremonial life had continued].

Others felt it important to leave their knowledge behind after their death, even though they suggested that many young people were uninterested in learning about it. In the words of one old man: 'that word where they [old people when he was younger] been tell me, I can't go turnim off, I gotta leavim la paper'. He saw both my research and the school culture program as a means of doing that.

The disagreement between those in Christian fellowship and those committed to Blackfella law surfaced quite graphically on some other occasions. In late 1978, during something of a revival of traditional secular dancing,[14] the group that had been holding dances in the evenings found that their venue one night would be adjacent to the men's Bible study group meeting in the village hall. Some village residents felt strongly that the latter meeting should not be disturbed by the loud singing from the dancing site, and many of the dancers and singers were extremely apprehensive about how the Christians (both Aboriginal and White) would 'take it'. After considerable prevarication, the main 'boss' for the dancing eventually held out against the pressure for him to move his group to 'bottom camp' at the back of the village (a move which incidentally would have meant leaving the well-lit area which promised to accentuate his personal singing prowess and controlling role). However, he agreed to delay the singing and dancing until the Bible study meeting had finished. The clash of the two events focused the public gaze on the tension between Christian practices and those associated with Blackfella law.

During the same period, a heated verbal exchange took place between a Christian man and two senior women who were preparing a group of girls for a dance. The man directed his two daughters to leave the group, as he would not allow them to participate in such affairs. This man was also discussed on several occasions as having informed certain senior missionaries that various rituals associated with the deaths of Aboriginal residents were about to be (or had already been) performed. He was said to oppose both the smoking out of the dwelling and belongings of recently deceased persons and square-up rituals involving the exchange of items among members of the deceased's family. He apparently sought missionary support in having such activities stopped.

Two further verbal exchanges reflect similar tensions. The first concerned two councillors talking of how best to deal with some young men who had recently come to Doomadgee from a station community in the Northern Territory, and had been causing trouble. One councillor pointed out that he had been informed by a local authoritative 'law' man that the young men had 'run away' from a forthcoming major cult ceremony, and that he therefore favoured directing the young men to go and talk to the 'law' man who would chastise them and send them back westwards. However the second councillor, who was a church elder, stated quite vehemently that he was not concerned with matters of Blackfella law but rather with the transgressions against 'Whiteman law' that had been perpetrated by the young men. The first speaker then moved off aggressively, saying: 'yeh but I'm listening to a lot of other word too', meaning that he regarded the requirements of Blackfella law as at least as important as those of White Australian law.

The second conversation began as something of a joking exchange, but finished with the two participants obviously very serious about what they were saying. The exchange took place near the 'old people's ground' where a number of 'law' experts were gathered; however, the first speaker was a committed Christian:

Speaker 1	I only want God's law — no other law.
Speaker 2	That's the White man law.

Speaker 1	That law *you* talking about, that's Devil business.
Speaker 2	Devil business brought you into the world! I'll have more to say to others [who oppose Blackfella law] directly [i.e. soon] too!

Speaker 2 was a man strongly committed to maintenance of Blackfella law. He was, for example, one among a number of senior men who innovatively composed new songs in Aboriginal languages, and was a major organiser of the 1982 initiation ceremony at the outstation to the west.

Non-Christians were often quick to accuse avowedly Christian Aborigines of hypocrisy when the two categories of people became embroiled in major disputes. Consider the accusation by a non-Christian woman against her Christian opponents during one conflict: 'You all Christian, you tell liar [lies] yet you all go to church!'. On another occasion, a woman was loudly lamenting the general state of affairs at Doomadgee, after her daughter had been involved in a fight. She addressed the following comment to the general listening public, but it was directed particularly at the Christian family with whom her daughter had been in conflict: 'I don't go to [Christian] meeting, like those people with double mind'. The non-Christian accusation has thus been that Christian Aborigines do not themselves live according to the behavioural standards that they preach. Several people made the point to me on different occasions that they were not Christians yet they were 'better behaved' than most of those who were. Of course, tension also arose when Christian Aborigines held strongly to their professed ideals. A woman returned home one evening soon after leaving for the 'gambling school' and explained the reason why: '[a recent convert] been baulking them — [be]cause he preacher man now, they waiting for him to go away [before commencing gambling activities]'.

Thus, the two perspectives on this question of appropriate world-view and religious life were widely divergent. However, the issue of syncretism between the two traditions must also be considered, since there is considerable evidence that Aboriginal residents have in fact not generally kept Christian doctrine and Blackfella law intellectually separate in any rigid fashion.

Christian doctrine and Blackfella law

A number of people known to be experts in matters of Blackfella law have been baptised over the years, and at least one was baptised and attended church fairly regularly during the research period. Similarly, 'square-up' rituals were held following the deaths of several avowedly Christian Aboriginal people, including the senior Aboriginal church elder who had consistently maintained that the two 'laws' could not be 'mixed up'. Furthermore, the use of Aboriginal languages for Christian preaching has not been perceived as inappropriate. Although such use of Aboriginal languages was said to have been carried out regularly only in the past, some people could relate several prayers in their language. For instance, in Garawa:

Wuluginya	*nyulu*	*junggu*	*ginggari*	*yarrayjba*
Father	he	sits	up	waiting

barrawuyadayjba	*ginggari*	*juju*	heaven
house made	up	long way	heaven

(God the father is a long way up in heaven waiting with a home prepared [for us]). (T7)

The Aboriginal people who in 1982 visited two Northern Territory settlements to observe Aboriginal leadership strongly approved of the use of Aboriginal languages there for such Christian discourse as hymn-singing.[15]

Even those Christian Aboriginal people who would state, when asked, that the two laws were mutually incompatible, sometimes indicated in unelicited discourse a mixing of concepts from Christianity and Blackfella law. For example, one such woman mentioned to me shortly before I was to leave with a group of people for coastal Ganggalida country, that it was all right for us to go there: 'as long as people don't swear in that country — it's holy country'. She meant that it was 'holy' because of the dangers from the extra-human being known as *Gurdidawa*, a dangerous and elusive totemic figure of short stature known to be ever-present in the area we were to visit and ever-ready to cause hardship to people, particularly strangers, if they engaged in inappropriate behaviour such as swearing. Another couple explained that church elders were the same as the old experts in Aboriginal law matters, in that both carried important 'law'.

Any adequate assessment of syncretism between Christianity and Blackfella law requires a detailed consideration of relevant aspects of Aboriginal intellectual life. Beliefs concerning sorcery and death are two dimensions of Aboriginal worldview that indicate a mixing of Christian doctrine with traditional concepts. For example, with reference to sorcery, the couple who commented on the important role of 'law'-carriers in both intellectual traditions also discussed how both 'laws' entailed a strong belief in 'spirits'. The man stated that there would not be one Aboriginal resident at Doomadgee who did not believe in 'Blackfella witchcraft', and indeed such belief was widespread among avowed Christians as well as others. I will not list here the many sorcery techniques known to be available within Blackfella law for both offensive and defensive use. It will suffice to say that most Aboriginal deaths were attributed to sorcery, although definite culprits were rarely designated. The reasons people may have had to desire to harm the deceased, or one of his or her close kin, were commonly discussed. As well, several 'Blackfella doctors' were consulted regularly for a wide range of ailments. Discourse and beliefs concerning sorcery and healing by 'Blackfella doctors' were usually completely insulated from the White domain, although there may have been rare occasions when Christian Aborigines discussed with White church elders some personal fear related to sorcery.

My point here is that Aboriginal belief in sorcery had its counterpart within Christian doctrine — namely the Brethren stress on the Devil as the ever-present agency that causes all evil in the world. The missionaries' constant references to the way the Devil works in devious ways to generate the downfall of Christians were related easily by Aboriginal people to the evil spiritual forces believed to operate according to Blackfella law. The fit is by no means a complete one: Blackfella law stresses mostly sickness and death as the result of evil sorcerers, whereas Christianity stresses mostly sinfulness and a subsequent horrific time after death as the result of the 'work of the Devil'.

Nevertheless, I believe that one Aboriginal Christian's comment on this matter is broadly correct. I was discussing with him his belief in an evil force in the world known as the Antichrist (some fundamentalist Christians apparently believe that the Antichrist is a force of the Devil, and seeks to develop evil influence over people everywhere; see Stanton 1980: 3–8). At the time of our conversation, belief in the devious activities of the Antichrist had been fuelled via the repetitive screening of a hired video cassette film entitled *The Final Conflict*, which develops a fictional plot about the activities of these evil forces. The film was apparently interpreted as a factual documentary account by many Aboriginal viewers. My informant mentioned widespread receptiveness among Aboriginal residents towards the idea of the existence of these forces. He recounted two examples of people believing that the numbers '666' were evidence of the Antichrist's evil activity,[16] neither of which I attempted to substantiate. The first involved a man 'sending back' a cheque he had received because it was made out for $666, and he therefore 'couldn't get it changed [i.e. cashed]'. The second was of a man who removed an insignia showing the number 666 from the outside of a car he had just bought in Mt Isa. But the comment that I wish to focus on particularly here is this man's statement that for him to believe in the Antichrist really amounted to believing in 'Whitefella witchcraft', and that this was 'easy' for him because he believed in 'Blackfella witchcraft' (i.e. sorcery). He saw the conception of evil forces in the world within both traditions as quite parallel.

Contemporary beliefs concerning death and its aftermath illustrate further the mixing of elements of Christian doctrine and Blackfella law. According to traditional beliefs,[17] the spirit leaves the body after death and proceeds to a particular site in coastal Ganggalida country. Songs once sung in a ceremony following the death are said to guide the spirit in its journey, as well as provide the musical accompaniment for certain dancing engaged in by the 'new spirit' together with other spirit-figures at various points along the route. This coastal site was apparently believed to be the initial destination of disembodied spirits from across a broad area, including at least the Ganggalida and Garawa linguistic territories. When the body was placed on a triangular platform soon after death, the head would always be faced towards this coastal site. It has also been said that at dusk one can sometimes see clouds of dust in the direction of the site, and that this results from new spirits being shown new dances there, the dust rising from the stomping feet of the dancers.

After climbing a particular tree and looking northwards (the direction in which it has to go), the spirit proceeds a short distance to a place nearer the beach; here it has a wash at a 'well', climbs a tree and then goes down to the beach. The spirit then encounters an 'old man' with a long *murrugu* (spearthrower), who is a 'sort of a gate'; this figure is said in some accounts to be a kind of bird, often a crow. Various informants then depict the 'old man' dividing new spirits between two places: one to the east with 'good water' to drink, and one to the north where the only available water is polluted. In some versions this division is done on the basis of gender, while others suggest that it depends on whether the deceased person was *nyilanyila* (or *ngabinyi*), i.e. a person whose front tooth (or teeth) had been ritually knocked out at an earlier stage of their life. Those with the tooth missing are able to proceed east to the place of 'good water'. Further variations on these accounts include the fact that the 'old man' Crow attempts to hurt the new spirit by poking it with a long, sharp or burning stick, but is 'blocked' by Hawk (or sometimes Pelican) who thus protects the spirit. Some have said that Crow does this in retribution for the disdainful attitude taken towards it by humans.

Certain individuals told me that Aboriginal people recognised the missionaries' account of what happens after death as the 'same story' as that entailed in traditional religious beliefs:

Our mob been talk about that story, bla this country, we been knew then when missionary been read that Bible for us, we been know then; that story, old story when dark people been used to talk about it, . . . same one . . . that same story now. (T80)

Thus, elements of Christian doctrine have been added to the account outlined so far. At the site on the beach, 'good people' were said to be separated from 'bad people', the former going 'up' to heaven and the latter being 'pushed down' to hell. Apart from some variation in designating where these two places are, there has been a strong association of heaven with the place of 'good water' and hell with the place of 'dirty water'. By some accounts, the separation of 'good people' from 'bad people' occurs via the agency of God or Jesus:

Jesus tell him to go up — 'you clean man you can come', and 'I don't want that [bad, dirty] man' — he pushim down: 'You go down na [to] hell'. (T80)

God or Jesus thus asks the new spirit if he is a 'good man' or a 'bad man'. The 'good man' is wanted: 'They havim that one, they no more [do not] pushim away':

He *wanjija walmuwa* [climb up]. That's the way those missionary, you know, was preaching about Jesus now, Jesus and God, one time well they [old-time Aborigines] been used to tell that part now before missionary been come along. (T80)

Other versions indicate that the 'old man' at the beach site is in fact Satan:

This *Wanggula* [Crow], that's the Satan . . . this Crow here, that's the Satan blanta Blackfella, you know spirit? You readim la Bible ind'it? Spirit, Satan, he wait [at the beach site] got a sharp stick, this Crow. (T69)

Aboriginal belief has thus come to incorporate elements of Christian doctrine concerning death and its aftermath into the traditional worldview. In fact, these 'traditional' beliefs about alternate places of good and bad water may well themselves have been influenced by Christianity. The significant point here is that Aboriginal people have not found it necessary to oppose Christian doctrine *in toto*, in order to maintain some continuity in those dimensions of Blackfella law that deal with this subject. As a further illustration of this point, we have the Aboriginal account of why animate things must die at all. A Garawa myth relates how Moon Dreaming gave humans the chance to 'die' and then return 'alive', in a parallel fashion to the way the moon waxes and wanes each month. In the myth this opportunity was lost and that explains why all living things must die 'for good'. Many Aboriginal people do not appear to have regarded the myth as necessarily inconsistent with the general Christian assertion that, like all else, death is due to the Lord's will.

Apart from these beliefs about sorcery and death, wide-ranging comments from people not in (nor seeking to be in) fellowship also indicated a routine attitude of toleration and in some cases acceptance of a number of Christian concepts and practices. Moreover, these people were often simultaneously quite committed to some of the precepts of Blackfella law. A 'law' man spoke of an old lady just after she had died, and appeared to accept without qualification the usefulness of the deceased's apparent Christian beliefs:

> She knew she was going to lose'im misal [die]; me'n old lady [his wife] went over 'nother day told her not to be frightened — [and that she would] meet all the other Christian people [when she dies].

One old woman, very knowledgeable about Blackfella law matters, attended a brief *ad hoc* prayer meeting at a village house, organised by several White missionary women. In response to my asking her why she had participated when she had not maintained any fellowship in the Assembly (at least not during the past few years), she replied simply that: 'they read Bible for us'. This perhaps indicated her sense of the occasion as one where the missionary women expressed affection for the Aboriginal women participants; and her following remark certainly indicated some annoyance with my suggestion that her attendance was inconsistent with her more general lack of participation in the affairs of the Assembly: 'don't ask too many question, boy [i.e. son]!'.

A further example is of a middle-aged man who was clearly knowledgeable about, and a believer in, dimensions of Blackfella law; he explained many details of ceremonial life to me over the years. While this man was often drunk, he nevertheless claimed to 'believe in God'. He explained on one occasion: 'God is only the one person today, because country would of been lonely'; and I interpret this sentiment as in part an association between what he perceives as the spirituality of God and the spirituality of the totemic landscape.

Finally, I present below a lengthy quotation from a man who at times argued quite avidly in support of Blackfella law. Yet he also pointed out that his beliefs partly derived from Christian doctrine:

> From the beginning, like after the creation . . . when the moon and star and dirt and night and everything been all together — I got the paper down there with me and I'll show you, I got tape too you can play it, see

> it [reference to Christian doctrine in written form and on tape, circulated by the missionaries] . . .
>
> [D. Trigger]: Where this come from? [Is] this missionary way?
>
> Yeh missionary way now, and the creation, the starting of the business when father, like the God and son you know Lord Jesus was in heaven, before we. All right, and then we come then. The other lot of people before us first been come, and then oh they been too bad, all right he been punish'em . . . and they in heaven now. Then he been try 'nother lot of people now, all this country been under water, see saltwater, you go up the hill anywhere now you see all the sea shell . . . out on the side of the hill anywhere, butt of the Bloodwood tree or anywhere at all you know.[18] Well we call'im lang this country, . . . *Wuluginya* [Father], like God the Father. (T7)

And again, referring to an area in Ganggalida country:

> Out in the bush here, he just like Father in heaven. You'n me go out there and we might be curse [swear] something, we get lost, [then] you can't see anyone track or you can't hear no-one sing out . . . When you go out there, you gotta be just like in the mission [White domain at Doomadgee], like you gotta [be]'have yourself, you can't swear, you can't row with dog anything like that, just like mssion out here in the scrub yeh them *Gurdidawa* ['short people'] they make you get lost. (T7)

After explaining in some detail the 'old' beliefs about death and its aftermath:

> That's one time ago before missionary discovered the country like. [D Trigger: What happen now this missionary came here?] Oh well they [Aborigines] followed the . . . trust one Lord because — like the idea what was going on in this country, and they want give that ['old' beliefs] away, because Lord went to the cross and he died for you and me and God the Father himself and even the Lord [Jesus] they created this world in the beginning like for us to live in and therefore we must go one way, to get there sort of thing. [D. Trigger: Where you can get to now then, if you die?] Well I think I'm believe in the Lord, I think I'll be with the Lord, I'm a Christian man and I been baptised long time over ten years . . . I don't think I'll go to . . . [place of 'good water'], I'll go *ginggari* [up, i.e. to heaven]. (T7)

It is clear that adequate assessment of the operation of Christianity as a body of beliefs and practices cannot deal solely with the small number of people in fellowship in the Assembly at any one time. The incorporation into Aboriginal consciousness of aspects of Christian doctrine has proceeed throughout a much broader number of village residents. Of particular significance in the pattern of Aboriginal/White power relations has been the quite pervasive integration of Christianity into aspects of settlement administrative life.

Christianity in the administrative process

From the earlier discussion of the historical role of Christianity in the administrative process (chapter 4), it is clear that the White-controlled administration has routinely avowed a Christian basis in seeking to legitimate its operation. In chapters 7 and 8, we have seen that at least some Aboriginal people appear to have not perceived any realistic possibility of a non-Christian administration. One quotation from a man who was council chairman for several years illustrates this point excellently. He was quoted before, when speaking at a public meeting, as forcefully distinguishing Doomadgee residents from those non-reserve Aboriginal people who in his terms had never been 'under the Act'. When expressing a similar opinion to me on another occasion, he referred to the antagonism commonly shown towards the Doomadgee missionaries (and Christianity generally) by many non-reserve Blackfellas (though more usually in his terms, Yellafellas). He reported his response to a group of these people in Mt Isa on one occasion: 'You rubbish the church and the missionary. I got my civilisation from church! You got your civilisation from *Mandagi* [Whitefella]!'. His point was that as a Doomadgee resident he came to learn what he knew of White society from a specifically Christian administration which has historically been the constant mediator of the relationship with White society for Aboriginal residents of Doomadgee. This man's criticism of the non-reserve Aborigines, who in his view had benefited from a broader range of contact with White society, was that they did not seem to understand the essential protective and instructive role of the missionaries in the remote institutionalised reserve setting.

In chapter 7, I described considerable opposition to missionary control. However, comments like those of the chairman constitute expression of approval for certain protectionist elements entailed within this pattern of control, and this is fused with approval for the evangelical tutelage of the missionaries. I also presented in chapter 8 this man's publicly stated opposition to (predominantly young) unmarried couples living together in sexual relationships. We saw that his 'responsibility', stemming from his secular administrative position as chairman, was experienced as fused with his 'responsibility' as a Christian 'in fellowship'. On that occasion he went on to express his (and the council's) opposition to this behaviour in terms of local understandings of Christian doctrine:

> When God been make Adam first, he looked down and he said like this: 'Oh well, I got to make a mate for you Adam'. And he took a rib out of Adam, one side you know one rib, so that Eve can be 'longside of Adam, be the right person for Adam. And today married life is a vow on the Bible. I take my wife as so-and-so as my beloved wife, and it's all upon

> the Bible, and it's a respect and it's shown before God. If the Lord Jesus had to call a trumpet tonight and those of you who are living like this now, I don't know how you're gonna stand before God's judgement. I don't want to speak or preach out here tonight, I want to bring some effect. It's going through me day by day and how to go about it by law. And only one law I can use tonight that is God law, God law, not the law of the land, not the law of anything else, not even Aboriginals' law . . . the law that God has made — man and woman. Those of you who are prepared tomorrow, like properly man and properly woman, show yourself out, nothing'll stop you tomorrow to coming up there [to the office in the White domain] signing a paper saying look I want to sign a paper for marriage. You realise again tonight, you gonna be in sin. When the Lord gonna come, all the Christian people . . . been married [are] gonna go to heaven, and you behind here — don't look about marriage then it'll be all over. Tribulations, tribulations, big tribulations, that word's a big word that tribulations, mean all sorts of . . . torment, all sorts of violence, not the little thing today that we see, they're only small, compared to that day to come. (T71)

It is true that in normal social interactions the chairman was much less effusive in his admonition of non-Christians and their sinful behaviour. His speeches at public meetings at times appeared deliberately tailored to fit the White manager's expectation of an appropriate (and therefore necessarily demonstrably Christian) leader. As I have already made clear, the manager was usually present at such meetings. Having noted this qualification, I can further state that I elicited similar opinions from the chairman in conversations where the manager was not present.

That was also the case with the senior Aboriginal church elder's statements (quoted in chapter 7) concerning the biblical basis for Black people necessarily 'coming under' White people in the administrative process. Those statements were made early in 1978. Some three and a half years later I discussed the same issue with him, and (as is clear in the excerpt presented below) his views had not changed substantially. The church elder first explained how, in contrast to the appropriate behaviour of his two brothers, one of Noah's sons had seen his father's 'shame' by looking at him directly when he was drunk and naked. The other two sons walked backwards into Noah's tent and covered him with a sheet. The difference between the account given in late 1980 and the one quoted in chapter 7 is that on the earlier occasion the cursed son was Ham and on the later occasion he was said to be Japheth. The fundamentalist interpretation in fact concerns the curse on Ham as the ancestor of dark-skinned peoples (see Buckland 1929: 189; Pettingill 1971: 338–9), but the speaker's error on the occasion of our discussion is irrelevant to the substance of his beliefs on this issue.

D. Trigger	How that coming about now today, you still see that part there, or what? It's a very hard thing.
Respondent	It's a hard thing. You can't believe it now [i.e. you can't understand how it could have happened], it's puzzling a mind to know a man, a White man [i.e. Noah] to have three different coloured sons. Shem was a White man; Ham was a half-caste man, he was in between that's where the Chinese and the Yellow man comes from; . . . and Japheth was the Black man. So there's three colour people in the world today.
D. Trigger	And that Japheth, all his descendants must be under?
Respondent	Yeh. God says: 'now from now on Japheth because you saw your father's shame you gotta come under'.
D. Trigger	Now, it's really say that . . .?
Respondent	Yeh, it says it right there in Genesis . . .
D. Trigger	It's a very hard thing you know, because lot of Christian people will say that that passage doesn't really mean that too you know. You know what I mean because they don't like to think of Black people being under White people anything like that.
Respondent	But it really happen ind'it [didn't it]? They can't deny . . .
D. Trigger	Well when I seen that passage there, . . . but I never seen that word 'black' or 'white' . . .
Respondent	No not 'black', I think it's 'dark' . . .
D. Trigger	See, who believe that round here . . .?
Respondent	Oh all who read it, I know I've read that and I just can't place on it just now [i.e. give the precise biblical reference] . . . but I know.

D. Trigger	I know I talked to old . . . [a man once but no longer at Doomadgee as a missionary, who was manager for a period] one time. I think he believe that way . . .
Respondent	Yeh.
D. Trigger	But where it lead him in his practical life, working with Aboriginal people . . . if he gonna think Black people gotta be under . . .?
Respondent	Well, that's where they got it from [i.e. such missionaries got the idea from the biblical passage], and it been happening all over the world, all over Australia.
D. Trigger	You think they still got it here, like the White Christian people, you think they're still believing that way?
Respondent	No, they're coming in to the point now where, they believe that . . . the Black should be up now equal, working together with the White. Now there's a good illustration in a piano accordion. You can make good music just playing the white buttons . . ., you can make good music just playing the black buttons . . . sweet music. But, if you play the black and the white together, that sort of harmonise it, that's more better, black and white together make the better harmony of all . . . They starting to that point now where Black can come into better harmony with the White. I don't know whether these fellas [Doomadgee missionaries] thinking that, but I know everywhere else, I've spoken to a lot of Whitefellas. (T75)

Note the emic notion here that Noah was White. I did not directly question Christian Aborigines about whether in their view God and Jesus were also White, however I would expect their perspective to be that this was so at least in the case of Jesus. Note too that the church elder consistently maintained his interpretation of the passage of Genesis in the face of my repeated confirmatory questions. Yet he concludes by indicating that he simultaneously believes that 'Black and White' should be 'equal'; perhaps this phrase should be interpreted to mean 'complementary' while yet unequal. I have already used several statements by this man as illustrative of the way some Aboriginal residents were not consistent in their expressed attitudes on the issue of acceptance of missionary administrative control. The further point is that the analogy with the black and white notes on a piano accordion was made in almost identical terms by the White manager at a public meeting two years earlier (T62). This is simply another indication of the manager's great influence over Aboriginal people in Christian fellowship.

Most of the manager's face-to-face dealings with Aborigines in the White domain were with those who were incorporated into the administrative apparatus and were avowed Christians. Of fourteen individuals recorded as having occupied the office of councillor for some time between early 1978 and late 1983, ten were committed Christians 'in fellowship'. Given the relatively small number of adult Aboriginal residents 'in fellowship' at any one time, this figure illustrates a strong tendency for those who became councillors to be committed Christians. The fact of greater participation by Christians in the formal affairs of the White domain was recognised openly by both Aboriginal and White residents. For example, among the Whites, the school principal told me that the school Parents' and Citizens' Association meetings were attended predominantly by 'the church people'. And among Aborigines, it was known quite widely that one council chairman consulted the senior Aboriginal church elder (who was not a councillor) on various administrative matters. In fact, the chairman himself explained that: 'I don't put myself in front of [X], he's an elder of the church'.

The final issue to be considered here is whether Christian Aborigines were favoured in material terms through the administrative process. As well as some allegations by non-Christians that Christians were advantaged, some relevant quantitative data were obtained. Of those adults living in newer European-style houses in late 1980, the senior Aboriginal church elder was able to say of 56 of them that 42 (75 per cent) were baptised. Of those living in the old mission huts and humpies, he was able to say of 243 of them that 121 (50 per cent) were baptised. The more meaningful figures concern the cross-tabulation of attendance at Christian meetings with type of dwelling. Of those said by the Aboriginal church elder in 1980 to be attending meetings regularly, 59 per cent lived in the newer houses, as compared to 14 per cent of those said to be not attending regularly. Of those said to be attending regularly or irregularly, 43 per cent were in the new houses as compared to only 13 per cent of those not attending. Tables 3 and 4 present these cross-tabulations. The best estimate derived from these figures is thus that those attending Christian meetings regularly were just over four times as likely to be living in the newer houses as were those not attending regularly; and those who attended at all (either regularly or irregularly) were three times more likely than non-attenders to be allotted a newer style house.

Table 3
Regular attendance at Christian meetings by house-type (late 1980)
(Column percentages, Chi square = 38.95, p < .001)

House type	Church attendance	
	Attending regularly (N = 34)	Not attending regularly (N = 72)
New	20 (59%)	39 (14%)
Old	14 (41%)	233 (86%)

Table 4
Attendance (regular and irregular) at Christian meetings by house-type (late 1980)
(Column percentages, Chi square 31.75, p < .001)

House type	Church Attendance	
	Attending (regularly or iregularly) (N = 67)	Not attending (N = 239)
New	29 (43%)	30 (13%)
Old	38 (57%)	209 (87%)

While these data support the hypothesis that those attending Christian meetings were favoured in the allocation of new housing, I have already discussed (in chapter 8) a number of other variables that must be taken into account when considering administrative decisions in relation to new housing. Foremost among these variables was employment, and I was also able to cross-tabulate this variable with baptism and attendance at Christian meetings.

Table 5
Regular attendance at Christian meetings by employment withing the settlement (late 1980)
(Column percentages, Chi square 8.27, p < .01)

Employment	Church Attendance	
	Attending regularly (N = 32)	Not attending regularly (N = 269)
Employed	19 (59%)	90 (33.5%)
Unemployed	13 (41%)	179 (66.5%)

Employment rates among those baptised and others were about the same in late 1980; samples of 160 baptised and 128 others both showed an employment rate of approximately 36 per cent. However, as Table 5 shows, a higher proportion of those attending Christian meetings regularly (according to the senior Aboriginal church elder) were employed on the settlement, than were those who were not attending regularly.

I present these figures as a means of showing that those 'in fellowship' were somewhat more likely to obtain employment than others. However, this may well result from greater conformity among these people to the White ideal of a reliable sober worker. Indeed, it could be that committed Christian Aborigines actively sought employment more than others. It cannot be concluded without such qualifications, that the senior missionary staff and/or the council directly favoured Christians in the allocation of available jobs, solely because of the latter's commitment to Christian belief and participation in meetings.

Christian consciousness and political accommodation

I have described in this chapter the process of becoming a Christian and the behavioural routine in which those 'in fellowship' participate. Dimensions of tension between those 'in fellowship' and others have been illustrated, as well as aspects of syncretism between the two traditions in the worldview of Aboriginal residents. I have sought to show, too, that Aboriginal acceptance of Christianity has involved commensurate acceptance of White administrative authority. This can be perceived firstly in relation to the small group of those 'in fellowship' at any one time, consisting of a permanent core and some who move in and out of fellowship through successive 'downfalls' and 're-dedications'. These people see the practices of White authority as intricately entwined with the practice of Christian doctrine, and as they quite avidly embrace the latter it becomes difficult to reject the former. One major aspect of this process has been that commitment to a Christian worldview and social identity has involved an attitude of alignment with the church elders, and two of the three White elders (the manager and the school principal) have been simultaneously in key positions of secular administrative authority. Thus, in the case of converts, Christianity has operated as a powerful legitimating ideology for White authority.

To this extent, Christianity has operated hegemonically, in that it has led a small number of village residents to embrace a system of authoritarian administrative control which has been antipathetic to their broad interests as members of a colonised minority within

Australian society. The minimal material advantage achieved by those 'in fellowship' cannot be said to have worked against their own short-term interests, but these gains have not enabled Christian Aborigines to avoid the more general process of pauperisation. Furthermore, the active collaboration of Christians in particular has assisted in reinforcing and re-endorsing the superordinate tutelary role of missionary authority.

While the majority of non-Christians have not directly supported White authority, neither have they actively rejected Christianity itself, or the missionaries in their role as the purveyors of Christian belief. As has been shown, there has certainly been considerable hostility expressed at times about the missionary staff, whether as individuals, factions, or as an entire group. This hostility has arisen through the kinds of administrative issues discussed in chapters 7 and 8. But Aboriginal people have certainly never aggressively and totally rejected Christian doctrine in a way similar to the Brethren rejection of Blackfella law. While the Brethren may be said to have quite clearly and consistently regarded Blackfella law as illegitimate, the widespread Aboriginal attitude towards Christianity has not mirrored this ethnocentric intellectual intransigence.

Those not 'in fellowship' have not alleged that Christian doctrine should not be attributed legitimacy by the missionaries, though their acceptance of the relevance of Christian belief has been minor compared with the commitment of those 'in fellowship'. The non-Christian Aboriginal majority has in general terms thus accepted White administrative authority to a much less extent than those 'in fellowship', but Christianity as a legitimating ideology for that authority must be seen as having a broader range of influence than just over the small group of Aborigines participating actively in the church assembly at any one time.

Notes

1 Pastor Ben Mason was an Aboriginal evangelist (apparently affiliated with the Aborigines Inland Mission) who travelled through Doomadgee on several occasions during the research period. During at least one of his visits (in 1980), approximately seventeen people were 'saved' following an open air evangelical meeting at which he spoke. He appeared to have considerable impact on such occasions.

2 This is a biblical reference (Luke 8: 4–15, and elsewhere) to passages containing the parable of the sower sowing his seed, where the seeds falling on rocky ground represent those who: 'for a while believe, and in time of temptation fall away'.

3 Figures provided by a White church elder. A proportion of the 260 baptised persons would have been living away from the settlement. Another

indication of the number of Christian Aborigines was obtained by systematically questioning the senior Aboriginal church elder about the residents of households. Of 301 adults for which he provided information, he stated that 164 (54%) were baptized; of 308 adults for which he provided information about church meeting attendance, he stated that 34 (11%) attended regularly, 33 (11%) attended 'sometimes', and 241 (78%) did not attend. It appeared to me at the time that he may have exaggerated the number of regular attenders among those we discussed. Nevertheless, these figures are consistent with those provided by the White church elder, to the extent that they indicate a large number of people once baptised but no longer attending Christian meetings.

[4] This is a reference to a biblical passage (Luke 5:19), where a handicapped person had to be let down through the roof of the house in order to get near Jesus, because of the multitude all around him.

[5] It is actually entitled *The Coming World Holocaust* (Don Stanton, Maranatha Message No.38, July 1980).

[6] These included: *Awake, The Aim, Today* and *Australian Missionary Tidings*.

[7] However, this was not the case in 1983 after the manager had left, when Aboriginal Christians were becoming more assertive at such meetings.

[8] These were in fact the two men who sequentially occupied the office of council chairman throughout the study period.

[9] Cf. Calley's (1964: 50) point for his New South Wales setting, that the missionaries:

> did not persuade their proselytes that the old gods were unreal, but only that they were evil. For this reason conversion to Christianity left much of the old system of belief intact.

[10] Cf. the work on the re-invention of *kastom* in Melanesia (Tonkinson 1982b: 304), where the same point is made.

[11] The first degree of male initiation (involving circumcision) is known by this phrase, which refers to a critical part of the ritual.

[12] See Trigger (1982: 112–3) for further quotations from this tape recording, a transcription of which was exhibit 29 in the Nicholson River (Waanyi/Garawa) land claim proceedings.

[13] The speaker is implying that a long time ago the country was under water. Several other older people expressed a similar notion.

[14] This occurred following my screening of the film *Lockhart Festival*, about a dance festival at Lockhart River settlement in northeast Queensland.

[15] *Aboriginal Leadership: sharing impressions on Aboriginal community leadership*, (p. 10), by Aboriginal leaders from Doomadgee and Mornington Island, June 1982, published by Aboriginal Training and Cultural Institute, Sydney. Although some parts of the Bible have been translated into Garawa and Yanyula by Summer Institute of Linguistics linguists at Borroloola over the years, these translations were not used at Doomadgee.

[16] Among fundamentalist Christians who hold these views, this number is said to be the mark of the Antichrist as stated in Revelations 13:18 (see, e.g., Stanton 1980: 4).

[17] The following data on beliefs about death and its aftermath were obtained mainly from Tapes 7, 17, 69, 80 and 83.

[18] The speaker is most likely alluding to the story of the flood in Genesis, although the notion of the country having once been flooded was also expressed in other contexts (see note 13).

CHAPTER TEN

Coercion, resistance and accommodation in colonial social relations

Throughout this study, I have explored an analysis of power relations and social action in the life and history of an Aboriginal settlement. The book began with a brief narrative account of my first experiences at Doomadgee — experiences which quickly led me to the problem of the complex interplay between resistance and accommodation in the lives of Aboriginal people. In beginning, I introduced the theoretical issue of the relationship between structural constraints and individuals' capacities for social action. In these terms, my foreshadowed task was to examine the extent to which Aboriginal consciousness and practices have been constrained by the coercive political and economic structures of Australian colonialism. Thus, the study has been guided by two major questions: Have Aboriginal people been dominated hegemonically as well as structurally? Does fine-grained ethnographic study reveal everyday forms of resistance similar to those that have been identified as part of cultures of resistance in the lives of various subordinate peoples?

I have firstly developed the argument that life outside the mission settlement entailed much less of a struggle over ideas than was the case once Aboriginal people became institutionalised at Doomadgee. The material on Wild Time suggests that on the frontier and immediately after pastoral settlement was established, the colonising society achieved broad domination over Aboriginal society, primarily through the use and threat of physical force. During this period, Whites faced a degree of physical resistance, though its effectiveness was seemingly dissipated by the use of Aboriginal men as native police and later as police trackers. Collective or organised military resistance was rendered problematic by the decentralised nature of traditional Aboriginal political life, as well as by various violent encounters among Aboriginal groups as the integrity of an economy built around hunting/gathering bands broke down under pressure from the invading society. Throughout the pattern of Black/White conflict, there were also occasional alliances between Aboriginal and non-Aboriginal individuals, seemingly based on relations of personal familiarity.

The introduction of 'rations' by the colonisers established a material basis for the beginning of a prolonged process of pauperisation among Aboriginal residents of camps fringing towns, cattle stations and police depots. However, over a period of several decades, there was considerable diversity in the degree of Aboriginal compliancc with the intrusive system of White economic activity and political authority. Thus, Whites distinguished 'station blacks' from 'bush blacks' (who remained comparatively independent of direct coercion). While there was tension between pastoralists and local government officials over appropriate ways of controlling Aboriginal people, all Whites shared an ideology that regarded such control as necessary. Neither oral historical accounts nor archival documents for this period provide evidence indicating attempts by Whites to convince Aborigines of the appropriateness of colonial control. Even Aboriginal agents of the White police are best thought of as equivalent to paid mercenaries rather than ideologically incorporated agents of the White apparatus of coercion. During Wild Time, colonial domination operated through the use and threat of physical force, not through hegemonic constraints.

In the decades after Wild Time, the economic dependency of Aborigines within sedentary camps on stations and the fringes of towns was consolidated. As wage labourers they had little control over their working conditions or income. Again, certain individuals worked, not as agents of Whites, but as brokers. These were the 'kings', regarded by other Aboriginal people as able to draw on powerful Whites for support, but not perceived to be part of the ruling apparatus. The brokerage of the 'kings' did not lead Aborigines to concede legitimacy to the structures and processes of White domination. Relationships of familiarity and mutual support developed between Aboriginal workers and White 'bosses' in some cases, but this did not entail entrenched hegemonic constraint over Aboriginal thinking. It appears that, intellectually, Aboriginal people did not embrace capitalist work values; nor were White 'bosses' accepted as providing appropriate moral tutelage. Furthermore, neither station Whites nor police protectors sought actively to eradicate Aboriginal culture in any total fashion.

However, from the early 1930s onwards, many of those working on stations would also spend part of their year at Doomadgee Mission. As the number of Aboriginal people based at Doomadgee increased over the decades, authoritarian administrative practices developed among the Brethren missionary staff. The authority of the staff was underpinned by state laws, and Aboriginal practices were subject to considerable coercion. The missionaries sought to constrain Aboriginal thinking in terms of an ideology based simultaneously on Christian Brethren doctrine and notions of what constituted responsible attitudes towards work and obedience to properly constituted laws.

Both the treatment of Doomadgee's history and the ethnography presented in subsequent chapters depict the nature of Aboriginal compliance with the missionaries' authoritarian rule. Equally, though, I have attempted to describe forms of Aboriginal resistance. Through intensive study of routine aspects of everyday life, I have argued that maintenance by Aboriginal people of a socially closed Blackfella domain constitutes a degree of resistance to the intrusive administrative and evangelical access sought by the White staff. The domain is constituted by a spatial locus (the 'village'), and by distinctive practices and modes of thought. To use Bourdieu's (1977) concept of habitus, this Aboriginal domain of social life is underpinned by a system of habitual predispositions, tendencies, propensities and inclinations to think and behave in particular ways. In describing and analysing the Blackfella domain, I have paid close attention to much routinised social action that implicitly reinforced and re-endorsed the fundamental social distance between Aboriginal and White residents of the settlement. This material depicts much of the 'oppositional character' of village life at Doomadgee, as Beckett (1987:9) puts it when introducing his study of the Torres Strait Islanders. Or, as in the case of the Aboriginal people of rural New South Wales, the exclusion of Whites from the Aboriginal domain at Doomadgee indicates 'an oppositional sense of identity' that forms part of a 'culture of resistance' (Morris 1988; Cowlishaw 1988).

This is not to overstate or romanticise the theoretical significance of the Blackfella domain. Its effective maintenance among Aboriginal people does not empower them politically or economically in the face of Australian colonialism; at least not in any direct or clearly discernible fashion. Furthermore, the 'weak' in this instance have no monopoly on the 'weapons' of withdrawal and exclusionary social closure as tactics in the broad pattern of Aboriginal/non-Aboriginal relations (cf. Scott 1986: 6–7). Nevertheless, tactical management of social distance from White society, on the part of structurally subordinate Aborigines constitutes a non-trivial form of resistance because its consequences are the denial of results sought by local White staff (and more generally by the Australian state). The staff have failed to achieve desired evangelical access and success in any fashion that has been embraced throughout the Aboriginal population. Furthermore, as the local agents of the state, staff have failed to convince Aborigines of the legitimacy of the bureaucratic mode of administering the settlement. White ideals about how people should work for a living, plan for the future, and generally subscribe to the worldview of Western rationality have not been embraced. Thus, in refusing to live in their domestic domain in the way Whites do, and by excluding Whites from participation in that domain, Aborigines have dulled the full impact of colonial forces which would otherwise become all encompassing and result in the homogenisation of Aboriginal people into Australian society.

The distinctively Aboriginal forms of politicking that have been maintained in the face of incomprehension and ethnocentrism by Whites are further evidence of cultural resistance. The Aboriginal manner of attributing status has not come to emulate the class-based criteria institutionalised in the broader society. Yet the competitive nature of status relations deriving from Aboriginal tradition may be viewed as inhibiting the development of an articulated and unified political consciousness throughout the village; and hence, we see 'accommodation within resistance', as Genovese (1974: 598) puts it.

The 'organic connection' between resistance and accommodation has emerged consistently throughout this study. On the one hand, deeply felt resentment and bitterness towards the staff was expressed generally among village residents. This sentiment of opposition in Aboriginal consciousness was typically focused on individuals' dissatisfaction with the way personal matters were handled by various staff. It was opposition usually expressed in terms of particular matters of self-interest, which only occasionally assumed an idiom that stressed general opposition to the White system of administration. Thus, it is oppositional sentiment which is diffuse and not articulated into any collective expression of political consciousness or action that might challenge that system in an organised manner. However, this is not to say that such resistance offers no challenge at all to the prevailing system of power relations. It is part of a consciousness and set of practices that enable subordinate people to survive and persist in the face of ethnocentric and assimilationist colonial ideology and practice. The fact that Aboriginal oppositional sentiment and action are typically fused with self-interested motives does not render them trivial in our analysis of colonial social relations.

On the other hand, foremost among the accommodatory aspects of Aboriginal social life are the sentiments of support and affection expressed by some residents for long-serving individuals among the White staff. The long entrenched paternalism of the missionaries thus linked individual staff and Aborigines in relationships of familiarity, thereby helping to legitimise relations of inequality (cf. Genovese 1974: 5–6). Paternalism may also be said to thus further inhibit and undermine solidarity and the development of a unified Aboriginal political consciousness. Yet the support expressed for the missionary administration was due to more than the networks of familiar personalised social relationships among individuals. For Aboriginal people have been enmeshed within a pattern of consumption of commodities and services that have come to be regarded as essential. And the treadmill of consumption, with its experienced immediacy of material needs, is important in understanding the development of Aboriginal consciousness. As White staff have historically organised the ongoing provision of commodities and services, realistic alternatives to the system of paternalistic White authority were not easily framed within Aboriginal consciousness. To the extent that this view represents accommodation in Aboriginal thinking, it is best construed as a resignation to what are thought to be the inevitable conditions of life. When village residents express support for the missionary administration, they do not thereby provide evidence of a duped consciousness, nor of a worldview that is necessarily penetrated hegemonically by the beliefs and values of the wider dominant society.

Those indicating a belief in the legitimacy of existing power relations were often among the small group of people incorporated into the administrative apparatus through the office of councillor (particularly the chairman) and Aboriginal policeman (particularly the sergeant). These people commonly expressed grave apprehension about alternatives to the system of White tutelage, basing their support for existing laws and administrative arrangements on their personal experiences of having to deal with bureaucratic matters as presented to them via the White manager. To this extent, occupying such an office appears to have disproportionately encouraged attribution of legitimacy to the system of authoritarian rule; at the least, it has typically engendered only very ambiguous rejection of that legitimacy.

We might note in the case of these individuals, and some others, a degree of hegemonic influence of aspects of colonial ideology; for example, this is particularly so when the thinking of councillors appears to emulate that of the authoritarian White manager. However, the necessary qualification is that ethnographic evidence of hegemonic domination of Aboriginal thinking should be available from contexts free from the influence of Whites with secular and religious authority. And we have seen that when away from the arena of public action in power-laden situations (such as at public meetings), councillors and others were not always consistent in their support for the White system. Thus, in positing hegemony, we must be careful to distinguish from real ideological domination, a 'pose of the powerless' that may be tailored for the consumption of familiar paternalistic Whites (cf. Scott 1985: 317, 321–2).

In any case, the institution of the council did not facilitate ideological containment broadly across the village. For the widespread perception of councillors was that they sought advancement for themselves and their close kin, and in the process were coopted by the manager (and his faction) into enforcing the latter's will. Rather than winning general support for the bureaucratic system of administration, the operation of the council provided a focus for a discourse of Aboriginal disquiet, and thus reinforced an understanding of that system as illegitimate and non-nurturant (cf. Myers 1986: 268). Village residents were typically not prepared to accept that the interests of councillors, and of the administrative system that underpinned their office, were congruent with the general interests of the broader Aboriginal population.

Similarly, colonial ideology about the significance of colour did not win broad-based Aboriginal consent. To the extent that the conceptual category 'Yellafella' is associated with individuals having achieved material advantage and a sense of separateness from other village residents, this is largely a result of the history of White attempts to separate mixed-descent people from other Aborigines. Colonial racial ideology and practices have thus certainly led to substantial tensions between the mixed-descent minority and others; tensions that cannot be regarded as serving the broad interests of either group. However, this material effect is not equivalent to Aborigines embracing the mystifications intrinsic to European racial ideology. Again, an analysis positing hegemonic domination of Aboriginal thinking would risk confounding grudging resignation to the consequence of colonial ideology with active intellectual support for it.

Finally, I have argued that Christian consciousness has engendered political accommodation. Christian doctrine does not in itself constitute dominant ideology; Christianity has had different political significance in different colonial contexts. However, at Doomadgee Christian morality has not been appropriated in order to condemn the moral basis of White authority, as occurred, for example, among pentecostalist Aborigines in northeast New South Wales (Calley 1964). Nor has it provoked strong adherence to traditional religion as in the case of a Western Desert Aboriginal settlement (Tonkinson 1974). Also, unlike the Torres Strait case (Beckett 1987), Christianity has not been blended into the customary life of the Aboriginal domain. Far from being a basis for resistance in any of such ways, Aboriginal responses to Christianity at Doomadgee have entailed parallel and commensurate political accommodation to White administrative authority. This is especially evident among the comparatively small group of those in fellowship at any one time, and their expressions of support for White authority constitute the strongest evidence in this study of hegemonic constraint upon the worldview of Aboriginal people. This analysis rests on my broader argument that the system of paternalistic White administrative authority is ultimately not congruent with the interests of the general Aboriginal population.

Furthermore, the majority of village residents not in Christian fellowship have passively tolerated Christian doctrine, with many people regarding some of the key issues addressed by Christianity as fundamentally important, death and its aftermath being prime among these. The high proportion of people participating in baptism (with its powerful symbolism of being 'born again') at some point in their lives, attests to this fact. Some individuals have nostalgic memories of times when they have themselves been in fellowship. In this way, certain aspects of Christian ideology have come to penetrate the consciousness of a wide range of Aboriginal people in a lasting fashion.

In the context of relations of familiarity stemming from missionary paternalism, there has thus been a fusion between passive toleration of key concepts within Christian doctrine and passive accommodation to missionary secular authority. This widespread (almost affectionate) tolerance for certain aspects of the Christian worldview has not, in the case of the majority, given rise to the kind of legitimation of missionary authority found among the minority in fellowship. Yet it has moderated the degree of active rejection of that authority, which prompts the generalisation that, by virtue of their consistently paternalistic promulgation of a religious worldview, the missionaries have gained greater acceptance of their administrative role than they would have if their administrative practice had been purely secular in character.

Like the many other aspects of colonial social relations discussed in this study, Aboriginal responses to Christianity have occurred within a broad pattern of contestation and struggle over appropriate ways to behave and think. In the course of pursuing understanding of the dialectic between coercion and consent, I have examined the cultural processes of 'lived' dominance and subordination. Equally important has been the task of understanding Aboriginal resistance within the general consensus that has been imposed through colonial domination. Through pursuing the theme of resistance and accommodation, I have sought to make clear the effects of the political and economic structures of colonialism on people in a region of northern Australia. The study is thus an ethnography that seeks to reveal the political implications inherent in the cultural processes of daily life.

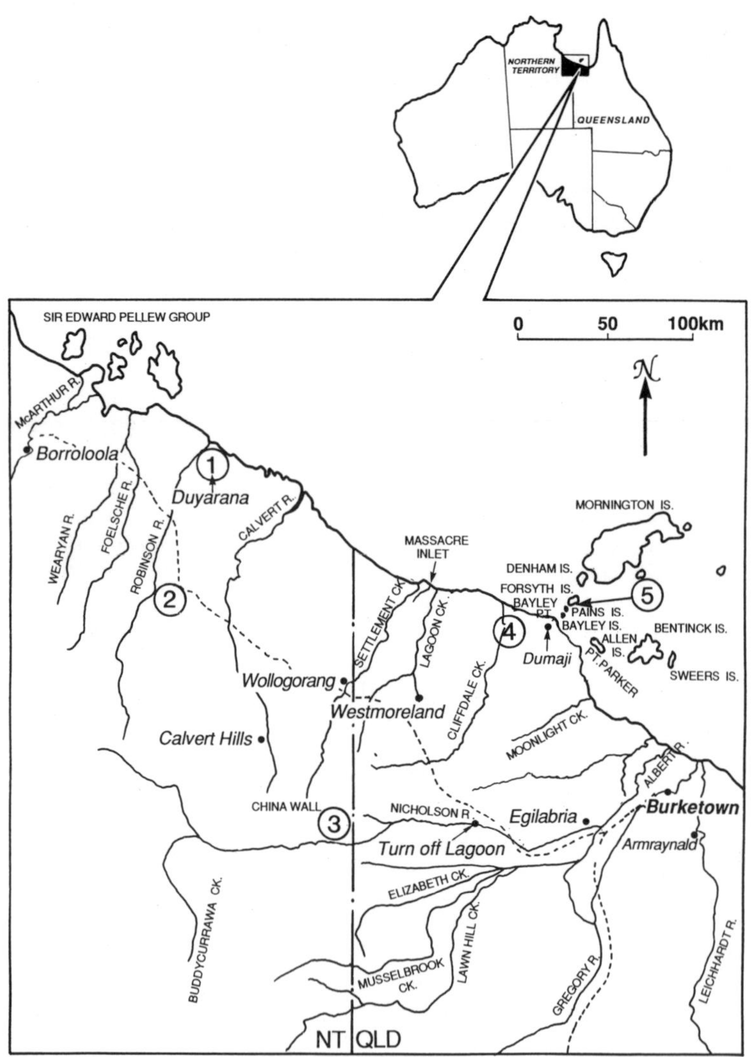

Map 4 Example groups: estates and movements

Appendix A: Historical movements of five example groups

On the following five genealogical charts (figures 2-6), individuals have been designated by a letter of the alphabet (though the names of well-known men who became 'kings' are given). Map 4 shows the approximate locations of the estates to which these cognatic groups trace ties. In case 1 (showing people affiliated with an area in coastal mainland Yanyula country known as Duyarana), *Garinjamaji* or Peter (designated by the letter *A*) travelled east into Queensland in Wild Time and eventually became 'king' of Westmoreland Station, obtaining seven wives and much influence during his lifetime. He was shot in the shoulder by 'Yella Paddy' in 1897 (in the event near Wollogorang described in chapter 2), was later caught by him again and held captive for two days, and (with one of his wives) would have been killed but for the intervention of a mixed-descent kinsman who had been reared by a White couple at Westmoreland. *A*'s sister's son, *B*, travelled east as a young boy from the same area, with his mother and others, 'when everything been settle down' (*c.* 1910). He saw *A*, his uncle, for the first time at Westmoreland. One of his brothers was 'caught' by a policeman in Ganggalida country after having been 'put up' by a local Aboriginal man working as a police tracker (who thereby assisted in his capture). It can be noted that the approximate distances over which these people initially relocated themselves were 130 km (Duyarana area to Wollogorang, and another 30 km to Westmoreland) and a further 150 km from Westmoreland to the Burketown area. The arrows on the genealogy for this case indicate that the descendants of the old people shown in case 1 now live predominantly at Doomadgee, but also at a number of other widespread places.

In case 2 (showing people affiliated with an area in Garawa country), the senior man is said to have lived in the vicinity of his

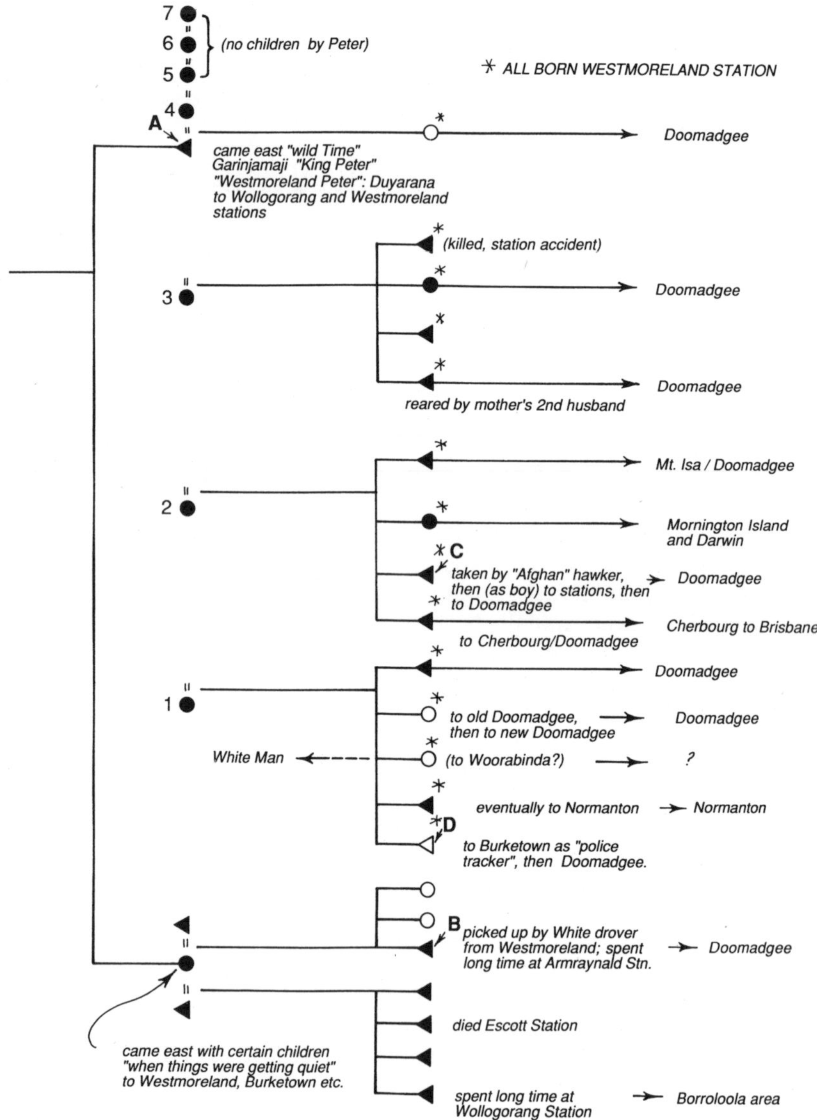

Figure 2 Case 1 showing people affiliated with an area in Yanyula country

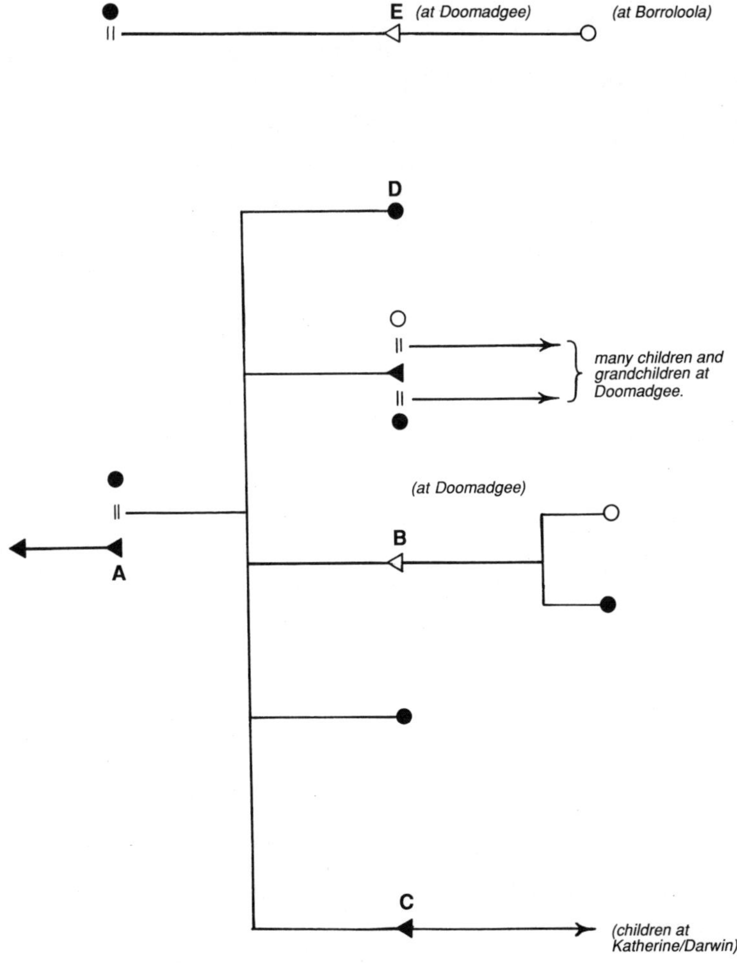

Figure 3 Case 2 showing people affiliated with an area in Garawa country

patriclan estate on the Robinson River. His son *A* was apparently born in the area and spent his early life there. *A* 'worked Wild Time' with a White man who had established a cattle enterprise in the area, having 'followed' his son *B* in after he had been 'picked up' by this White 'boss'. *B*'s approximate birth date is 1906 (as given in Doomadgee Mission records) and his father (*A*) probably came in to camp at the White man's station towards the end of the second decade of this century. During *B*'s youth, periods of residence and work at the station were interspersed with periods spent in the bush. *C* was taken as a young boy from the Robinson River area westwards by a 'surveyor', and has not been seen by his family since that time. *D* died (in 1933) when in the charge of a White policeman; it is said that she was made to walk with chains around her legs from the Calvert Hills Station area towards Borroloola, was fed only with salt, and eventually died at a site on the Wearyan River. Old people allege that the policeman on this occasion also beat several Aboriginal people with a stick, in order to obtain an apparently false confession from them that the group had killed and eaten a cow.[1]

In case 3 (showing people affiliated with an area in Waanyi country) the senior man is said to have lived in the vicinity of his patriclan estate on the upper Nicholson River. *Gundawarinya* (or 'George') and his brother *A* are known to have come east in Wild Time, to have both been wounded (probably by a police party) at a site on Cliffdale Creek, but saved from being killed by a local Aboriginal man who was working as a police tracker. Dymock (1982: 87) states that 'Gundawari' was captured about 1907 on the Nicholson River, escaped, then was 'captured again and persuaded to "come in" to Turn Off Lagoons or else be shot'. Oral accounts indicate that *Gundawarinya* finally came to Turn Off Lagoon, was made 'king' there, and acquired five wives and much influence. However, his brother *A* travelled northeast into coastal Ganggalida country, and eventually married, had children and died there. He did visit Turn Off Lagoon occasionally. Both *Gundawarinya* and his sister *B* (born approximately 1899 according to Doomadgee Mission records) had their children at Turn Off Lagoon, as social life 'settled down'.

In case 4 (showing people affiliated with an area in coastal Ganggalida country), the most senior generation (like the one below it, represented here by only one man in this extract from a much larger genealogy) had died prior to White contact. The next generation experienced first contact and while they lived in the vicinity of their estate for most of their lives, some died in a fringe camp at Burketown. In the third generation down, both *A* and *B* were born at the patriclan estate area. The woman (*A*) travelled occasionally to the Burketown camp, and spent time at the site known as Dumaji (before it became the site for the Old Doomadgee Mission). The

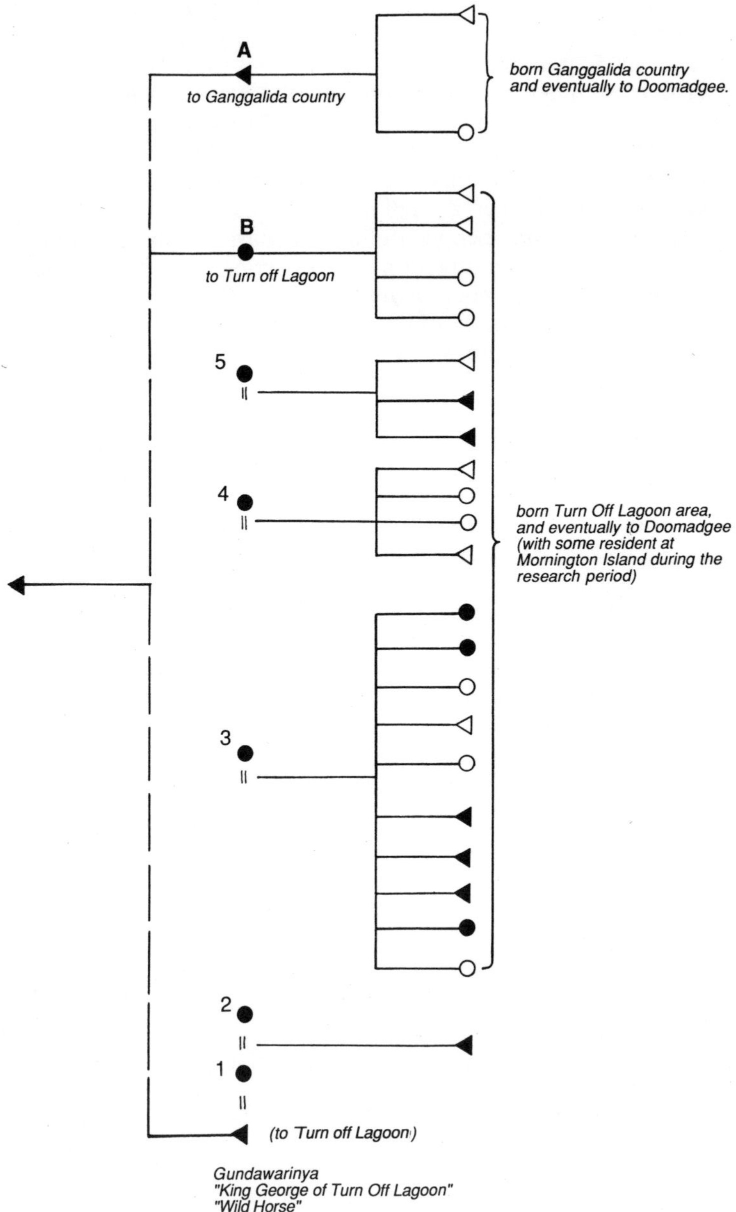

Figure 4 Case 3 showing people affiliated with an area in Waanyi country

man (*B*) spent some time working for a White man in the Burketown area. In the next generation down, people spent most of their early lives at Dumaji on the coast, Burketown and stations in the region. At this time things had mostly 'quietened down'. *C, D, E* and *F* were born approximately 1900, 1910, 1914 and 1918 respectively (according to Doomadgee Mission dates); *H* was the child of a White man who had attacked and raped her mother in the bush. Like *G*, she was adopted by *A* when a small girl.

In case 5 (showing people affiliated to Bayley, Pains and Forsyth Islands), substantial interaction was occurring between the islands and the mainland in both precontact and Wild times; it can be noted that the patriclan country of the father of many of *B*'s children was nearby on the mainland. *B*, with some of her children, travelled by raft to the mainland to live when her mother died on either Bayley or Pains Island. *C* and *D* were taken a long way west (in 1897) by the Yanyula and Garawa people who had come on the revenge trip described in chapter 2. *E* was taken to Normanton (to the east of Burketown) by a police party, *F* and *G* spent a substantial part of their lives at the Burketown camp, and *H* was sent to Palm Island (off the east coast of Queensland), though the reason for this is unclear. The latter's two daughters were kidnapped on Allen Island off Point Parker by Bentinck Island men who were camping there. This event apparently occurred well after Wild Time proper in 1940 (Tindale 1962: 269), when the dinghy the two girls were travelling in stopped to obtain water. However, the contemporary Aboriginal historical perspective acknowledges the special case of the Bentinck Island people who remained 'wild' right up until 1948, when they were finally shifted from their bush camps and moved to Mornington Island Mission.

Notes

[1] McLaughlin (1977: 6–7) gives a newspaper extract which reports that eleven witnesses (ten Aboriginal and one White) alleged appalling brutality leading to the woman's death. The policeman involved was tried and acquitted. As McLaughlin (1977: 7) points out, 'more so than the contact massacres this incident has been raised, at least by Garawa people, as epitomizing injustice they have experienced under white authorities'. In 1979, Aboriginal people at Borroloola (including a few sometimes resident at Doomadgee) participated in the making of a film (entitled 'Two Laws') in which they present aspects of their oral history, and the death of this woman is one of the episodes acted out (see also Avery 1979).

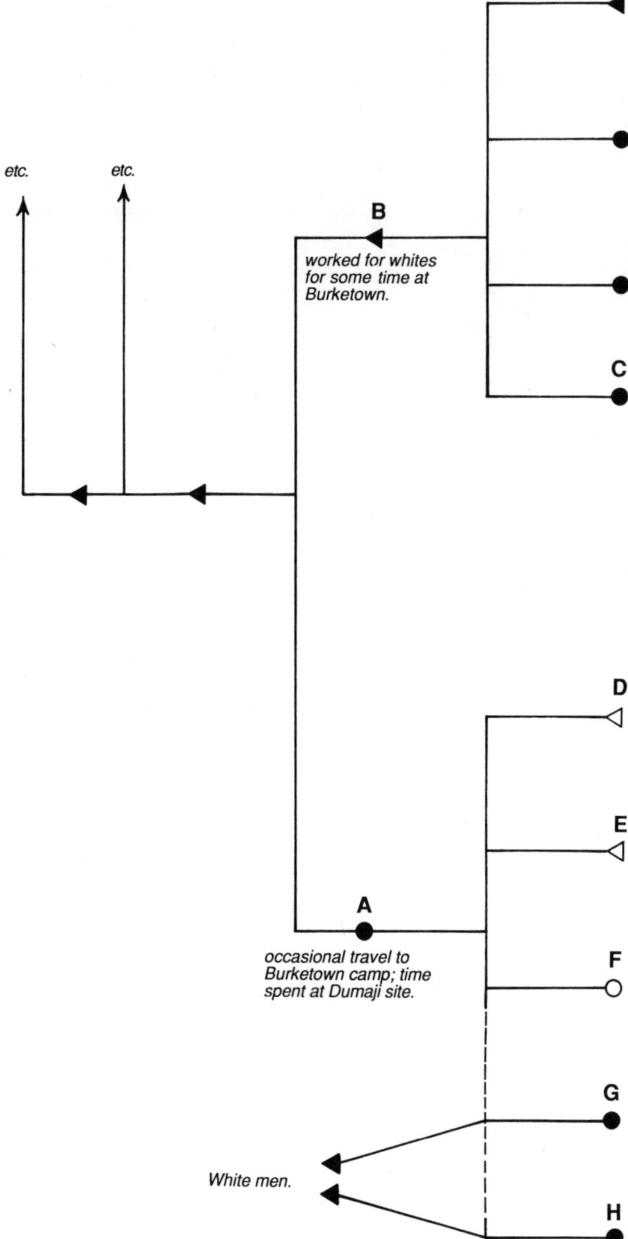

Figure 5 Case 4 showing people affiliated with an area in Ganggalida country

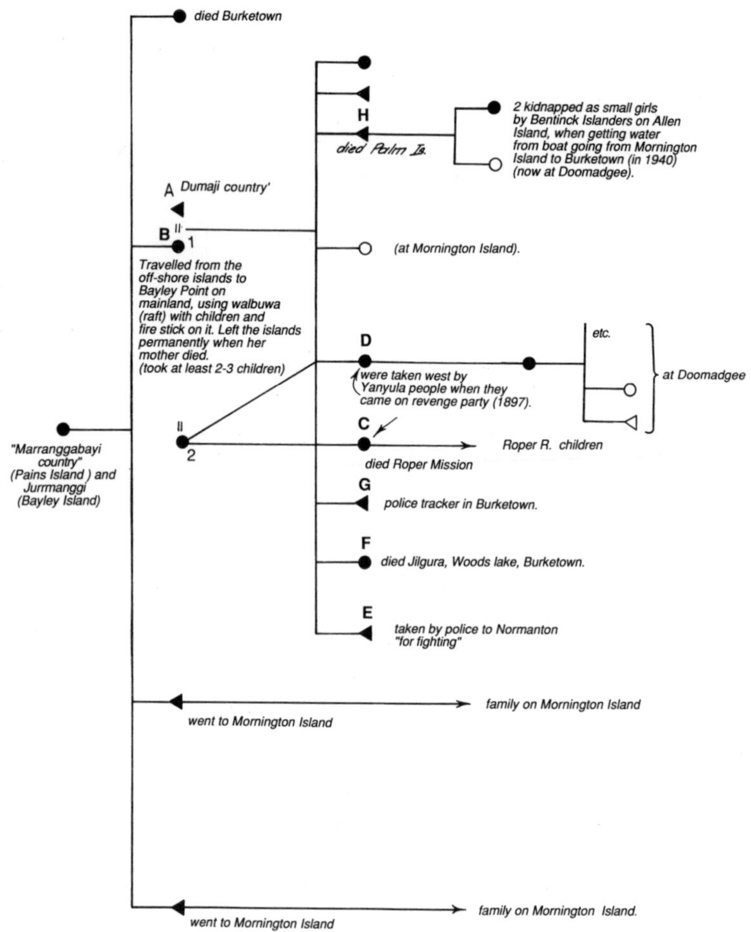

Figure 6 Case 5 showing people affiliated to Bayley, Pains and Forsyth islands

Appendix B: Incomplete list of individuals removed from Burketown, Turn Off Lagoon and certain stations

Year	From	To	Reason
1912	Burketown	Barambah	Going about armed and killing station cattle.
1914	Burketown	Mapoon	Reported bad character, refuses to work under agreement. Stirs up discontent amongst other Aborigines. Wife to accompany him.
1920	Burketown	Yarrabah	Threatening murder and immorality.
1929	Burketown	Mornington	Destitute; for their own protection.
1931	Burketown	Mornington	For their own protection and welfare.
1931	Burketown	Palm Is.	For her own protection.
1931	Burketown	Palm Is.	Suffering from severe skin disease; for treatment.
1933	Burketown	Palm Is.	Refuses to work and destitute [wife and child?] to accompany him.
1934	Burketown	Palm Is.	Convicted horse stealing in May 1933. Unable to obtain employment. Family destitute and in rags.
1934	Burketown	Palm Is.	Troublesome character absconding from employment and suspected of suffering from V.D.
1935	Burketown	Fantome Is.	For Medical treatment.
1935	Burketown	Fantome Is.	Suffering from V.D. To accompany parents.
1935	Burketown	Fantome Is.	Suffering from leprosy.
1935	Burketown	Palm Is.	Laziness, refuses to work and generally unsatisfactory conduct. To accompany husband and parents.
1930	Wood Lake [Burketown]	Mornington	Very lazy; continually interfering with other Aboriginals' wives.
1914	Turn Off Lag.	Barambah	Subject to morphia habits.
1919	Turn Off Lag.	Mornington	For his own benefit.

1919	Turn Off Lag.	Mapoon	For her own protection.
1919	Turn Off Lag.	Palm Is.	Very dangerous aborigines. Have threatened life of station manager.
1926	Turn Off Lag.	Palm Is.	Uncontrollable; general nuisance; to be made an example of.
1927	Turn Off Lag.	Mornington	Running wild in aboriginal camps. For their own protection.
1930	Turn Off Lag.	Palm Is.	Uncontrollable; for the good of other aboriginals.
1934	Turn Off Lag.	Mornington	Morally weak; children to accompany mother.
1935	Turn Off Lag.	Mornington	Destitute; immoral associations.
1935	Turn Off Lag.	Mornington	To accompany husband.
1935	Turn Off Lag.	Mornington	Children to accompany parents.
1935	Turn Off Lag.	Mornington	Immoral associations.
1935	Turn Off Lag.	Mornington	To accompany mother.
1935	Turn Off Lag.	Mornington	Immoral associations.
1935	Turn Off Lag.	Mornington	To accompany mother.
1935	Turn Off Lag.	Mornington	Destitute immoral association.
1935	Turn Off Lag.	Mornington	To accompany husband.
1935	Turn Off Lag.	Mornington	To accompany parents.
1935	Turn Off Lag.	Mornington	Immoral associations.
1935	Turn Off Lag.	Mornington	To accompany husband.
1935	Turn Off Lag.	Mornington	To accompany parents.
1935	Turn Off Lag.	Mornington	Immoral associations.
1935	Turn Off Lag.	Mornington	To accompany parents.
1936	Turn Off Lag.	Mornington	Unemployable/begging for food useless type unable to find employment/low moral character/ [wife] to accompany husband/ children to accompany mother.
1914	Lawn Hills	Mapoon	For her own protection.
1933	Gregory Downs	Mornington	Sick and nearly blind; unable to maintain himself.
1935	Gregory Downs	Palm Is.	Indecently interfering with female children. Wives to accompany husband; children to accompany parents.
1923	Gregory Downs	Mornington	Conduct has not been good.
1916	Escott Stn	Barambah	Stealing; terrorising residents.
1931	Marless Stn	Mornington	Mothers deceased; for their protection.
1913	Augustus Dns	Cape Bedford	Mother died and left children destitute.
1927	Augustus Dns	Mornington	Destitute; for their benefit.
1916	Wernadinga Stn	Mapoon	For her own protection.

1935	Donors Hill Station	Doomadgee	Sent to Mission to be cared for and educated instead of handing over to White employers

List in Gulf Country History File (Australian Institute of Aboriginal and Torres Strait Islander Studies library)

Bibliography

Abercrombie, N., S. Hill and B. Turner 1980. *The dominant ideology thesis*, London: George Allen and Unwin.

Aboriginal Land Commissioner 1982. Transcript of proceedings re the Nicholson River land claim Najabarra, 19-23 October and Darwin, 22-3 November, Canberra, Commonwealth Reporting Service.

Akehurst, Dorothy 1933. An outline of the work among Aborigines in north Queensland, *Australian missionary tidings*, 1st September 1933: 175–7.

Altman, J.C. and J. Nieuwenhuysen 1979. *The economic status of Australian Aborigines*, Cambridge: Cambridge University Press.

Anderson, Christopher 1983. Aborigines and tin mining in North Queensland: a case study in the anthropology of contact history, *Mankind* 13: 473–98.

Avery, J. 1977. The claims. In Submission by Northern Land Council to the Aboriginal Land Commissioner on the Borroloola land claim, J. Avery & D. McLaughlin, pp. 23–80, Darwin: Northern Land Council.

Avery, J. 1979. Police, combos and Aborigines: conflicts in the north eastern Gulf of Carpentaria in the period before World War II. Unpublished ms.

Banton, M. 1987. *Racial theories*, Cambridge: Cambridge University Press.

Barker, H.M. 1964. *Camels and the outback*, Melbourne: Isaac Pitman and Sons.

Bauer, F.H. 1959. *Historical geographic survey of part of northern Australia*, Part 1: Introduction and the eastern Gulf region, Canberra: CSIRO.

Beckett, J. 1987. *Torres Strait Islanders — custom and colonialism*, Cambridge: Cambridge University Press.

Bleakley, J.W. 1918. Annual report of the Chief Protector of Aborigines for the year 1917, *Queensland parliamentary papers* 1: 1671–81.

Bourdieu, P. 1977. *Outline of a theory of practice*, Cambridge: Cambridge University Press.

Buckland, A.R. (ed.) 1951 [1929] *The universal Bible dictionary,* London: Butterworth.

Calley, Malcolm J.C. 1958. Bandjalang social organisation, Unpublished PhD thesis, University of Sydney.

Calley, Malcom J.C. 1964. Pentecostalism among the Bandjalang. In *Aborigines now*, Marie Reay ed., pp. 48–58, Sydney: Angus and Robertson.
Cantle, Merle 1980. *Jewels of fine gold*, Sydney: Outreach Book Service.
Carrington, Len 1977. Reminiscences of Augustus Downs during the 20's and 30's. In *Gregory Downs hotel centenary 1977*, pp. 14–17, compiled by Gregory Branch Queensland Country Women's Association.
Chase, Athol Kennedy 1981. 'All kind of nation': Aborigines and Asians in Cape York Peninsula, *Aboriginal history* 5: 7–19.
Commissioner for Community Relations 1977. *Second annual report*, Canberra: Australian Government Publishing Service.
Cowlishaw, G. 1988. *Black, White or Brindle — race in rural Australia*, Cambridge: Cambridge University Press.
DAA n.d.*a*. Community study: Doomadgee Aboriginal community. Unpublished ms. completed 1979, Canberra: Department of Aboriginal Affairs.
DAA n.d.*b*. Doomadgee review. Prepared for Commonwealth Department of Aboriginal Affairs. Unpublished ms.
DAA 1982. Strategy paper — Doomadgee. Prepared for Commonwealth Department of Aboriginal Affairs. Unpublished ms.
DAIA 1968. *Annual report of the Director of Aboriginal and Island Affairs*, for the year ending 30th June, 1968, Queensland: Government Printer.
DAIA 1976. *Annual report of Department of Aboriginal and Islanders Advancement*, for the year ending June 30, 1976, Brisbane: Government Printer.
DAIA 1978. *Annual report of Department of Aboriginal and Islanders Advancement*, for the year ending June 30, 1978, Queensland: Government Printer.
DAIA 1983. *Annual report of Department of Aboriginal and Islanders Advancement*, for the year ending June 30, 1983, Queensland: Government Printer.
Douglas, J.D. 1974. *The new international dictionary of the Christian church*, Exeter: Paternoster Press.
Dymock, J. 1982. Historical material relevant to Nicholson River land claim. Unpublished report prepared for Northern Land Council, Darwin.
Genovese, E.D. 1974. *Roll Jordan Roll: the world the slaves made*, New York: Pantheon.
Genovese, E.D. 1975. Class, culture and historical process, *Dialectical anthropology* 1: 71–9.
Gerritsen, R. 1982. Blackfellas and Whitefellas. In *Service delivery to remote communities*, P. Loveday ed., pp. 16–31, Darwin: Australian National University North Australia Research Unit.
Goffman, E. 1961. *Asylums: essays on the social situation of mental patients and other inmates*, Harmondsworth: Penguin.
Hall, S., B. Lumley and G. McLennan 1977. Politics and ideology: Gramsci. In *On ideology*, Centre for contemporary cultural studies, pp. 45–76, London: Hutchinson.
Hiatt, L.R. 1984. Traditional land tenure and contemporary land claims. In *Aboriginal landowners*, L.R. Hiatt ed., pp. 11–23, Oceania Monograph No. 27, Sydney: University of Sydney.
Hockey, A.J. 1961–2. Appendix 6: Doomadgee Mission via Burketown. In 'Native Affairs: Annual report of Director of Native Affairs for the year ended 30th June, 1961', *Queensland parliamentary papers*: 1354–65.

Hoffman, J. 1984. *The Gramscian challenge: coercion and consent in Marxist political theory*, New York: Blackwell.

Keefe, J. (Senator) 1972. Commonwealth Parliamentary Debates (Senate) 9.3.1972.

Kolig, E. 1980. Captain Cook in the Western Kimberleys. In *Aborigines of the west: their past and their present*, R. and C. Berndt eds., pp. 274–82, Perth: University of Western Australia Press.

Long, J.P.M. 1970. *Aboriginal settlements: a survey of institutional communities in eastern Australia*, Canberra: Australian National University Press.

Lukes, S. 1977. *Essays in social theory*, London: Macmillan.

Mackinolty, C. and P. Wainburranga 1988. Too many Captain Cooks. In *Aboriginal Australians and Christian missions*, T. Swain and D. Rose eds., pp. 355–60, Adelaide: Australian Association for the Study of Religions.

McIntyre, J.N. 1921. Where ignorance is bliss — 'tis folly to be wise'. Chapter in ms. entitled 'Capabilities of the Gulf Country', Mitchell Library, Sydney.

McLaughlin, D. 1977. Part A. In Submission by Northern Land Council to the Aboriginal Land Commissioner on the Borroloola region land claim, J. Avery and D. McLaughlin, pp. 1–22. Unpublished report prepared for the Northern Land Council, Darwin.

Maddock, K. 1972. *The Australian Aborigines: a portrait of their society*, London: Allen Lane The Penguin Press.

May, D. 1983. *From bush to station*, Townsville: James Cook University.

Meggitt, M. 1962. *Desert people*, Chicago: University of Chicago Press.

Memmott, P. 1979. Lardil properties of place, an ethnological study of man-environment relations. Unpublished PhD thesis, University of Queensland.

Miller, D. and J. Branson 1987. Pierre Bourdieu: culture and praxis. In *Creating culture*, D. Austin ed., pp. 210–25, Sydney: Allen and Unwin.

Morris, B. 1988. Dhan-gadi resistance to assimilation. In *Being black*, I. Keen ed., pp. 33–64, Canberra: Australian Institute of Aboriginal Studies.

Murray, M. 1982. School based curriculum development Doomadgee State School, North West Region. Unpublished ms.

Myers, F.R. 1979. Emotions and the self: a theory of personhood and political order among Pintupi Aborigines, *Ethos* 7, 4: 343–70.

Myers, F.R. 1986. *Pintupi country, Pintupi self*, Washington: Smithsonian Institution Press.

Nettheim, G. 1981. *Victims of the law*, Sydney: George Allen and Unwin.

Ortner, S. 1984. Theory in anthropology since the sixties, *Comparative studies in society and history* 26: 126–66.

Parkin, F. 1982. *Max Weber*, Chichester: Ellis Horwood.

Parry-Okeden, W.E. 1897. Report on the north Queensland Aborigines and the Native Police, *Queensland votes and proceedings* 2: 23–46, plus map.

Pettingill, William L. 1971. *Bible questions answered*, Michigan: Zondervan.

Pryor, C. n.d. Doomadgee. In *Beyond the Act*, Les Malezer, Matt Foley and Paul Richards eds., pp. 147–8, Brisbane: Foundation for Aboriginal and Islander Research Action Ltd.

Reay, Marie 1962. Subsections at Borroloola, *Oceania* 33: 90–115.

Read, M.G. 1947–48. Appendix 15: Doomadgee Mission. In 'Native Affairs: Information contained in report of Director of Native Affairs for the twelve months ended 30th June, 1947', *Queensland parliamentary papers* 2: 1079–109.

Reynolds, Henry 1981. *The other side of the frontier*, Townsville: James Cook University of North Queensland.

Rienits, Rex and Thea Rienits 1968. *The voyages of Captain Cook*, London: Hamlyn.

Rootes, C. 1981. The dominant ideology thesis and its critics, *Sociology* 15: 436–44.

Rose, D. 1984. The saga of Captain Cook: morality in European and Aboriginal law, *Australian Aboriginal studies* 2: 24–39.

Roth, W.E. 1900. Report of the Northern Protector of Aboriginals for 1899, *Queensland votes and proceedings* 5: 581–95.

Roth, W.E. 1902. Report of the Northern Protector of Aboriginals for 1901, *Queensland parliamentary papers* 1: 1131–49.

Roth, W.E. 1903. Report of the Northern Protector of Aboriginals for 1902, *Queensland parliamentary papers* 2: 451–75.

Roth, W.E. 1904. Report of the Northern Protector of Aboriginals for 1903, *Queensland parliamentary papers* 1: 847–73.

Rowley, C.D. 1970. *The destruction of Aboriginal society,* Harmondsworth: Penguin.

Rowley, C.D. 1972. *The remote Aborigines*, Harmondsworth: Penguin.

Schaffert, Phil 1981. King Tabby could manage 3 wives but not the bottle, *The Northerner* 10: 4–5 (July).

Scott, J. 1985 *Weapons of the weak: everyday forms of peasant resistance*, New Haven: Yale University Press.

Scott, J. 1986. Everyday forms of peasant resistance, *Journal of peasant studies* 13 (2): 5–35.

Scott, J. 1987. Resistance without protest and without organization: peasant opposition to the Islamic *Zakat* and the Christian tithe, *Comparative studies in society and history* 29: 417–52.

Sharp, I.G. 1966. Report on the present wage position of Aborigines in the Northern Territory and the States. In *Aborigines in the economy*, Ian G. Sharp and Colin M. Tatz eds., pp. 145–73, Brisbane: Jacaranda.

Sharp, R.L. 1935. Semi-moieties in north-western Queensland, *Oceania* 6: 158–74.

Sharp, R.L. 1939. Tribes and totemism in north-east Australia. *Oceania* 9, 3: 254–75; 9, 4: 439–61.

Shaw, B. 1983. *Banggaiyerri: the story of Jack Sullivan*, Canberra: Australian Institute of Aboriginal Studies.

Sider, G. 1987. Why parrots learn to talk and why they can't: domination, deception and self-deception in Indian-White relations, *Comparative studies in society and history* 29: 3–23.

Stanner, W.E.H. 1965a. Religion, totemism and symbolism. In *Aboriginal man in Australia*, R.M. and C.H. Berndt eds., pp. 207–37, Sydney: Angus and Robertson.

Stanner, W.E.H. 1965b. Aboriginal territorial organization: estate, range, domain and regime, *Oceania* 36: 1–26.

Stanner, W.E.H. 1979. *White man got no dreaming*, Canberra: Australian National University Press.

Stanton, Don 1980. *The coming world holocaust*, Maranatha Message No. 38, Stapled booklet.

Stevens, C. 1989. *Tin mosques and Ghantowns: a history of Afghan cameldrivers in Australia*, Melbourne: Oxford University Press.

Stevens, Frank 1973. Industrial and race relations in northern Australia. Unpublished PhD thesis, University of New South Wales.

Stevens, Frank 1974. *Aborigines in the Northern Territory cattle industry*, Canberra: Australian National University Press.

Stevens, Frank 1980. *The politics of prejudice*, Sydney: Alternative Publishing Co-op.

Talbot, J. 1953–4. Appendix 7: Doomadgee Mission. In 'Native Affairs: Annual report of Director of Native Affairs for the year ended 30th June, 1953', *Queensland Parliamentary Papers* 2: 959–1011.

Talbot, J. 1956–57. Appendix 7: Doomadgee Aboriginal Mission. In 'Native Affairs: Annual report of Director of Native Affairs for the year ended 30th June, 1956', *Queensland parliamentary papers* 2: 1223–91.

Talbot, J. 1958–9. Appendix 4: Doomadgee Mission via Burketown. In 'Native Affairs: Annual report of Director of Native Affairs for the year ended 30th June, 1958', *Queensland parliamentary papers* 2: 1027–93.

Terwiel-Powell, F.J. 1975. Developments in the kinship system of the Hope Vale Aborigines. Unpublished PhD thesis, University of Queensland.

The Australian Law Reform Commission 1979. Aboriginal Customary Law Field Report No. 5, The Cape York Peninsula Queensland. Unpublished Report.

The Austalian Law Reform Commission 1986. *The recognition of Aboriginal customary laws: summary report* (Report No. 31), Canberra: Australian Government Publishing Service.

Tindale, Norman B. 1962. Geographical knowledge of the Kaiadilt people of Bentinck Island, Queensland, *Records of the South Australian Museum* 14, 2: 259–96.

Tonkinson, Robert 1974. *The Jigalong mob: Aboriginal victors of the desert crusade*, California: Cummings.

Tonkinson, Robert 1982a. Outside the power of the dreaming: paternalism and permissiveness in an Aboriginal settlement. In *Aboriginal power in Australian society*, M. Howard ed., pp. 115–30, St Lucia: University of Queensland Press.

Tonkinson, Robert 1982b. Kastom in Melanesia: Introduction, *Mankind* 13: 302–5.

Tonkinson, Robert 1988. One community, two laws: aspects of conflict and convergence in a Western Australian Aboriginal settlement. In *Indigenous law and the state*, B. Morse and G.R. Woodman eds., pp. 395–411, The Netherlands: Foris.

Trigger, D.S. 1981. Blackfellows, Whitefellows and head lice, *Australian Institute of Aboriginal Studies Newsletter* New Series 15: 63–72.

Trigger, D.S. 1982. Nicholson River (Waanyi/Garawa) land claim. Unpublished report prepared for Northern Land Council, Darwin.

Trigger, D.S. 1987. Languages, linguistic groups and status relations at Doomadgee, an Aboriginal settlement in north-west Queensland, Australia, *Oceania* 57: 217–38.

Trigger, D.S. 1989. Racial ideologies in Australia's Gulf Country, *Ethnic and racial studies* 12 (2): 208–232.
Turnbull, W. 1911 [1896]. Letters to A. Carroll, *Science of man* 13, 2: 39–41.
Van Sommers, Tess 1966. *Religions in Australia*, Adelaide: Rigby.
Weber, Max 1968. *Economy and Society*, 3 vols. New York: Bedminster.
Williams, R. 1977. *Marxism and literature*, Oxford: Oxford University Press.

Unpublished historical and archival sources*

Akehurst, D. n.d. Early days at Doomadgee, ms.
Akehurst, L. n.d. [Untitled ms. concerning missionary work at Doomadgee].
Akehurst, L. 25.4.1931. Letter to Chief Protector of Aboriginals, GCHF.
Bedford, B. and H. Rossow 1960. Extract from address at a missionary meeting (March 1960), Brisbane, ms.
Bowie, T.J. (Constable, Police Station Rankine River) 28.4.1944. Report re Nicholson patrol, to The Superintendent of Police, Alice Springs. Australian Archives (NT Branch) CRS F1 Item: 43/55.
Calligan, J. (Inspector, Police Station Cloncurry) 9.6.1943. Letter to Commissioner of Police, Brisbane. GCHF.
Casey, John (Acting Sergeant, Police Station Burketown) 3.10.1898. Report re M.G. Watson's letter to Commissioner of Police Brisbane complaining against Blacks, to Inspector of Police, Normanton. QSA Pol/J16 No. 13862.
Chambers, J.B. (Protector of Aboriginals, Burketown) 3.9.1948, 28.10.1948. Letters to Director of Native Affairs. GCHF.
Champney, H.D. (Protector of Aboriginals, Burketown) 31.1.1950. Telegram to Superintendent Doomadgee Mission; 1.2.1950. Letter to Director of Native Affairs; 1.3.1950. Letter to Director of Native Affairs. GCHF.
Chief Protector of Aboriginals n.d. Letter (to Queensland Minister for Lands?); 26.9.1936. Summary of matters concerning Doomadgee Reserve. GCHF.
Commissioner of Police (Brisbane) 1.3.1899. Letter to Inspector of Police Normanton. QSA POL/J20, No. 07785.
Cunneen, J.F. (Director, Westmoreland Pastoral Company) 8.2.1962. Letter to Manager, Westmoreland Pastoral Company. GCHF.
Davis, W. 19.9.1949. Report concerning Doomadgee Mission, to Deputy Director of Native Affairs, GCHF.
Dempsey, [?] 8.8.1913 Memorandum to Inspector Waters, Darwin. Northern Territory Archives F275/A325.
Deputy Director of Native Affairs 13.5.1952. Letter to Acting Superintendent Doomadgee Mission. GCHF.
Director of Native Affairs (Qld) 29.1.1943. Memorandum to Protector of Aboriginals, Borroloola; 14.11.1949. Letter to Deputy Director of Native Affairs; 5.4.1950. Letter to Superintendent, Doomadgee Mission. GCHF.
Director of Tuberculosis (Qld) 9.5.1950. Report on visit to Aboriginal Mission stations, Gulf of Carpentaria 12.4.1950–1.5.1950, GCHF.

Doomadgee: a report of the development of a work of God amongst the Aborigines in North Queensland, February 1953, ms.

Dunn, John (Acting Sergeant, Police Station Burketown) 15.5.1897. Report re establishing detachment of Native Police at Turn Off Lagoons, to The Inspector of Police Normanton. QSA POL/J20, No. 07785.

Forsyth, Jas. 30.12.1902. Letter to Under Secretary, Home Secretary's Department, Brisbane. GCHF.

Graham, C. (Sergeant, Police Station Alice Springs) 15.3.1943. Nicholson Patrol. Australian Archives (NT Branch), CRS F1 Item: 1943/55.

Graham, D. (Inspector, Police Station Normanton) 13.1.1897. Telegram to Commissioner of Police, Brisbane. QSA POL/J16 No. 00465.

Hagarty, R. (Protector of Aboriginals, Gregory Downs) 26.5.1943. Letter to Inspector of Police, Cloncurry; 15.6.1944, 8.6.1949. Letters to Director of Native Affairs Brisbane. GCHF.

Hockey, A. 1970. Assembly work amongst Aborigines at Doomadgee, north Queensland, ms.

Hockey, G. 1969. Doomadgee Aborigines, ms.

Hosier, W.J. (Protector of Aboriginals, Burketown) 19.9.1931. Letter to Chief Protector of Aboriginals. GCHF.

Jessen, A.J. (Protector of Aboriginals, Burketown) 6.2.1962, 27.6.1962, 15.12.1962, 15.6.1963. Letters to Director of Native Affairs; 16.5.1962. Letter to Inspector of Police, Cloncurry. GCHF.

Kyle-Little, S.H. (Patrol Officer, NT Department of Native Affairs) 16.12.1948. Report relative to mines and cattle stations employing native labour in the Borroloola district. Australian Archives (NT Branch) F315, 49/393 A II.

Kyle-Little, S.H. 21.12.1948. Report of patrol of Borroloola district to Wollogorang Station by way of Seven Emus Station and return by way of Robinson River Station. Australian Archives (NT Branch) F315, 49/393 A II.

Lamond (Inspector, Police Station Normanton) 7.2.1899. Letter to Commissioner of Police Brisbane. QSA POL/J20, No. 02921.

Lamond 10.2.1899. Letter to Commissioner of Police, Brisbane. QSA POL/J16 No. 02983.

Lamond 8.3.1899. Telegram to Commissioner of Police, Brisbane. QSA POL/J16, No. 03779.

Lamond 20.11.1899. Letter to Commissioner of Police, Brisbane. QSA POL/J16, No. 18105.

Little and Hetzer (Brodie Brothers' Pastoral Company) 8.6.1868. Letter to Colonial Secretary. QSA COL/A106, No. 1720.

Lyne, Timothy (Constable, Police Station Turn Off Lagoon) 1.6.1898, 30.11.1898. Reports re bush patrols to Lawn Hill Station, to Inspector of Police, Normanton. QSA POL/J20 Nos. 08060, 01473.

Macintosh, T.B. (Lawn Hill Station) 6.12.1902. Letter (No. 19398) to Jas Forsyth M.L.A. GCHF.

McKinnon, W. (Protector of Aboriginals, Borroloola) 9.4.1943. Letter to Director of Native Affairs, Brisbane. GCHF.

Murnane, B.J. (Alhambra Station) 2.4.1943. Letter to N. Smith, M.L.A. Brisbane; 7.3.1944. Letter to Mr Chandler, M.L.A. Brisbane. GCHF.

Nuss, H. (Protector of Aboriginals, Burketown) 12.11.1942. Letter re employment of Aboriginals, Westmoreland Station, to Director of Native Affairs. GCHF.

Old, James E. (Acting Sergeant, Police Station Burketown) 25.5.1899. Extracts from correspondence, Burketown Police Station, compiled by Dr P. Memmott (1975), Aboriginal Data Archive, University of Queensland.

Ordish, Lionel (Constable, Police Station Turn Off Lagoon) 19.10.1899. Reports re Blacks calling at Turn Off Lagoon; and 12.11.1899. Report re health and number of Blacks: to The Superintendent of Police Normanton. QSA POL/J16, No. 18105.

Progress report of the Chief Protector of Aborigines (Extract) May 1906. GCHF.

Read, D. n.d. Early history of Doomadgee, ms.

Read, M. (Superintendent, Doomadgee Mission) 7.6.1948. Letter to Director of Native Affairs; 5.2.1949, 21.4.1949. Letters to Deputy Director of Native Affairs; 14.6.1950. Letter re report by Director of Tuberculosis, to W. Davis (DNA). GCHF.

Read, M. 7.7.1946. Is Gospel work amongst the Aboriginals worthwhile?, ms.

Roth, W.E. 23.12.1898. (Northern Protector of Aboriginals) Observations of working of Opium Regulations . . ., Extract of letter to Commissioner of Police, Brisbane, GCHF.

Roth, W.E. 14.8.1901. The Northern Territory-Queensland border, north of Urandangie, GCHF.

Roth, W.E. 30.12.1902. Letter (No. 00106) to Under Secretary, Home Secretary's Department. GCHF.

Roth, W.E. 21.4.1903. Letter to Under Secretary, Department of Public Lands. GCHF.

Smith, E.P. (Constable, Police Station Turn Off Lagoon) 31.12.1905. Extract from Report to Inspector of Police Normanton. GCHF.

Talbot, J. (Acting Superintendent) 11.2.1950, 9.4.1952. Letters to Deputy Director of Native Affairs; January 1950, 9.7.1958. Letters to Director of Native Affairs. GCHF.

Watson, M.G. (Gregory Downs Station) 10.8.1898. Letter to Commissioner of Police Brisbane. QSA POL/J16 No. 10683.

Watson, M.G. 31.10.1898. Letter to Commissioner of Police, Brisbane. QSA POL/J16 No. 14519.

---

*The abbreviations QSA and GCHF stand for Queensland State Archives and Gulf Country History File (held at Australian Institute of Aboriginal and Torres Strait Islander Studies library, Canberra), respectively. Where no location is shown for a document, a copy of it is held in the author's possession.

Index